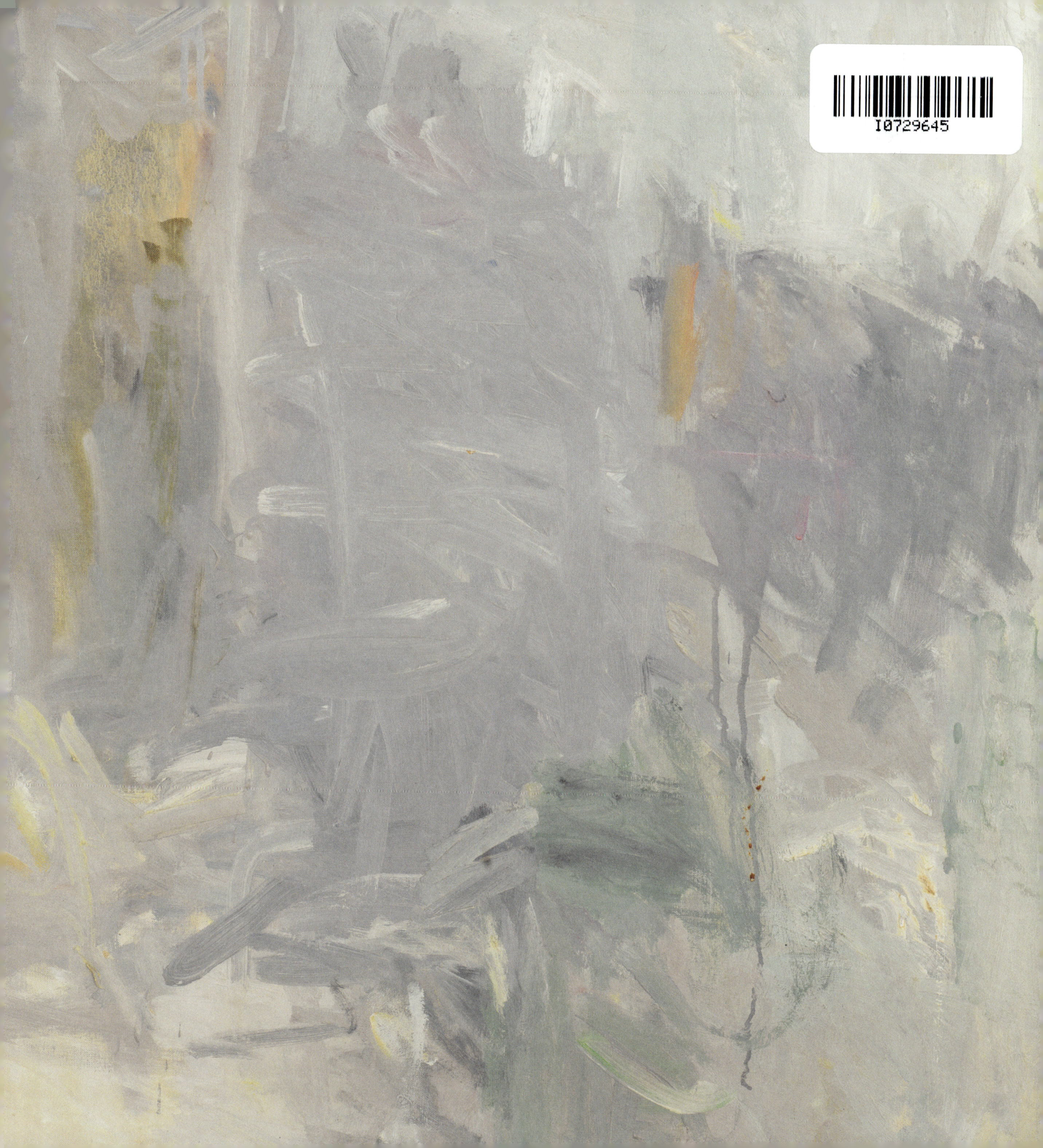

I0729645

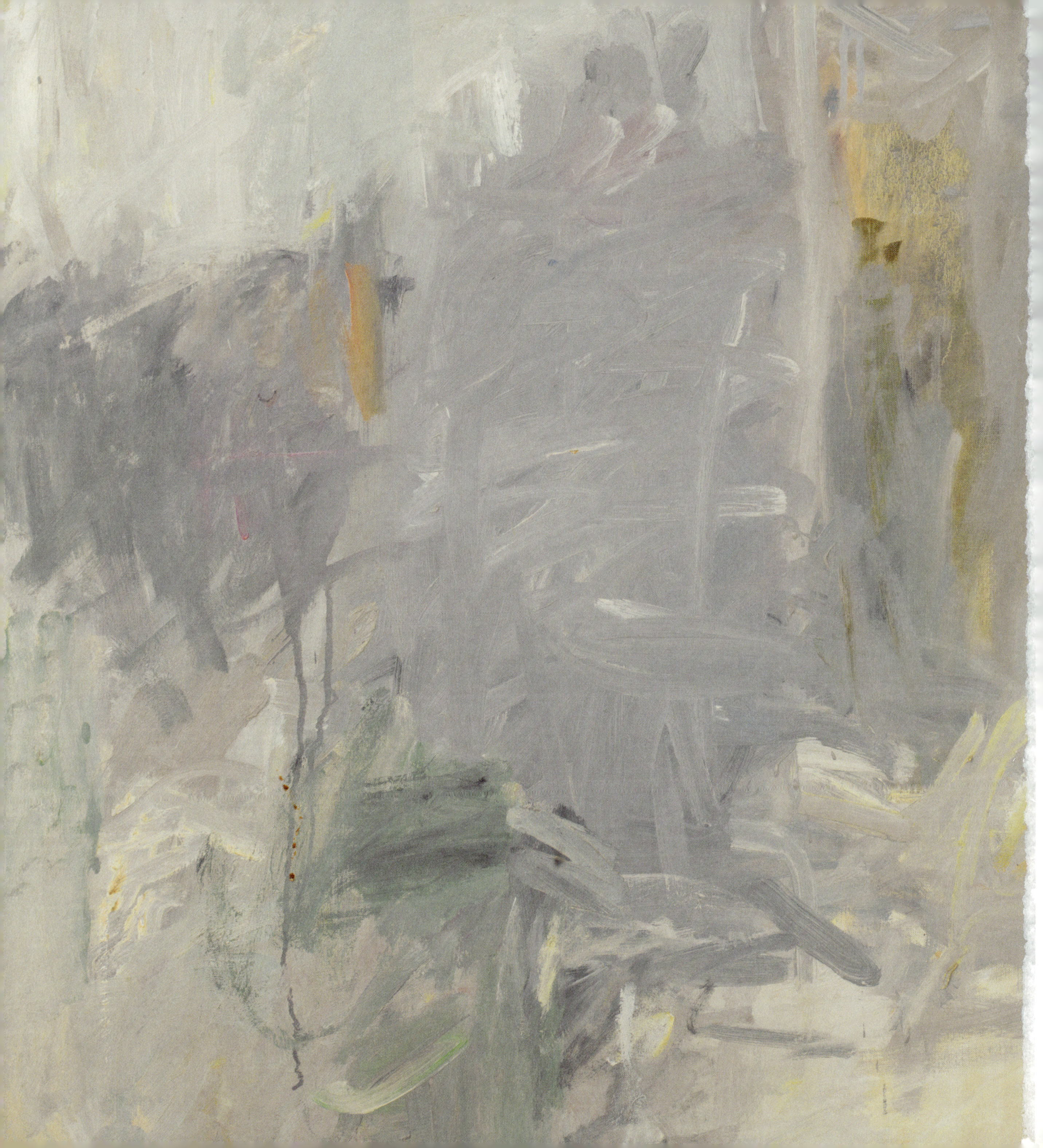

FIGURATION NEVER DIED

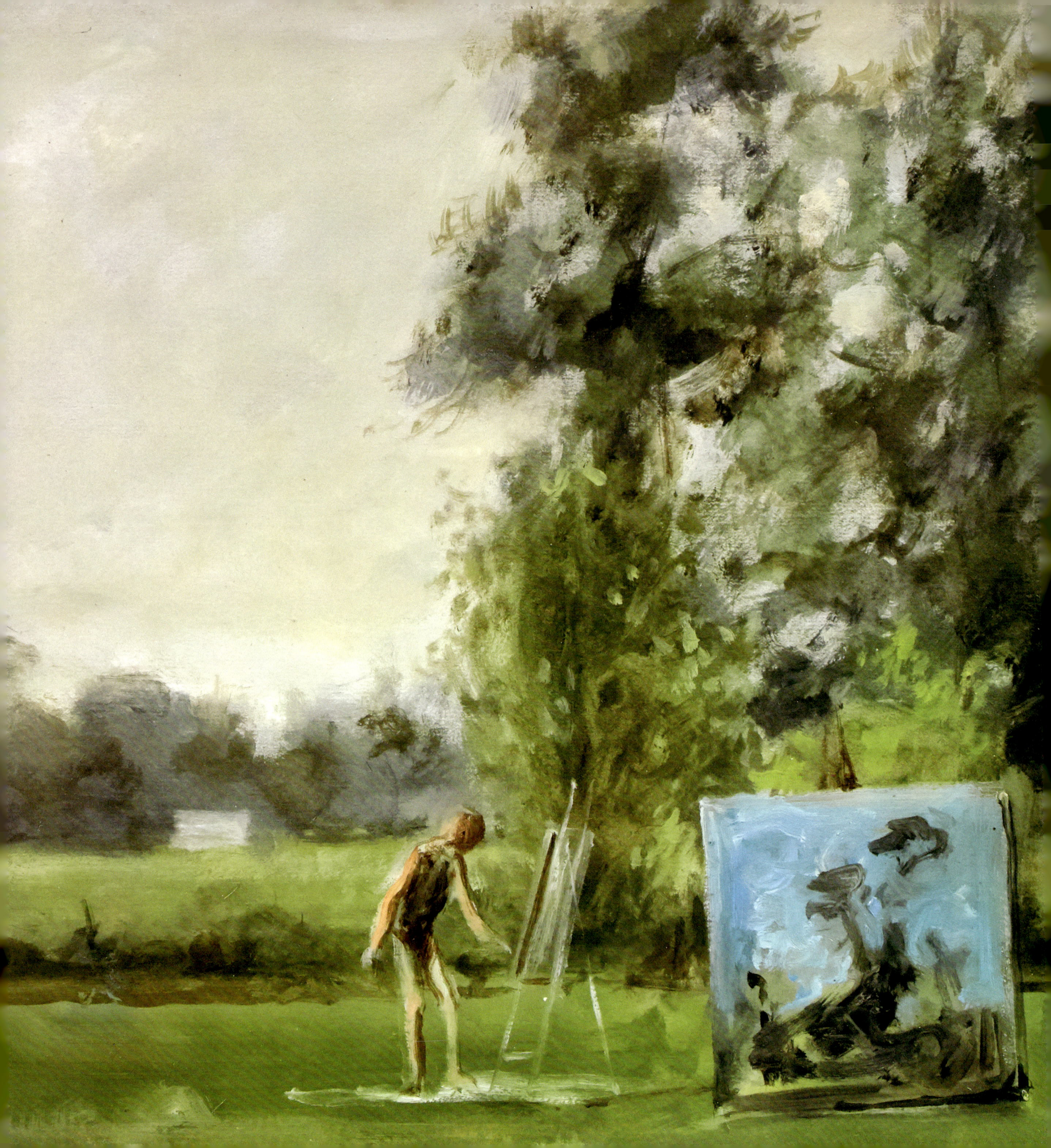

FIGURATION NEVER DIED

NEW YORK PAINTERLY PAINTING, 1950–1970

Karen Wilkin

FOREWORD BY BRUCE WEBER

THE ARTIST BOOK FOUNDATION

NORTH ADAMS

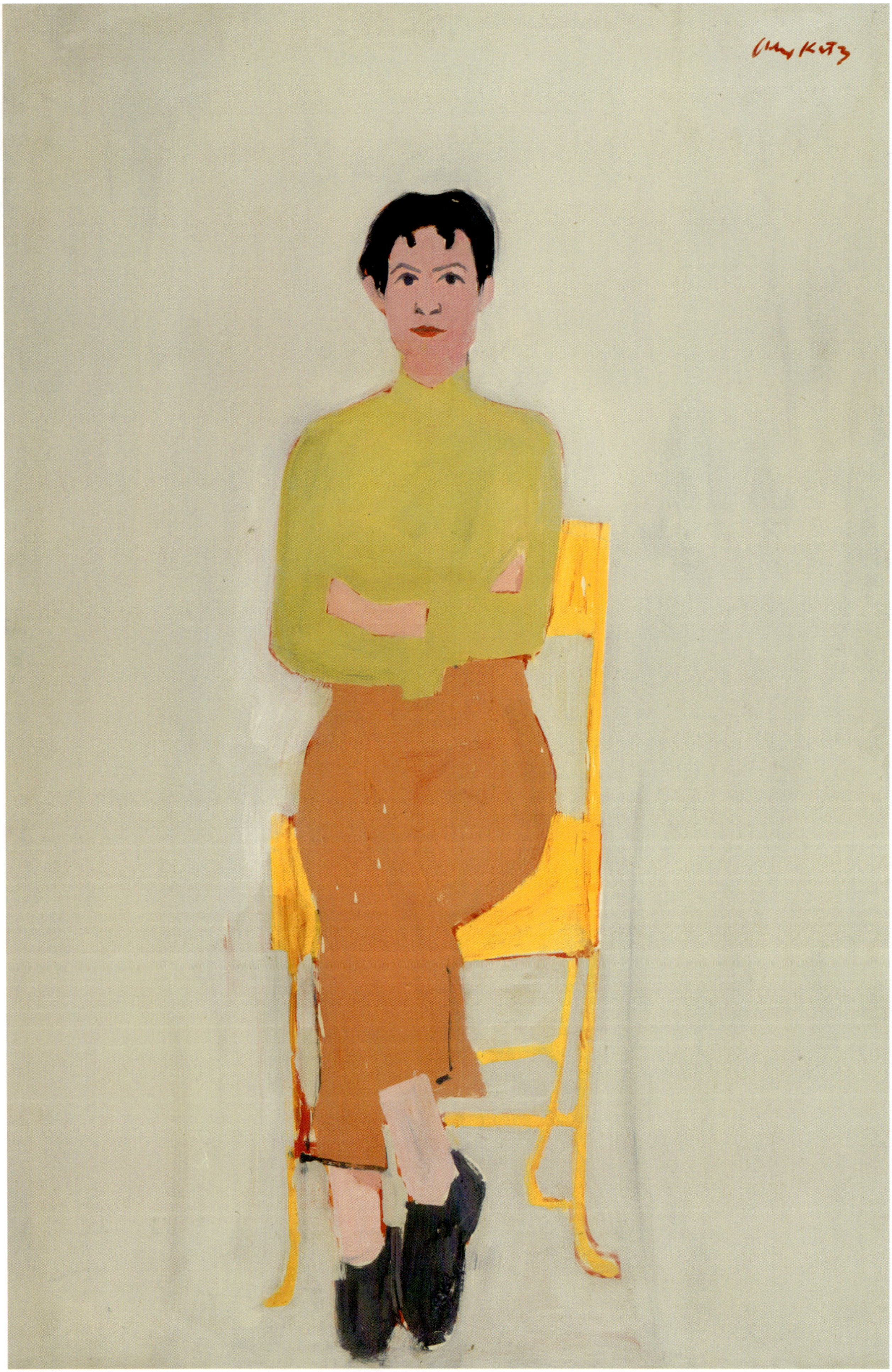

TABLE OF CONTENTS

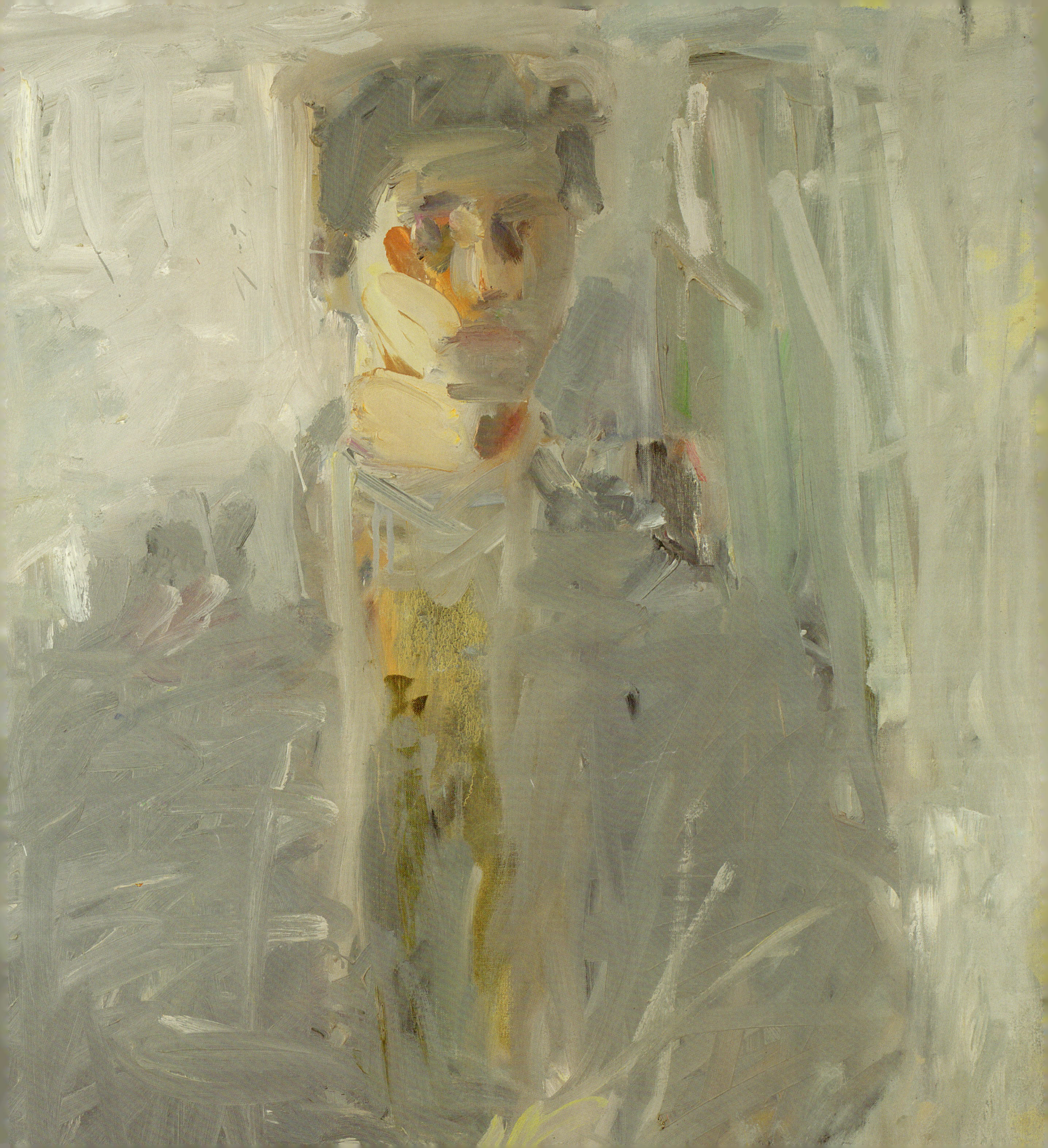

In 2014, Wolf Kahn stood at the podium in the Brattleboro Museum & Art Center, scanned the standing-room-only crowd assembled to hear his lecture titled *Control and Letting Go*, and pronounced, "Well, I guess I'm big in Brattleboro." By that time, Wolf had been spending summers in our southern Vermont town for nearly 50 years. He and his wife, Emily Mason, were beloved members of our tight-knit arts community. Many in the audience that evening knew Wolf well, and we understood that his opening remark was less aggrandizing than self-deprecating.

At 87, Wolf anguished over the fact that his place in the history of American art had not been clearly explicated. Although he obviously enjoyed the adulation he received in Brattleboro, he chafed at being called a Vermont artist. And he was ambivalent, at best, about being identified as a landscape painter or even a colorist. For someone so steeped in art history, so thoughtful about the influences of others on his work, the lack of scholarly clarity surrounding his relationships to his predecessors and peers gnawed at him.

Sometime soon after that lecture, I was discussing Wolf's plight with Stephen Hannock, who recounted that he had recently had similar conversations about the legacies of Robert De Niro, Sr., Al Kresch, and Paul Resika. It quickly became clear to us that there was a story to be told here—of a group of New York artists who came of age in the 1950s, absorbed the lessons of Abstract Expressionism, but never strayed from figurative painting, at least not for long. No sooner had the concept begun to materialize than it occurred to us that the incisive scholar and curator Karen Wilkin should be the one to tell that story. We were thrilled when she agreed to do so and could not be more pleased with how the exhibition has come to fruition.

As fate would have it, Wolf Kahn died six months before the exhibition opened. He is, none-theless, bigger than ever in Brattleboro, and all of us at the museum he helped bring into existence and nurtured until his final days are deeply gratified to have played a part in illuminating his legacy and those of the nine other remarkable artists featured in *Figuration Never Died*.

Danny Lichtenfeld, Director
Brattleboro Museum & Art Center
August, 2020

Wolf Kahn, detail of *Self-Portrait*, 1959.
Oil on canvas, 42 x 40 in. (106.7 x 101.6 cm).
Wolf Kahn and Emily Mason.

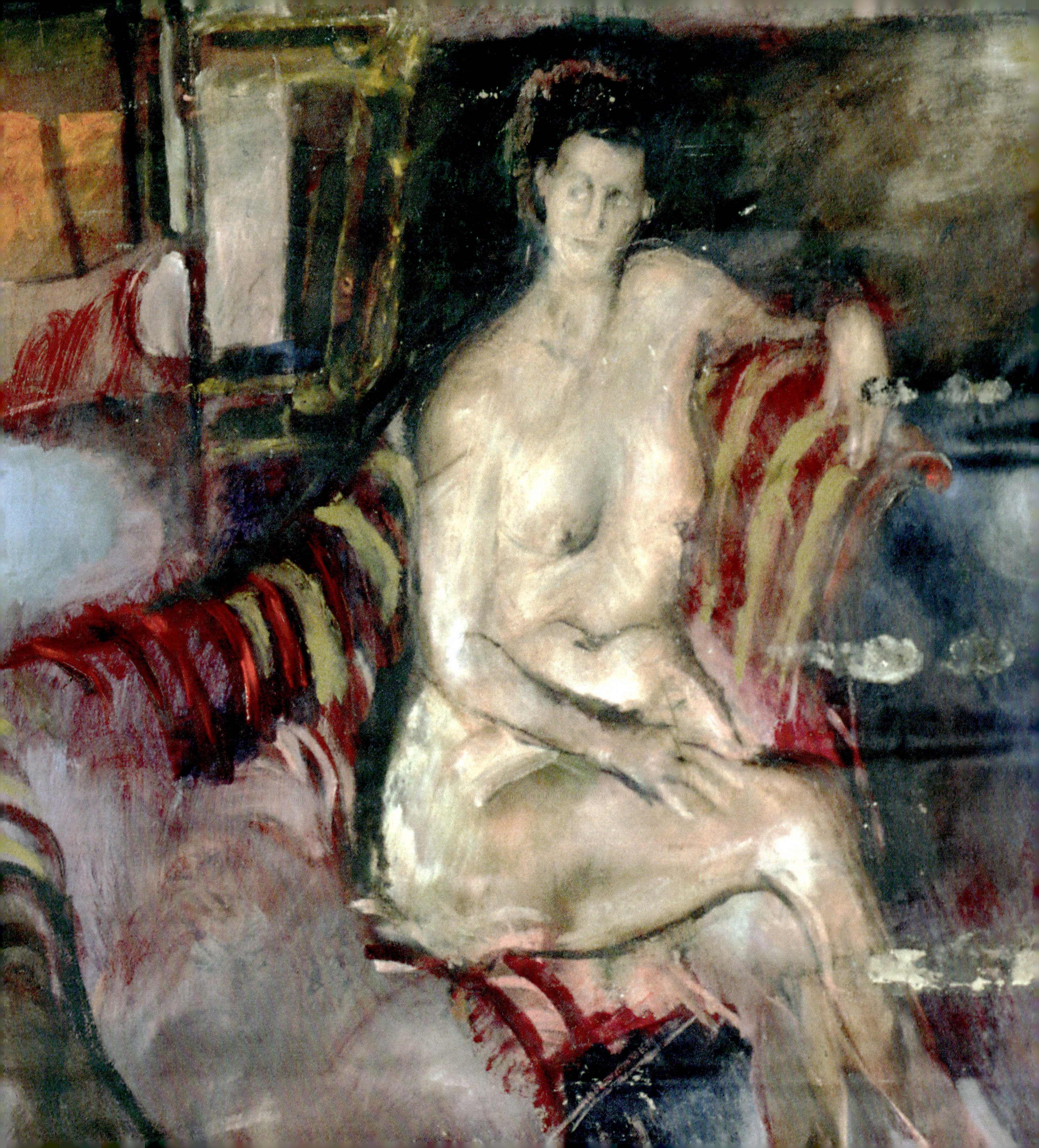

am deeply grateful to all the lenders to this exhibition for allowing their works to be seen by a larger public. Special thanks are due for their invaluable assistance to Philippe Alexandre and Marie Evans, Alexandre Gallery; James Barron, James Barron Art; Lori Bookstein and Joseph Bunge, Bookstein Projects; Eric Brown, Eric Brown Arts Group; Ulrika and Joel Citron, and Mary Anne Butler; Lorraine DeLaney; Colby College Museum of Art; Patricia Magnani, Registrar, and Tracy Fitzpatrick, Neuberger Museum of Art; the Paul Georges Estate; Costas Grimaldis, C. Grimaldis Gallery; Henry Justin, Center for Figurative Painting; Wolf Kahn; Albert Kresch and Elizabeth Kresch; Heidi Lange, D.C. Moore Gallery; Alicia G. Longwell, Parrish Art Museum; Jessica May and Jaime DeSimone, Portland Museum of Art, ME; David Moos, David Moos Art Advisory; Mariska Nietzman, Paul Kasmin Gallery; Hart Perry; Blair and Paul Resika; Nathan Resika; John and Tania Secor; Rex Stevens, Estate of Grace Hartigan; and Diana Urbaska. I am indebted to Stephen Hannock for initially involving me in this project and to Leslie Pell van Breen and Deborah Thompson of The Artist Book Foundation for their crucial expertise and hard work, and to Ahmad Yassir for his contributions. My thanks to Danny Lichtenfeld, director, and Mara Williams, chief curator, of the Brattleboro Museum & Art Center for their enthusiastic support of *Figuration Never Died*, and especially to Sarah Freeman, exhibitions manager, whose tireless efforts made the exhibition a reality.

Karen Wilkin
July 2020

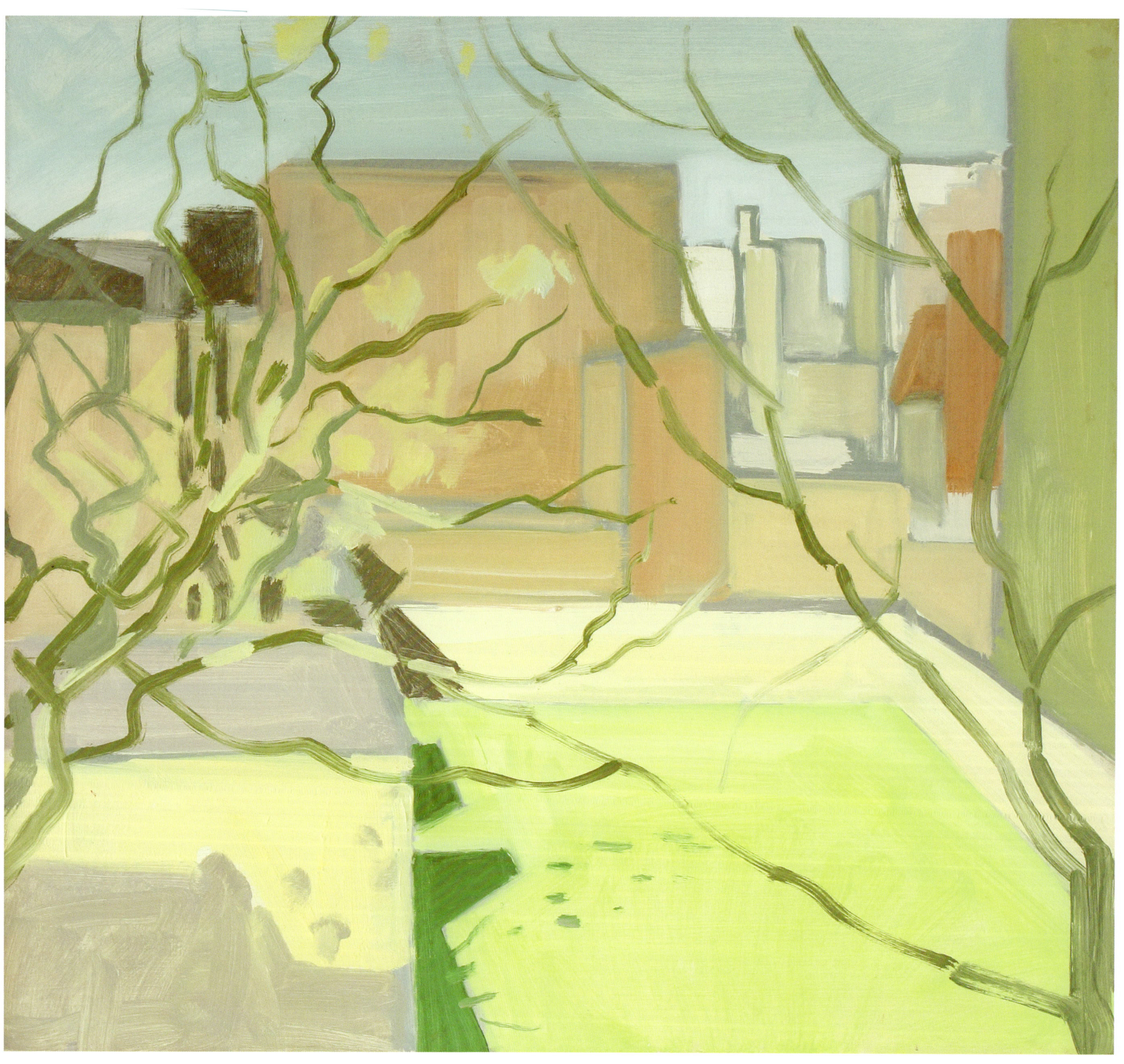

FOREWORD

I am excited to write this foreword to Karen Wilkin's publication that will accompany the Brattleboro Museum & Art Center's exhibition, *Figuration Never Died*. Her essay adds a new dimension to the history of a most significant chapter in recent Modernism, enlarging our conception of New York School painting and providing a fuller context for our greater understanding and appreciation of today's multiplicity of approaches to art. Wilkin has frequently touched on this topic in her extensive writing on twentieth-century American art, but this publication gives her a unique opportunity to further develop her insights and to bring together at the Brattleboro Museum & Art Center examples from two momentous decades of what she calls "New York painterly paintings."

Wilkin reveals to us how, during the days when Abstract Expressionism dominated the New York–centered international art scene, the very act of insisting on figuration was considered a gesture simultaneously radical and anachronistic—or at the least, hopelessly unfashionable. Yet, as she points out in her essay, that figurative "gesture" persisted, remaining both radical and unfashionable, throughout the movements of Color Field, Pop art, Minimalism, and Post-Modernism that followed Abstract Expressionism.

Focusing primarily on 10 artists, Robert De Niro, Sr., Lois Dodd, Jane Freilicher, Paul Georges, Grace Hartigan, Wolf Kahn, Alex Katz, Albert Kresch, Paul Resika, and Anne Tabachnick, Wilkin explains how many of them moved forward from their early interest in abstraction to engage in traditional painting genres while infusing an energetic, painterly approach into their work and continuing to ground their style and structure in abstraction. Many of the artists emerged from the shadow cast by Abstract Expressionism even as they continued to draw on numerous principles and precepts of that American school. The artists who dissented from abstract orthodoxy were united in their insistence on the enduring significance of figuration. Many embraced landscape and still-life painting specifically, even when these subjects also seemed irretrievably out of fashion. All felt in some degree limited by abstraction and were, in fact, part of a much larger group of American artists emerging at the time who wanted to go beyond it. They aspired, as the landscape painter and art writer Rackstraw Downes noted, to "enlarge and increase the resources of painting."[1]

Lois Dodd, *View from the Window, May, June*, 1968.
Oil on Masonite, 15½ x 17 in. (39.4 x 43.2 cm).
Private collection, Portland, ME.
© Lois Dodd, courtesy Alexandre Gallery, New York, NY.
© 2020 Lois Dodd / Licensed by VAGA at Artist Rights Society (ARS), New York, NY.

In 2013, I had the pleasure of organizing the exhibition *See It Loud: Seven Post-War American Painters* at the National Academy Museum in New York City and authoring the accompanying publication. The display featured the work of Resika, Georges, and Kresch as well as Leland Bell, Neil Welliver, Stanley Lewis, and Peter Heinemann. All began their careers at a time when abstraction and representation were polarized in the American art world, and all initially worked as abstractionists before embracing the possibilities of a more dialectical synthesis of the two approaches.

The 2013 show occupied the academy's entire exhibition space and featured paintings on loan from the collection of the Center for Figurative Painting in New York City. The center had been established in 2000 by the collector Henry Justin for curators, researchers, painters, gallerists, writers, teachers, and students as well as the public to view the assembled works. In short, it was meant to be seen by anyone interested in the art of painting. Justin hoped that the center would highlight directions in American figurative, landscape, and still-life painting of the second half of the twentieth century, but today the collection can be accessed only by appointment. And that is in part why this new exhibition and its accompanying publication are so important. Like *See It Loud*, it has been organized with the hope of encouraging a meaningful reassessment of postwar American representational painting that will contribute to restoring balance to the historical view of American art in the second half of the past century.

Looking back on the exhibition and catalogue of *See It Loud* and now reading the pages of Karen Wilkin's study, I am again stirred by an appreciation of the courageous and pioneering roles played by Paul Resika and Paul Georges, who turned from abstraction and toward representation at the height of the New York School's global triumph in the early 1950s. Critics and public alike saw Abstract Expressionism as a kind of conquest over the past, a victory of strictly modern, purely American invention. Resika and Georges, however, led a dissenting vanguard who acknowledged the new movement but nevertheless refused to break with European artists of the past, whom they regarded as beloved ancestors. At the very crest of the Abstract Expressionist wave, Resika and Georges developed their own representational and painterly directions that were inspired by their close study of the work of such Old Masters as Titian, Rembrandt van Rijn, Francesco Guardi, and Canaletto, as well as such nineteenth-century European painters as Gustave Courbet, Edouard Manet, and Jean-Baptiste-Camille Corot.

Resika and Georges studied with Hans Hofmann in the late 1940s. They were among the first of his students in America to recognize that Hofmann's teaching, based on an amalgam of formalist principles, could be applied equally to abstract and representational painting. They recognized that his openness to nature and working from a still life or a model opened a door the orthodox worshippers of abstraction had rudely slammed shut. It was a door to new painterly possibilities. As the art writer Cynthia Goodman has observed, Hofmann "was adamant that others express themselves in relation to nature. Otherwise, the artist's work would risk lapsing into mere decoration and repetition."[2]

Clearly, Hans Hofmann wanted his students to comprehend the figure as well as the landscape and object as a system of intersecting planes. He wanted them to develop the ability to convey the dynamic play of tensions in space that surrounded and intersected with these forms. He instructed his students to look at the planes and to establish them through geometric shapes that expanded the space, and taught that the relationship of these planes had to be subordinated to the overall rhythm of the work. In fact, his resonant message to those who would listen was that the making of abstract form is a grammar driving all visual expression, whether American, European, modern, traditional, abstract, or representational.

This publication is an important contribution to telling the fuller story of the development of postwar American painting. Karen Wilkin's essay provides a welcome, broad, and engaged understanding figuration's richness and depth of achievement in the United States following in the wake of Hans Hofmann and Abstract Expressionism.

Bruce Weber
Saugerties, New York
November 24, 2019

ENDNOTES

1 Rackstraw Downes, "What the Sixties Mean to Me," *Art Journal* 32, no. 2 (Winter 1974/1975): 127.
2 Cynthia Goodman, "Hans Hofmann as Teacher," *Arts* 53 (April 1979): 124.

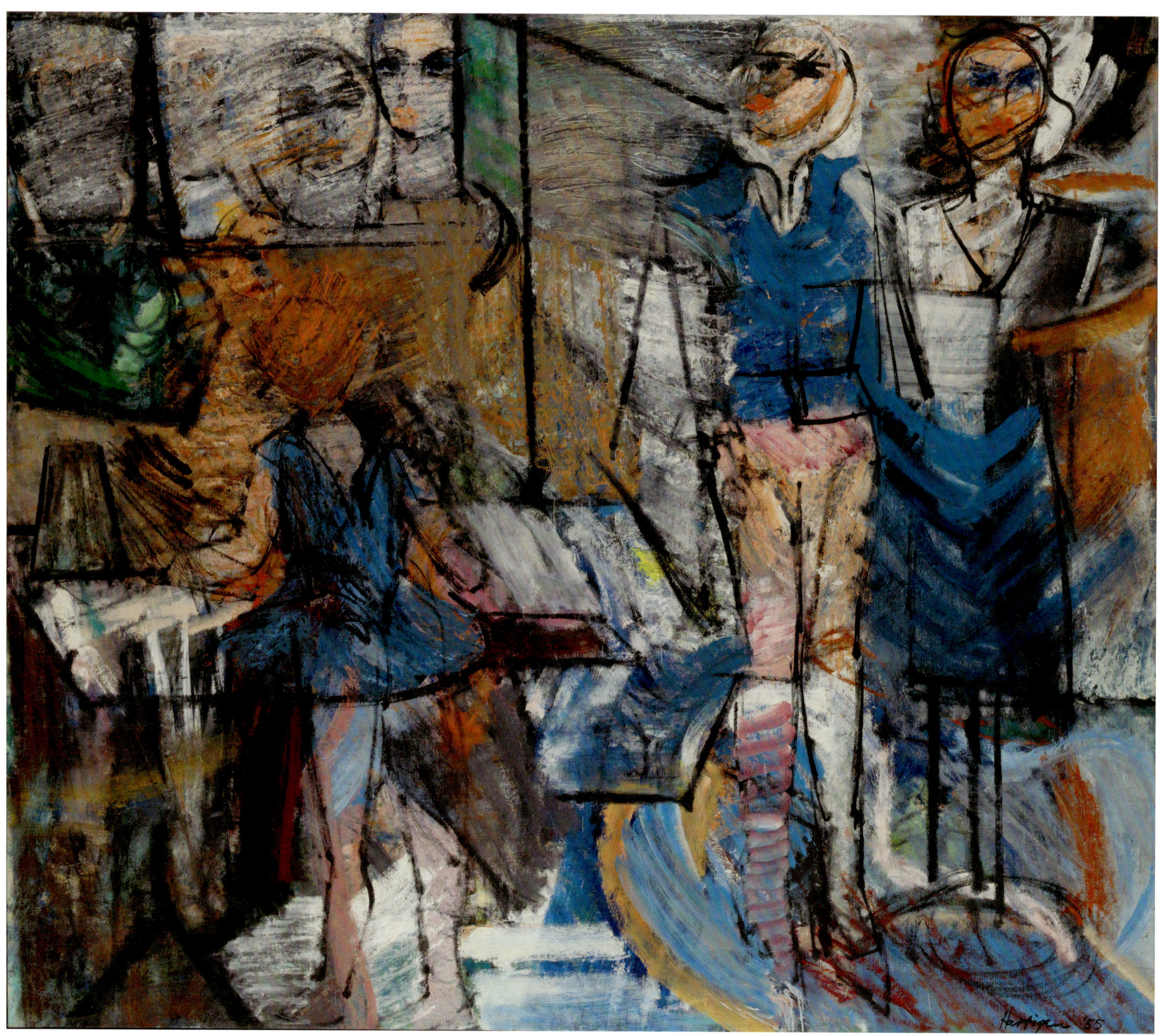

FIGURATION NEVER DIED

I n May 1962, *Recent Painting USA: The Figure* opened at the Museum of Modern Art (MoMA), a major exhibition selected by the museum's director, Alfred H. Barr Jr., from an open call. The museum's last large overview of current art, shown in early 1951, was *Abstract Painting and Sculpture in America*. Nonrepresentational art dominated the selection, as the title promised, although there were three paintings by Stuart Davis who always insisted that he was not an abstract artist, as well as works by John Marin that, while hardly literal, included recognizable elements.

MoMA's focus had largely been on abstraction during the decade between *Abstract Painting and Sculpture in America* and *Recent Painting USA: The Figure*, but it could be argued that current figurative art was not entirely ignored. Dorothy C. Miller's surveys of the contemporary scene—beginning with *15 Americans*, in 1952, and *Twelve Americans* in 1956—stressed abstraction; William Baziotes, Jackson Pollock, Mark Rothko, and Clifford Still were featured in 1952; and James Brooks, Sam Francis, Philip Guston, and Franz Kline in 1956. But artists who made explicit reference to perception and the figure, including Edwin Dickinson, Grace Hartigan, and Larry Rivers, were also part of the mix. In 1959, however, *16 Americans* was devoted exclusively to abstract artists, including Jasper Johns, Ellsworth Kelly, Louise Nevelson, and Frank Stella. The 1963 iteration, titled simply *Americans*, tilted heavily toward abstraction but also included unabashedly figurative work by Richard Lindner, Marisol, and James Rosenquist. Nonetheless, most of MoMA's shows in the 1950s and 1960s favored the nonobjective and the invented over the perceptual, and the few solo exhibitions awarded to painters in those years included Pollock, Rothko, Arshile Gorky, and Hans Hofmann. *Recent Painting USA: The Figure* seems to have been intended to redress the imbalance.

Not everyone was convinced. Previewing *Recent Painting USA: The Figure*, the painter and writer Fairfield Porter wrote in *Art in Its Own Terms*:

> The exhibition opening at the Museum of Modern Art in May has the purpose of "exploring recent directions in one aspect of American painting: the renewed interest in the human figure." Since painters have never stopped painting the

Grace Hartigan, *Showcase*, 1955.
Oil on canvas, $69^{7}/_{16}$ x $80^{5}/_{16}$ in. (176.1 x 204.3 cm).
The Metropolitan Museum of Art, New York,
NY. Purchase, Roy R. and Marie S. Neuberger
Foundation Inc., gift, 1956, 56.199.
Image copyright © The Metropolitan Museum of
Art. Image source: Art Resource, NY.

figure, and since the exhibition shows no change on the part of particular painters from a non-objective to a figurative style, it could be said to represent a renewed interest in the figure on the part of critics and the audience rather than among painters.[1]

Since Porter himself had never stopped painting the figure, he must have felt that he spoke with special authority, but the exhibition itself also reinforced his point as it included 74 painters who worked with the figure in diverse ways, chosen from submissions by 1,841 artists from across the entire country.[2] Those selected came from 18 states, mainly New York and the surrounding area and California, with a few expatriates based in Europe and Mexico. The number of submissions suggests that even though figurative work was occasionally in exhibitions during the decade preceding *Recent Painting USA: The Figure,* MoMA's curators and director may not have been paying enough attention to what was happening in the studios. As Porter suggested, it was their interest that had flagged, not the artists'.

Yet there may have been reasons for their lack of enthusiasm. Few of the names of the painters chosen from that vast pool of submissions resonate today, even though we must assume that they appeared to be the best of the lot at the time.[3] We note Elmer Bischoff, Elaine de Kooning, Richard Lindner, Robert De Niro, Sr., Leon Golub, Nathan Oliveira, Larry Rivers, and Paul Wonner as we read the checklist, plus a few individuals known mainly to specialists, but the great majority of the 63 men and 11 women remains unfamiliar. Porter acknowledged that the exhibition "does not pretend to survey all the figurative work that is being done,"[4] and regretted the absence of Alex Katz and Paul Georges. Many other inventive artists could be listed among the noteworthy omissions. Of course, since the exhibition catalogue states that "the selection was determined by the entries received,"[5] curatorial shortcomings may not be the only explanation.

Even if we acknowledge Porter's contention that "painters have never stopped painting the figure," adventurous painting in New York during the 1950s was generally seen as synonymous with abstraction, especially with highly charged, gestural Abstract Expressionism

Fairfield Porter (American, 1907–1975), *Laurence at the Breakfast Table, No. 4*, 1953. Oil on canvas, 40⅛ x 30 in. (101.9 x 76.2 cm). Parrish Art Museum, Water Mill, NY. Gift of the Estate of Fairfield Porter, 1980.10.58. © 2020 The Estate of Fairfield Porter / Artists Rights Society (ARS), New York, NY.

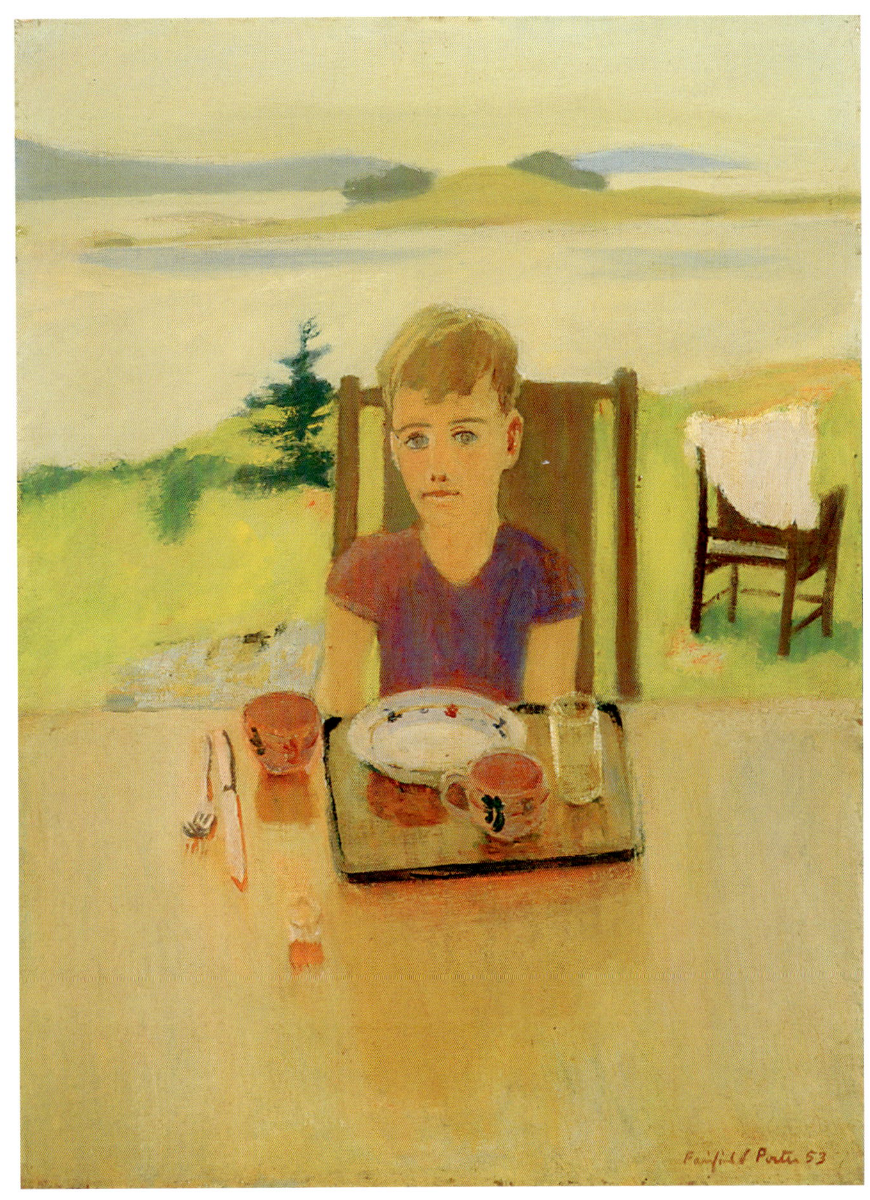

and the contingent, wet-into-wet approach of Willem de Kooning. The story is familiar: the most forward-looking artists of the period, both recognized and aspiring, gathered in Greenwich Village at the Cedar Tavern, the Artists' Club, and neighborhood cafeterias, to hold forth about their shared conviction that abstractness was a necessity and that the source of art was the unconscious. They were equally certain that an "authentic" painting was infused with every aspect of its author's personality and that the history of a painting's evolution was an important part of its meaning. Assertive gestures were not only declarations of individuality, like handwriting, but were also carriers of emotion. Layering was essential to "authenticity" as an indication of the painting's previous state and possible future, a sign of the artist's anxiety in the face of the existential instability of the moment. For many of them, a sense of expansiveness and "all-overness" was also as crucial as the evidence of past states and the implications of future possibilities. It announced that the painting was a continuous surface of a particular dimension, inscribed with a record of the artist's willed and unwilled intentions. All-overness implied that the painting was a fragment of a larger continuum, suggesting boundlessness and endless possibility. If the dragged layering of gestural abstraction evoked the agonized indecisions of the present, all-overness could be read as emblematic of a desire for the infinite, even the eternal.

These ideas, more or less articles of faith among the first generation of Abstract Expressionists, remained seductive to younger artists, many of whom looked to de Kooning as their model. Gestural, layered, emotionally charged abstraction—"painterly" abstraction, to borrow a term from the Swiss-German art historian Heinrich Wölfflin—was so common among second-generation hopefuls that Clement Greenberg coined the term the "Tenth Street touch" to describe their approach, complaining that it had "spread through abstract painting like a blight during the 1950s."[6]

Some dissenting younger artists were immune to the blight. One faction, taking its cue from "nonpainterly" senior artists such as Jackson Pollock, Barnett Newman, and Mark Rothko, while following the lead of their contemporary Helen Frankenthaler, whose luminous, disembodied stain/soak abstractions pointed the way to other directions, rejected not only the facture and appearance of gestural Abstract Expressionism but also its overt drama. Their dispassionate, opulent investigations of the eloquence of color were later labeled Color Field. The Pop artists shared the Color Field painters' desire for detachment, adding irony and adopting the imagery, conventions, and anonymous handling of materials associated with advertising and mass culture. Still other nonconformist young painters of the period carved out territory of their own. Although many had begun as abstract artists, they abandoned abstraction to make the world around them the basis of their work, painting from direct observation and memory, and often looking to the history of art as a starting point. Like the first generation of Abstract Expressionists, and in contrast to the Color Field and Pop painters, these artists remained enthusiastic about the physicality of oil paint, using a fluent, urgent touch to translate their perceptions into a variety of individual languages, almost all informed by the hand. Yet for all their appreciation of the sensuality and responsiveness of oil paint, they resisted the dragged "Tenth Street touch." Instead, they detached gesture from the overt emotion it signaled for the previous generation, inventing a new kind of "painterly" painting more indebted to Edouard Manet's early work than to de Kooning.

This exhibition at the Brattleboro Museum & Art Center focuses on 10 inventive artists from this generation, whom we could describe as painterly: Robert De Niro, Sr. (1922–2003), Lois Dodd (1927–), Jane Freilicher (1924–2014), Paul Georges (1923–2002), Grace Hartigan (1922–2008), Wolf Kahn (1927–2020), Alex Katz (1927–), Albert Kresch (1922–), Paul Resika (1928–), and Anne Tabachnik (1927–1995).[7] They are linked not only by their mutual fascination with making reference to the visible, but also by their closeness in age, friendships, and shared experiences in the small New York art world of the 1950s and 1960s.

There seem to have been multiple triggers for their stubborn attraction to figuration. Many—De Niro, Freilicher, Georges, Kahn, Kresch, Resika, and Tabachnick—were students of Hans Hofmann and so thoroughly absorbed his ideas about the dynamic construction of pictures that they always remain apparent no matter how referential their imagery. That former Hofmann students were exploring painting from perception is not altogether surprising. Kahn noted that Hofmann "was interested in people who were interested in representation. He used to say that the problem with modern art is, it has no human content."[8] For Georges, Kahn, and Resika, encounters with Old Master art and with the specificity of place during extended sojourns in Europe—Georges in France, and Kahn and Resika in Italy—were also crucial to their evolution. Georges had a lifelong aspiration to the Grand Manner, while Resika's work of the 1950s and 1960s is particularly informed by the masters he studied closely in Europe, just as it echoes the characteristics of locations in southern France, Mexico, Cape Cod, and more that he got to know well in those years. The same could be said of Kahn's landscapes that for decades have reflected his deep familiarity with rural New England where he worked for part of every year. Kahn traced the beginning of his awareness of the effect of place to living in Venice in 1958. "My style changed…. For the first time I discovered a peculiar light. I mean, you might say a local kind of light. Which I tried very hard to capture."[9]

Dodd's and Katz's formations were different, although she also spent a considerable amount of time in Italy as a young painter studying Old Master art as a firm underpinning to her plainspoken Yankee sensibility. She and Katz were involved early on with the 10th Street Tanager Gallery, which Dodd helped to found, and they showed there together. They had also been at the Skowhegan School of Painting and Sculpture in Madison, Maine, at the same time; it was a summer session of plein-air painting, with long-lasting repercussions for their work that soon led them both to spend part of every year in the state. That ambitious young New York painters such as Katz and Dodd were painting figures, farm animals, and pastoral landscapes in rural Maine in the 1950s might seem unexpected, yet the explanation is simple. Georges summed up the general attitude of his colleagues at the time when he told an interviewer, "I was bored to death with Abstract Expressionism, even though I liked some of it."[10]

Despite their rejection of what was seen in progressive circles as the dominant mode of painting, many of the younger generation were part of the downtown vanguard scene, frequenting the Club, the Cedar Tavern, and the Waldorf Cafeteria. Katz called the Club "a fantastic education for me." He maintained that "it hardened the thinking a great deal hanging around all those guys. There were an awful lot of bright guys. Someone would say something and some would look at him and they'd jump on it. You know, it was like you were sloppy. And you weren't sloppy again that way."[11] Hartigan told an interviewer that when she lived in her downtown studio, after painting all day "I'd walk over to the Cedar Bar and just see who I'd run into."[12] Kahn remembered a cross-generational "sense of camaraderie, which has since, kind of, gone by the boards."[13] Porter, a contemporary and friend of the first generation of Abstract Expressionists, was particularly friendly with younger artists who shared his interest in figuration. He occasionally painted with Georges on Long Island, sometimes joined by Resika. Hartigan, who showed at the recently established Tibor de Nagy Gallery, was also in close contact with Porter; he exhibited there and wrote reviews of the gallery's exhibitions. Katz, recalling his contemporaries' generally negative reaction to his 1959 show at Tanager Gallery—paintings of "solitary figures on the ground" that he described as his "first really adult show"—said that "the older guys were terrific. You know, de Kooning came in and he was terribly sweet. He said 'They're like photographs but they're paintings. Don't let them knock you out of it.' …Guston was just terribly nice to me, and Jack Tworkov and all the guys down there were very nice."[14] Hartigan remembered that when she first started to move away from abstraction and spent a year working from Velázquez, Goya, and Rubens with a "fairly free, open brush,"[15] her friends thought she was reactionary. "Bill de Kooning was nice about it because Bill had tremendous training in Europe, of course, and he knows that young artists go through times like that." Others, she recalled, "felt that I had lost my nerve."[16] They didn't change their minds when she began basing her compositions on displays in shops and shop windows in her downtown neighborhood, anchoring her free-wheeling paintings in quotidian experience.

It is worth remembering that independent-minded as these young explorers of the figurative were, they were neither unique nor unprecedented. De Kooning sent a shockwave through the art world in 1953 with the first exhibition of his *Woman* series (which he

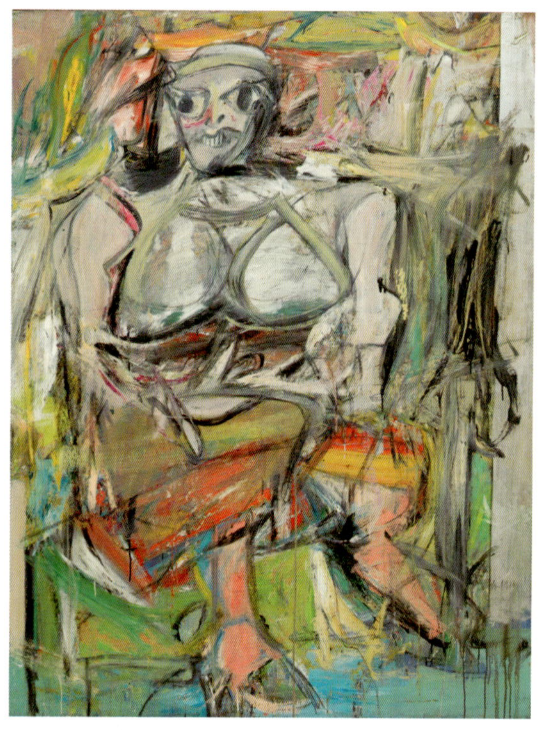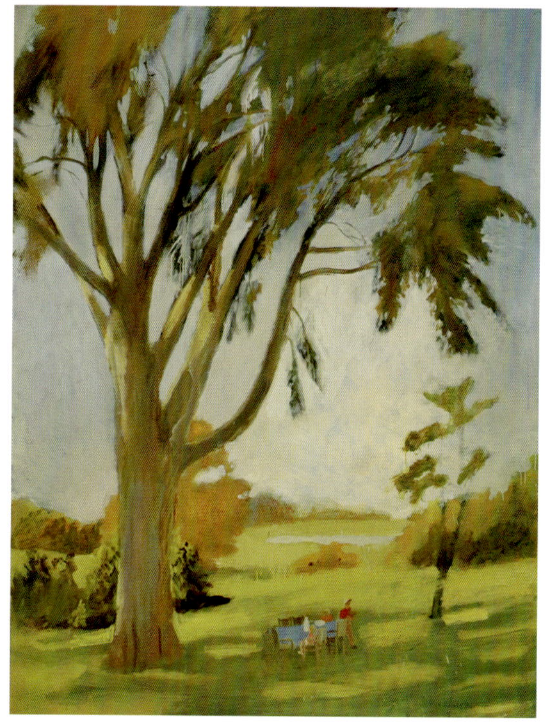

began painting in 1950) at Sidney Janis Gallery. Porter had been painting perceptual land-scapes, interiors, and figures since the late 1940s, although he later said that he had been provoked by Greenberg's declaration, in response to the *Woman* series, that it was no longer possible to paint figuratively. "I thought," Porter recalled, 'If that's what he says, I think I will do just exactly what he says I can't do.' I might have become an abstract painter except for that."[17]

LEFT: **Willem de Kooning** (American, 1904–1997), *Woman I*, ca. 1950–1952.
Oil and metallic paint on canvas, 75⅞ x 58 in. (192.7 x 147.3 cm).
Museum of Modern Art, New York, NY. 478.1953.
© 2020 The Willem de Kooning Foundation / Artists Rights Society (ARS), New York, NY. Digital Image © The Museum of Modern Art/Licensed by SCALA / Art Resource, NY.

RIGHT: **Fairfield Porter** (American, 1907–1975), *Lunch Under the Elm Tree*, 1954.
Oil on canvas, 78 x 59⅞ (198.1 x 152 cm).
Parrish Art Museum, Water Mill, NY. Gift of the Estate of Fairfield Porter, 1980.10.65.
© 2020 The Estate of Fairfield Porter / Artists Rights Society (ARS), New York, NY.

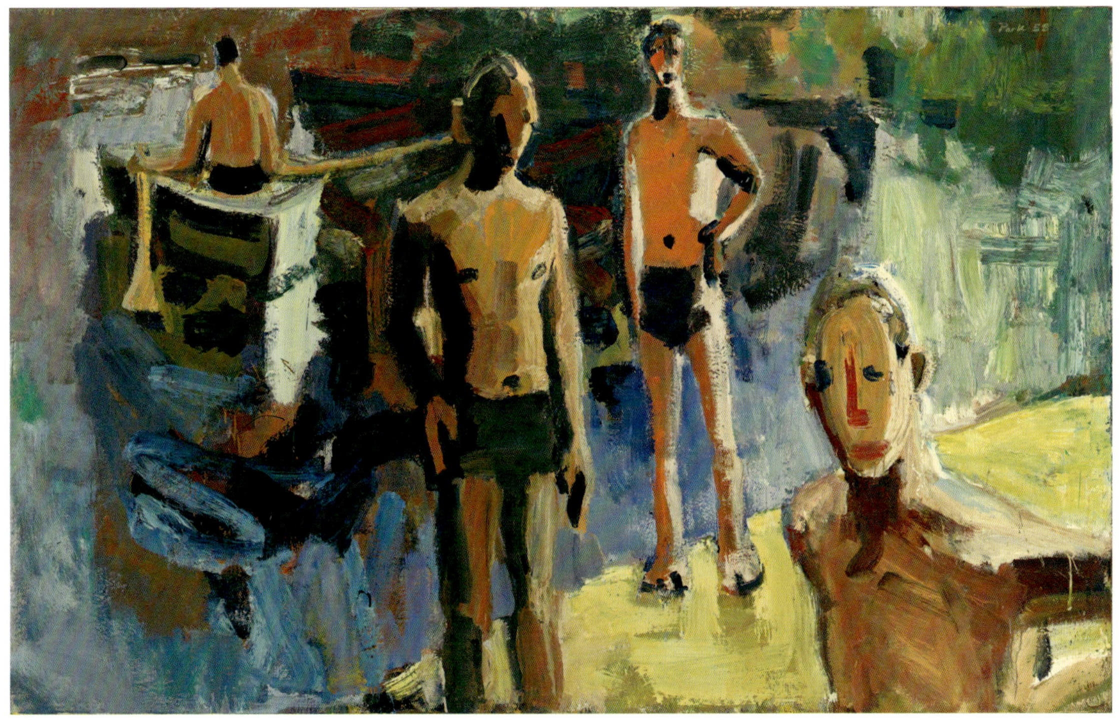

David Park (American, 1911–1960), *Four Men*, 1958. Oil on canvas, 57$\frac{1}{8}$ x 92$\frac{1}{16}$ in. (145.1 x 233.8 cm). Whitney Museum of American Art, New York, NY. Purchase, with funds from an anonymous donor, 59.27. Courtesy of Hackett Mill, representative of the Estate of David Park. Digital image © Whitney Museum of American Art / Licensed by Scala / Art Resource, NY.

Something similar was happening in California. At some point in 1950, David Park (1911–1960) took a load of his abstract paintings to the dump in Berkeley. A statement he made in 1952 helps to explain his action:

> I believe the best painting America has produced is the current non-objective direction. However, I often miss the sting that I believe a more descriptive reference to some fixed subject can make. Quite often, even the very fine non-objective canvases seem to me to be so visually beautiful that I find them insufficiently troublesome, not personal enough.[18]

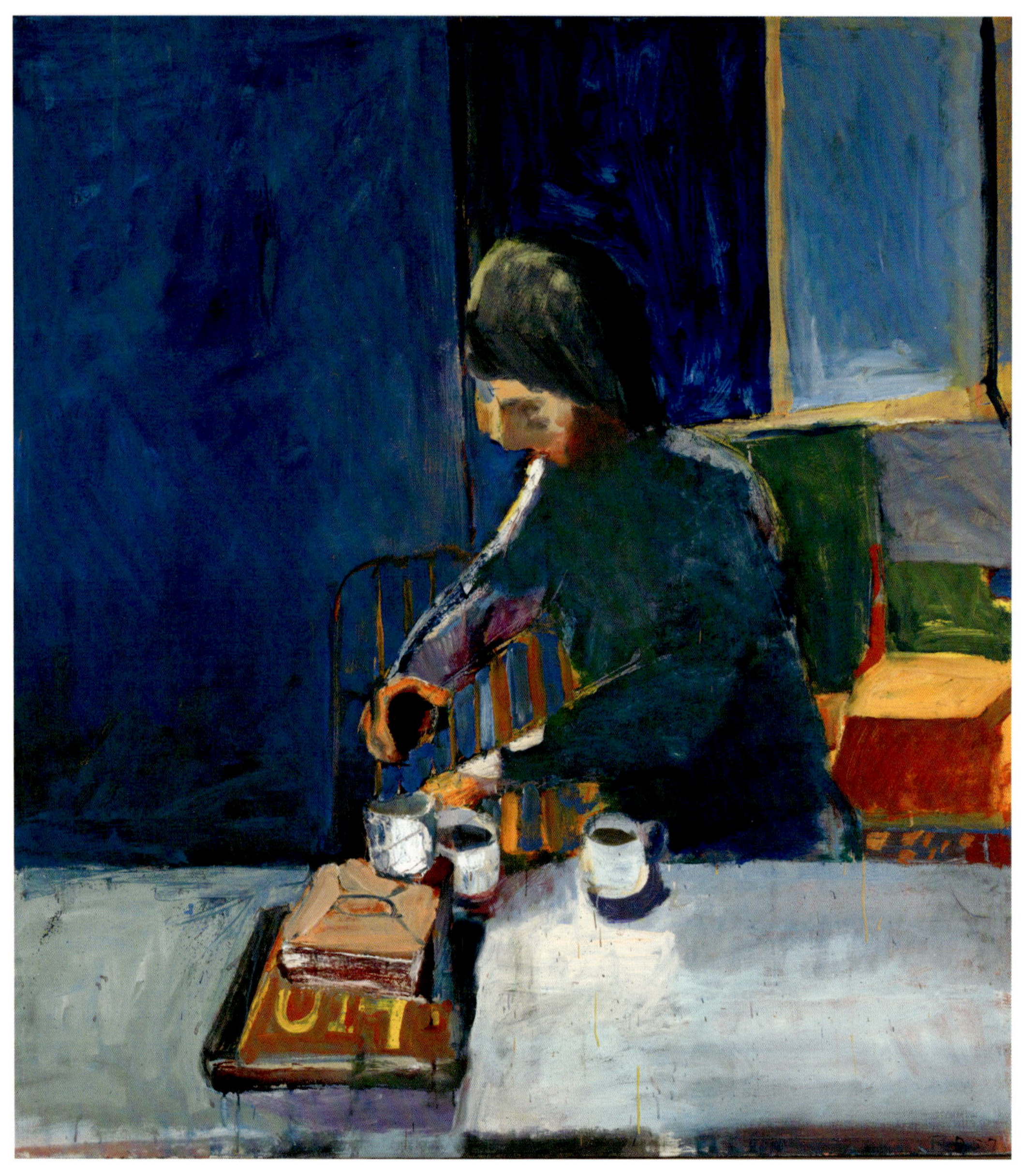

After repudiating his previous work, Park began making the broadly stroked figurative paintings for which he is known, co-opting Abstract Expressionist gesture for the image. Park's friends, including Elmer Bischoff, Joan Brown, Richard Diebenkorn, and Paul Wonner followed suit, banding together for life-drawing sessions and exploring similar territory in their canvases. When their work was first seen in New York, beginning with Park's solo exhibition at Staempfli Gallery in 1959, it was seen as a challenge to the primacy of abstraction.

Despite the tangled cross-connections and overlaps in the histories, formations, and friendships among the 10 artists in this exhibition, each is obviously a distinct individual. And for all their common commitment to reference, for some, memory and allusion often are as important as perception in generating their imagery. De Niro's way of constructing his paintings of the 1950s and 1960s with generous planes of saturated color and superimposed line boldly describing the image announces his debt to Hofmann, his understanding of Henri Matisse, and his powers of invention. The canvases of De Niro's fellow Hofmann alumnus, Kahn, from the same period are loosely stroked, flickering evocations of the light and atmosphere of place, rather than descriptions, yet for all their unstable accumulations of strokes, they are remarkably specific. Like De Niro's, Tabachnick's economical, improvisatory paintings reveal her admiration for Matisse, as well as what she learned from Hofmann about activating space. At times, she allows drawing—with a varied touch—to play an important role in conjuring up her images, while at others, the edges of colored planes function as a kind of line.

Despite also having been Hofmann students, Freilicher's and Georges' approaches are different yet again. Freilicher toggled between abstraction and figuration in her early working life, while Georges was committed to perception. Freilicher's still lifes and landscapes seem artless and spontaneous, as if she were reconstituting what was before her as energetic marks on canvas, directly, without calculation. Her works read as intimate, modest records of her pleasure in looking and in manipulating paint. Georges' paintings, while frequently rooted in his daily experience of the studio, his family, and the familiar, are notably theatrical. His large, energetically brushed and dramatically lit tableaux turn domestic subjects into modern-day history paintings.

Richard Diebenkorn (American, 1922–1993),
Girl with Cups, 1957.
Oil on canvas, 59 x 54 in. (149.9 x 137.2 cm).
Yale University Art Gallery, New Haven, CT. Gift of
Richard Brown Baker, B.A. 1935, 1975.110.1.

Kresch and Resika both work broadly and directly, simplifying forms and constructing with vigorous brush marks, as if paying homage to the dynamic, clearly defined space that Hofmann advocated. Yet their paintings could not be more dissimilar. Resika, in the 1950s and 1960s, combined what he learned from Hofmann with his study of Old Master painting and his fascination with landscape, an approach developed and enriched by his extended stays in Europe. Kresch's work, by contrast, has an expressionist flavor. Yet neither artist settles for a single way of making a painting. The character of their nominal subjects seems not only to influence color and tonality, but also affects touch and structure, making each work a wholly new invention.

Hartigan, like Freilicher, shifted between reference and abstraction for much of her earlier working life. In the 1950s and 1960s, she often seems to have been most stimulated by visually fragmented subjects that justified complex arrangements of planes in multiple colors. Her paintings of the period sometimes teeter on the brink of abstractness without losing a potent sense of reference. For both Katz and Dodd, the light and landscape of Maine were significant elements in their commitment to figuration. Some of Dodd's most ambitious paintings of the 1950s take the bucolic settings of Maine summers as their point of departure, prefiguring much of her future work. Her early works are generally looser and brushier than her later, crisp improvisations on buildings, windows, reflections, flowers, landscape, and the like, but the cows that punctuate her canvases of the 1950s are clearly recognizable. "I was thinking about pattern," Dodd says. "At that time I spent the summer in Lincolnville, Maine. There were a lot of cows in the area. They seemed to be in a place between pattern and representation. They made a good shape: white with big black patches."[19] Katz's paintings, like Dodd's, became increasingly specific in the 1950s and 1960s, but he never completely eliminated the evidence of the hand in them, as he would in the pristine, anonymous surfaces of his later works. During these crucial years, he also began to concentrate on the figure, painting his friends and colleagues, and beginning in 1957, repeatedly depicting his muse, Ada Del Moro, whom he married in 1958. "I figured," Katz says, "well, if I get Ada right, if you only get one person right—if you get a women or a man right—it's universal."[20]

In the decades following their rebellious beginnings, each artist's work evolved differently. Some dug more deeply into their initial pursuits; others sought more clarity, intensified color, and sometimes heightened fidelity to perception. None abandoned the contrarian impulse that led them to do exactly what was supposed to be impossible for ambitious young artists in the early 1950s—an attitude that could be said to anticipate and even lay the groundwork for the current art world's multiplicity of conceptions and ways of working. It seems an appropriate moment to reconsider the work of these daring pioneers, not only for its own merits, but also for its prescience and its opposition to the norms of the time. Of course, they simply may not have been able to do otherwise. As Dodd disarmingly observed, recalling the early 1950s, "We all settled down to start a life of art…I guess none of us was fit for anything else."[21]

Karen Wilkin
New York, NY
January 2020

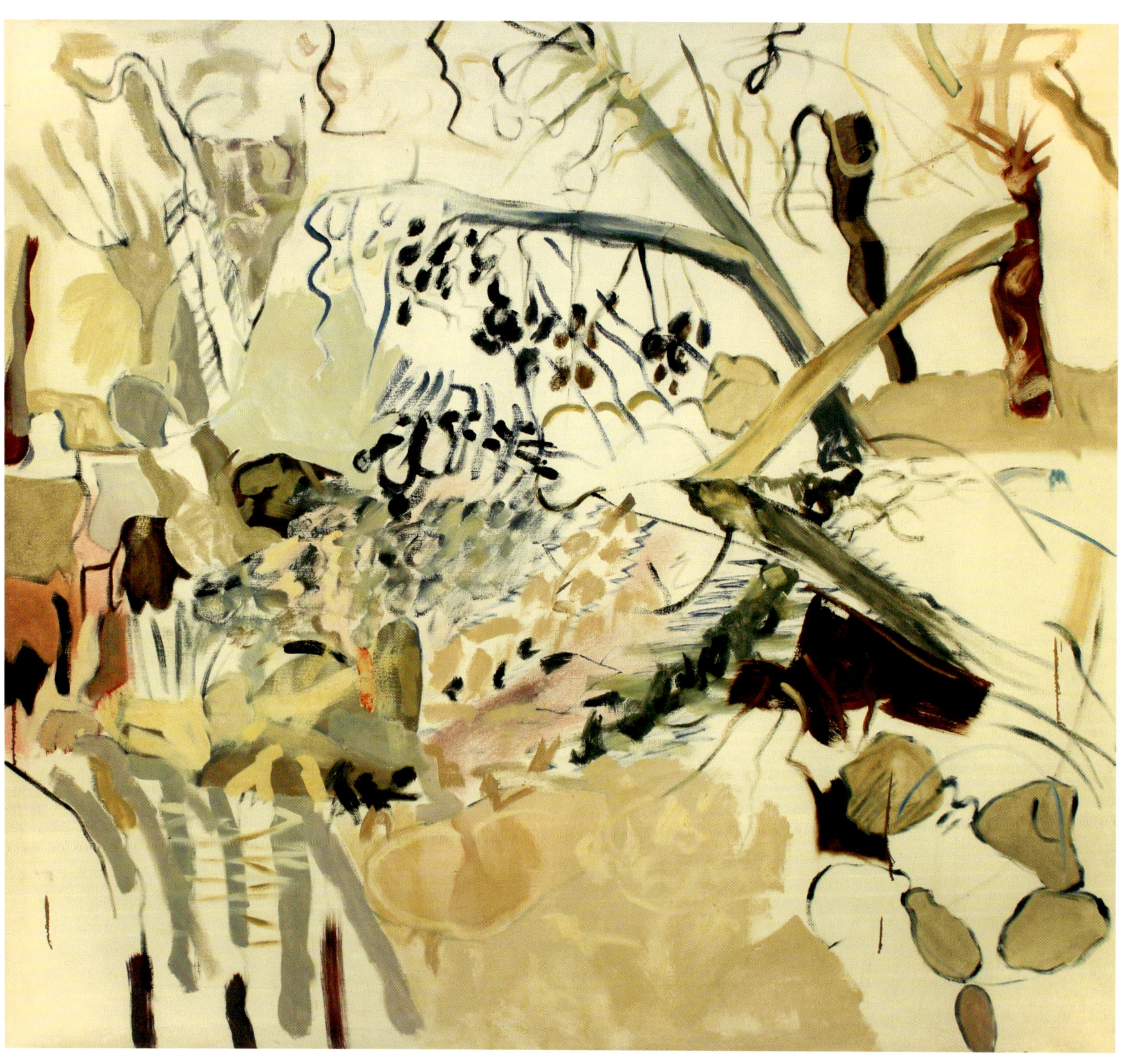

ENDNOTES

1   Fairfield Porter, "Recent American Figure Painting," in Fairfield Porter, *Art in Its Own Terms: Selected Criticism 1955–1975*, ed. Rackstraw Downes, (Cambridge, MA: Zoland Books, 1979), 69–70.

2   Foreword, *Recent Painting USA: The Figure*, an exhibition catalogue (New York: Museum of Modern Art, 1962). The unpaged catalogue's foreword states that 1,841 artists submitted photographs and slides. These were reviewed by the museum staff members Dorothy C. Miller, William S. Lieberman, and Frank O'Hara, who selected 150 artists to send work for further study—a total of 335 paintings. The museum's director, Alfred H. Barr Jr., then selected one work by each of 74 artists for the exhibition.

3   Ibid.

4   Porter, "Recent American Figure Painting," 73.

5   Foreword, *Recent Painting USA: The Figure*.

6   Clement Greenberg, introduction to *Post-Painterly Abstraction*, an exhibition catalogue (Los Angeles: Los Angeles County Museum of Art, 1964).

7   Obviously, these 10 were not the only ambitious, gifted painters interested in figuration during the period under review. Leland Bell, Nell Blaine, Elaine de Kooning, Philip Pearlstein, and Larry Rivers, to name only a few, could all be considered in this context. But their work seems to spring from a different set of assumptions and attitudes toward materials, even though they traveled in circles that closely overlapped with those of the 10 artists in this exhibition.

8   Wolf Kahn, "Interview with Wolf Kahn, 1977 November 28–1978 January 6," interviewed by Paul Cummings (Washington, DC: Smithsonian Institution, Archives of American Art, Oral History Program, 1978), 40.

9   Ibid, 69–70.

10 Paul Georges, "Interview with Paul Georges, 1965 December 28," interviewed by Bruce Hooton (Washington, DC: Smithsonian Institution, Archives of American Art, Oral History Program, 1965), 29.

11 Alex Katz, "Interview with Alex Katz, 1969 October 20," interviewed by Paul Cummings (Washington, DC: Smithsonian Institution, Archives of American Art, Oral History Program, 1969), 17.

12 Grace Hartigan, "Interview with Grace Hartigan, 1979 May 10," interviewed by Julia Haifley (Washington, DC: Smithsonian Institution, Archives of American Art, Oral History Program, 1979), 14.

13 Kahn, interviewed by Cummings, 53.

14 Katz, interviewed by Cummings, 15.

15 Hartigan, interviewed by Haifley, 11.

16 Ibid, 15.

17 Porter, "Recent American Figure Painting," 28.

18 Quoted by Janet Bishop, "A Picture as an Event," in *David Park*, an exhibition catalogue (San Francisco: San Francisco Museum of Modern Art, 2019) 17.

19 Lois Dodd, interviewed by Jennifer Samet, hyperallergic.com/194330/beer-with-a-painter-lois-dodd/ (accessed January 10, 2020).

20 Katz, interviewed by Cummings, 19.

21 Lois Dodd, interviewed by Ada Katz in *Eight Begin: Artists' Memories of Starting Out*, ed. Ada Katz. (New York and Waterville, ME: Libellum Books and Colby College Museum of Art, 2014), 31.

Lois Dodd, *Pond*, 1962.
Oil on linen, 58 x 64 in. (147.3 x 162.5 cm).
Alexandre Gallery, New York, NY. © Lois Dodd,
courtesy of Alexandre Gallery, New York, NY.
© 2020 Lois Dodd / Licensed by VAGA at Artists
Rights Society (ARS), New York, NY.

TEN NEW YORK PAINTERLY PAINTERS

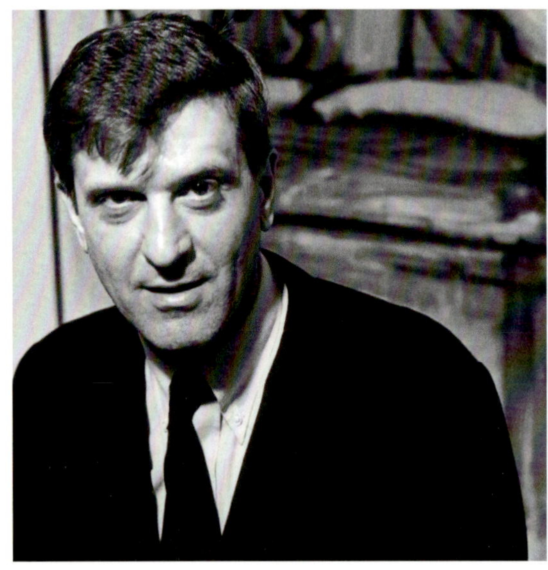

ROBERT DE NIRO, Sr.

b. 1922, Syracuse, NY; d. 1993, Manhattan, NY

Robert De Niro, Sr.'s mother, Helen O'Reilly, an Irish American, encouraged him to pursue a career in art, unlike his Italian-American father, Henry Martin De Niro, who opposed the idea. De Niro studied at the experimental Black Mountain College under Josef Albers from 1939 to 1940, and then with Hans Hofmann, with whom he enjoyed a close friendship. Hofmann's emphasis on dynamic structure and his enthusiasm for Henri Matisse had a lasting influence on De Niro. A self-proclaimed perfectionist, De Niro painted and repainted his canvases and, unlike Hofmann who worked spontaneously, he executed hundreds of studies before deciding on a particular subject. De Niro married fellow painter and poet Virginia Admiral in 1942, with whom he had his only child, the actor Robert De Niro, Jr.

De Niro traveled from 1961 to 1964, establishing himself in Paris and painting landscapes. Later, he taught at The Cooper Union and the School of Visual Arts in New York City, and was a visiting artist in Michigan State University's art department in 1974. He was the recipient of a Longview Foundation Award in 1958 and a Guggenheim Fellowship in 1968. De Niro's work is in the collections of the Hirshhorn Museum and Sculpture Garden in Washington, DC; The Metropolitan Museum of Art, the Whitney Museum of American Art, and the Brooklyn Museum in New York City; and the Denver Art Museum in Colorado, among many others. He is represented by DC Moore Gallery, New York City.

Selected Solo Exhibitions

2019: *Robert De Niro, Sr.: Intensity in Paint: Installation of Six Works*, DC Moore Gallery, New York, NY

1986: *Robert De Niro*, Crane Kalman Gallery, London, England

1981: *Drawings by Robert De Niro*, Foster/White Gallery, Seattle, WA

1971: *Robert De Niro*, Brenner Gallery, Provincetown, MA

1946: *Art of This Century Gallery*, Solomon R. Guggenheim Museum, New York, NY

Selected Group Exhibitions

2020: *Figuration Never Died*, Brattleboro Museum & Art Center, Brattleboro, VT

1998: *Seeing the Essential: Selected Works by Robert De Niro, Sr., Paul Resika, and Leland Bell*, Hackett-Freedman Gallery, San Francisco, CA

1982: *The 46th Annual National Midyear Show*, The Butler Institute of American Art, Youngstown, OH

1971: *A New Consciousness*, The CIBA-GEIGY Collection, Ardsley, NY

1961: *Artist's Equity Association Exhibition*, Colorado Springs Fine Arts Center Annual, Colorado Springs, CO

1956: *Second Generation New York*, Whitney Museum of American Art Annual, New York, NY; Stable Gallery Annual, New York, NY; The Jewish Museum, New York, NY

Collections

Brooklyn Museum of Art, Brooklyn, NY

Denver Art Museum, Denver, CO

Hirshhorn Museum and Sculpture Garden, Washington, DC

The Metropolitan Museum of Art, New York, NY

Parrish Art Museum, Water Mill, NY

Smithsonian American Art Museum, Washington, DC

Whitney Museum of American Art, New York, NY

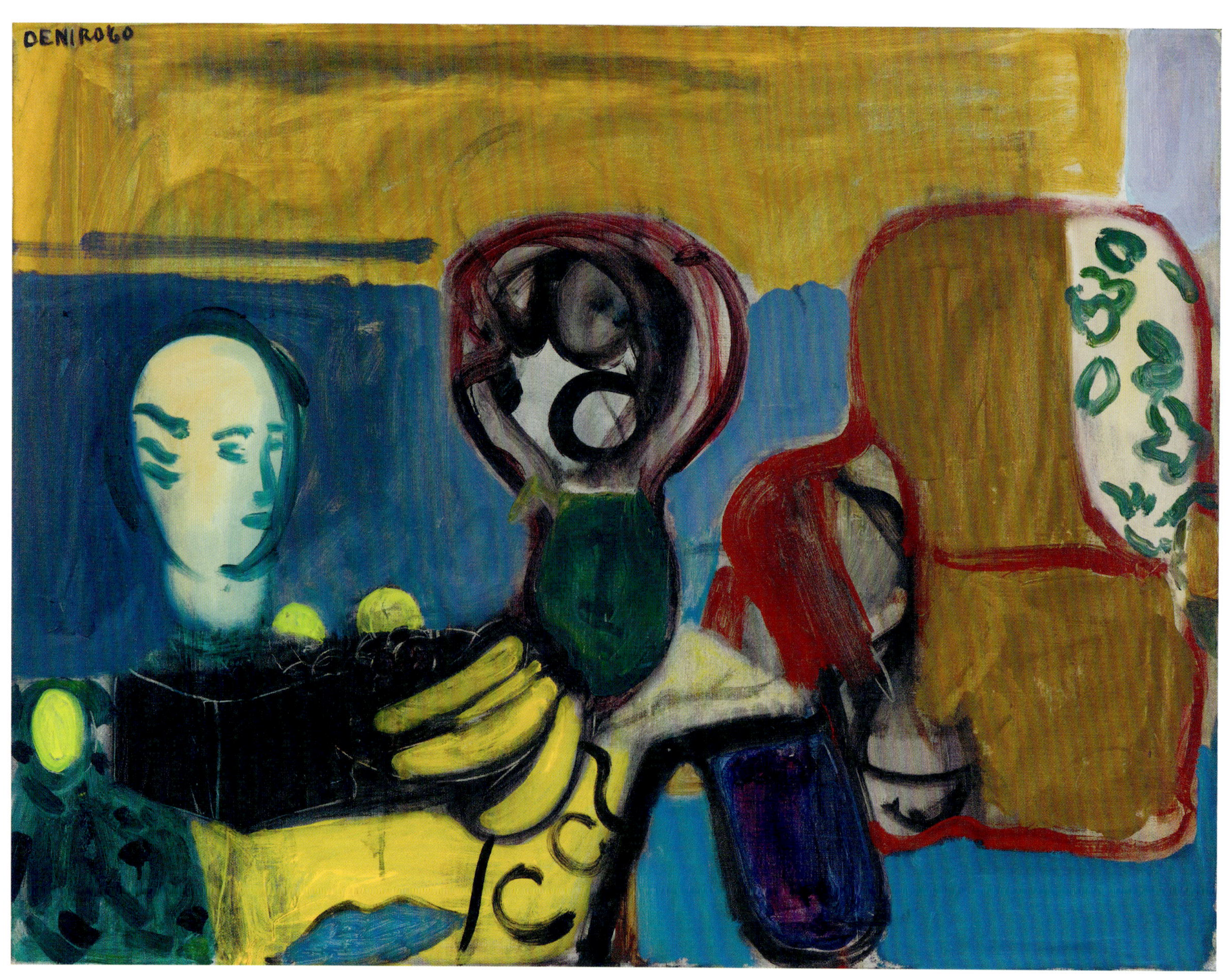

■ *Untitled Still Life*, 1960.
  Oil on canvas, 30 x 40 in. (76.2 x 101.6 cm).
  Private collection.

    ■ indicates a work in the exhibiton

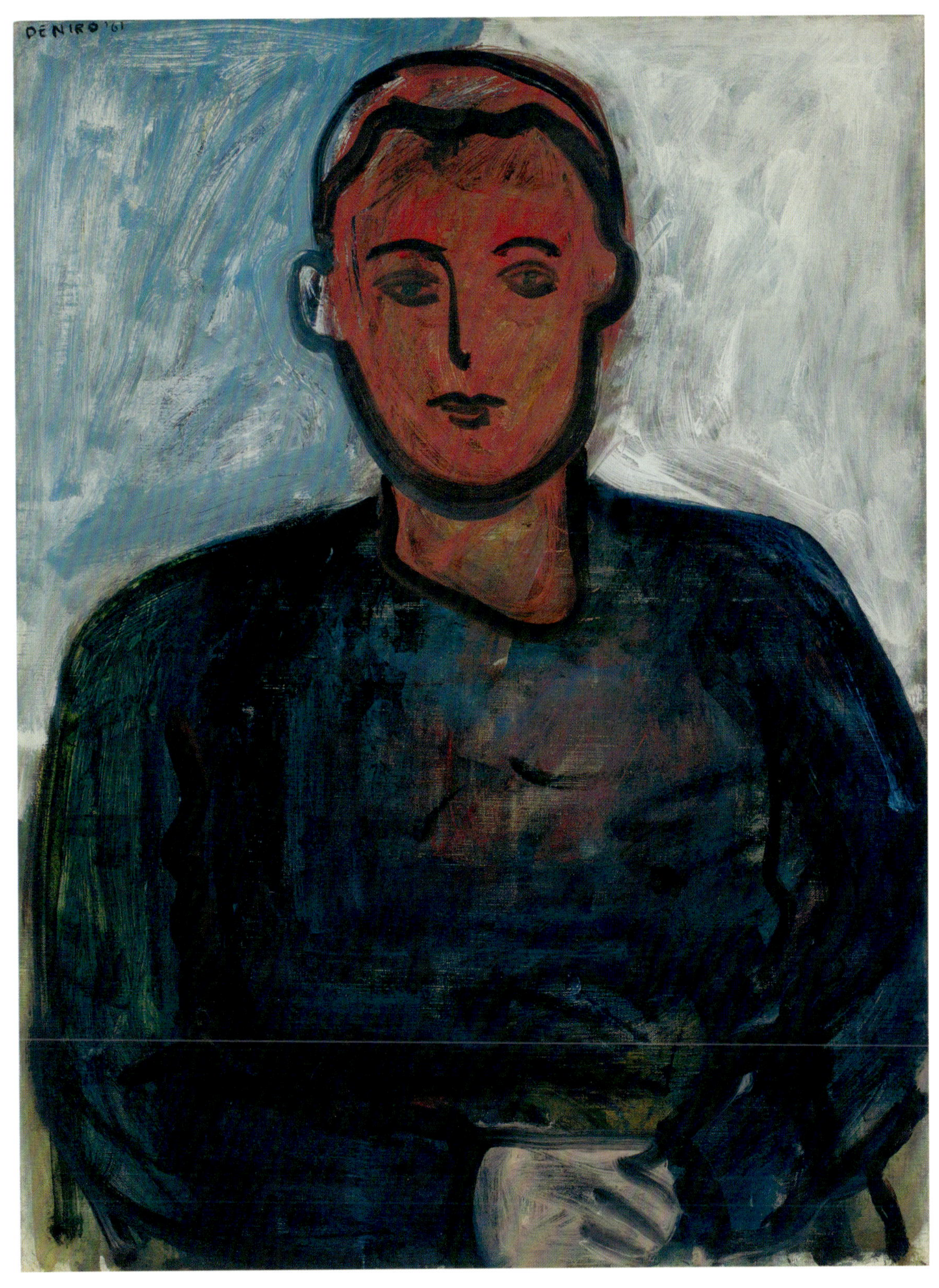

■ *Portrait of a Young Man with a Red Face*, 1961.
Oil on canvas, 40 x 30 in. (101.6 x 76.2 cm).
D.C. Moore Gallery, New York, NY. © 2020 Estate of Robert
De Niro, Sr. / Artists Rights Society (ARS), New York, NY.

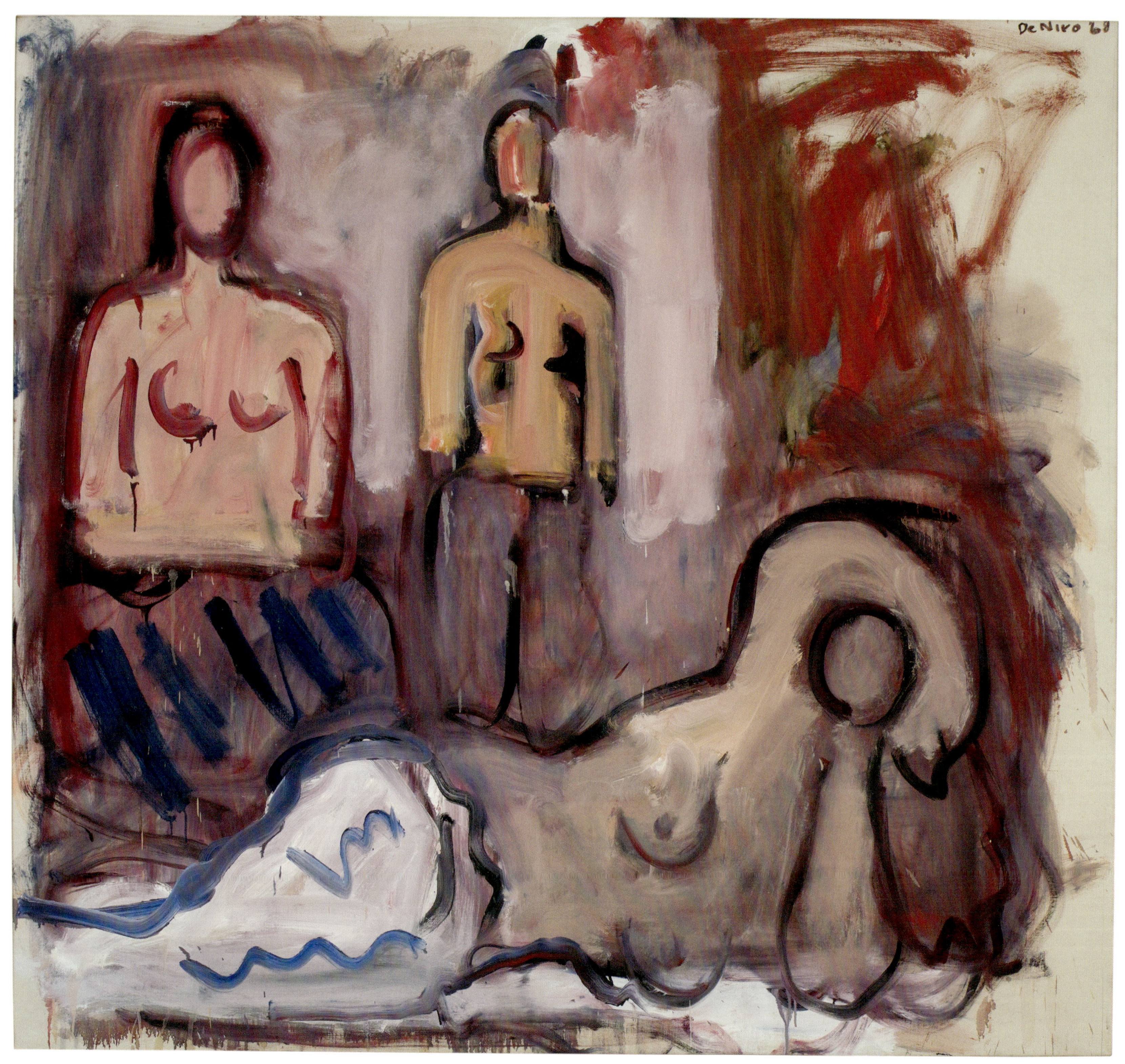

■ *Three Women*, 1968.
Oil on linen, 64 x 70 in. (162.6 x 177.8 cm).
D.C. Moore Gallery, New York, NY. © 2020
Estate of Robert De Niro, Sr. / Artists Rights
Society (ARS), New York, NY.

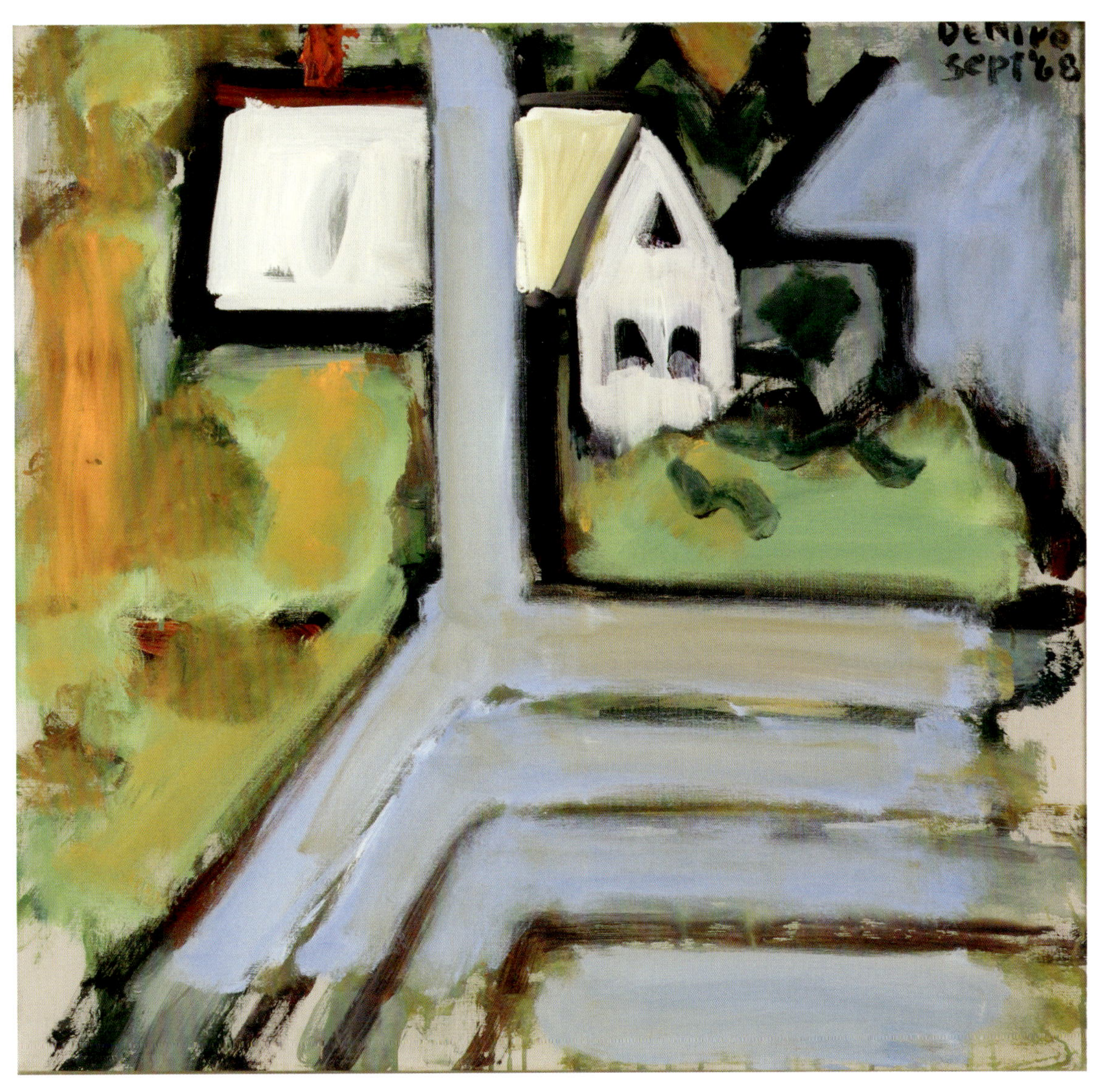

White Building, Blue Porch, 1960.
Oil on canvas, 30 x 32 in. (76.2 x 81.3 cm).
Estate of the artist. © 2020 Estate of Robert De Niro, Sr. /
Artists Rights Society (ARS), New York, NY.

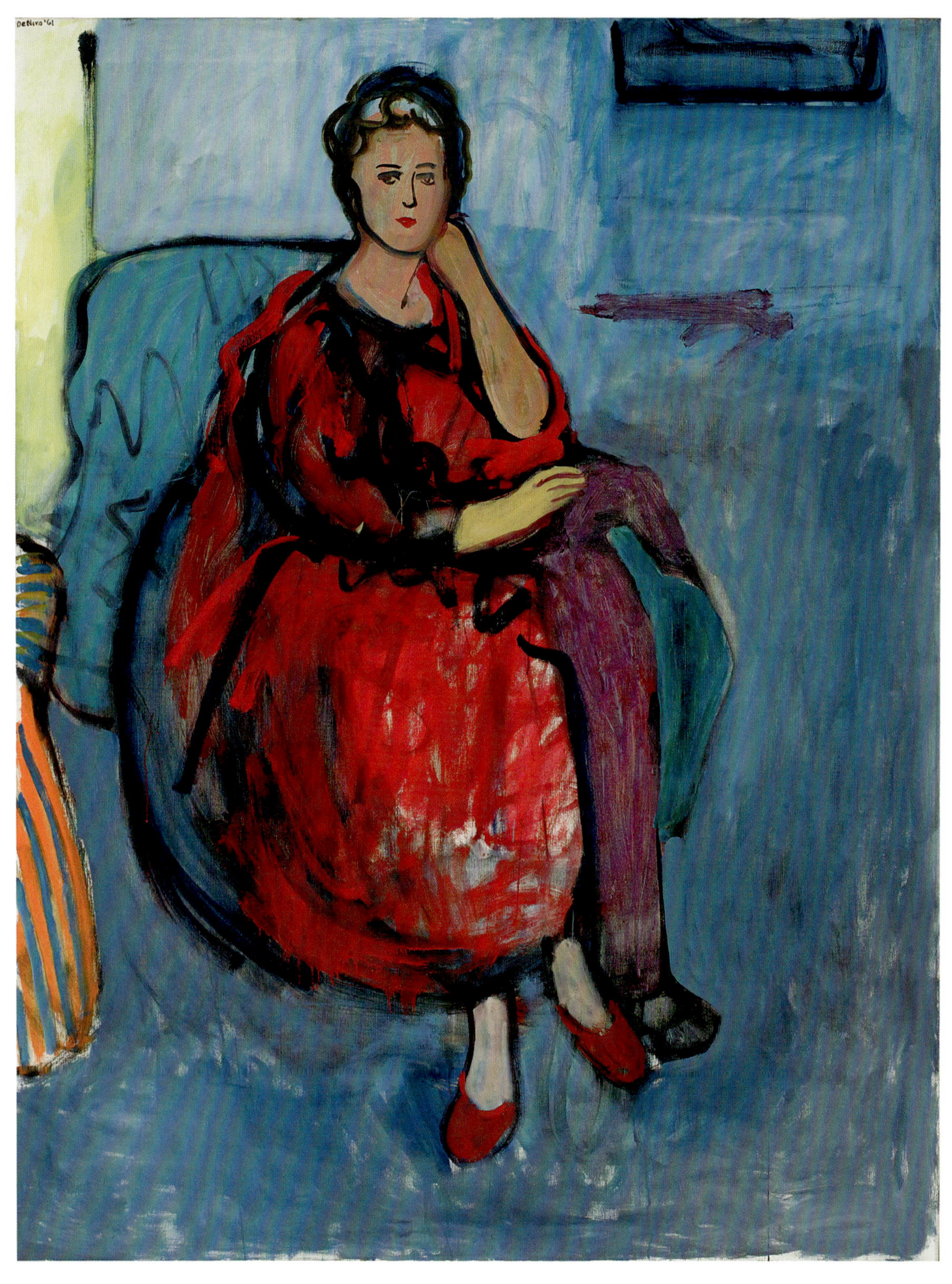

Woman in Red, 1960.
Oil on canvas, 70⅛ x 52¼ in. (178.1 x 132.7 cm).
D.C. Moore Gallery, New York, NY. © 2020 Estate of Robert De Niro, Sr. /
Artists Rights Society (ARS), New York, NY.

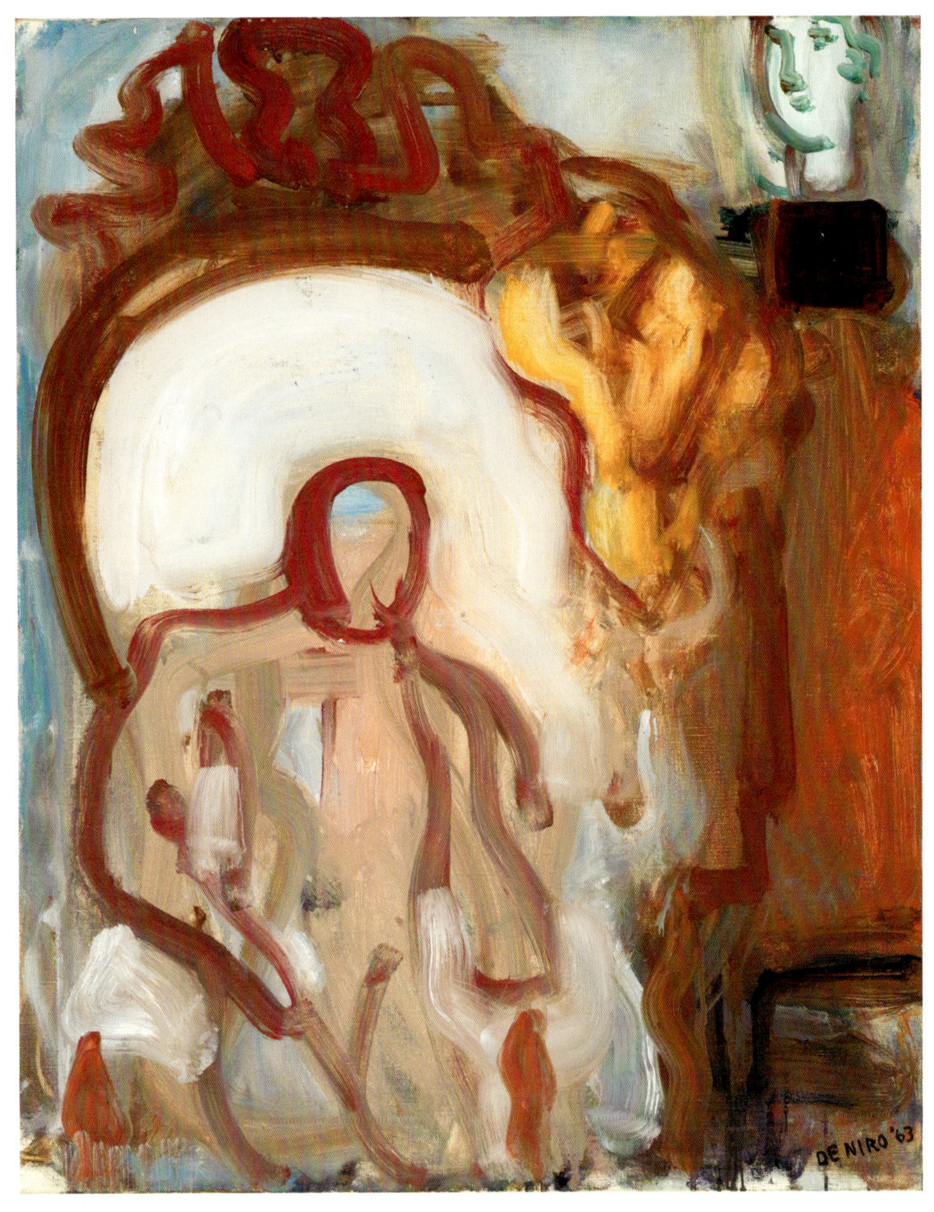

Nude in Armchair, 1963. Oil on canvas,
32¹/₈ x 25⁵/₈ in. (81.6 × 65.1 cm).
The Whitney Museum of American Art, New York, NY.
Gift of the artist. 98.46. © 2020 Estate of Robert De Niro, Sr. /
Artists Rights Society (ARS), New York, NY.

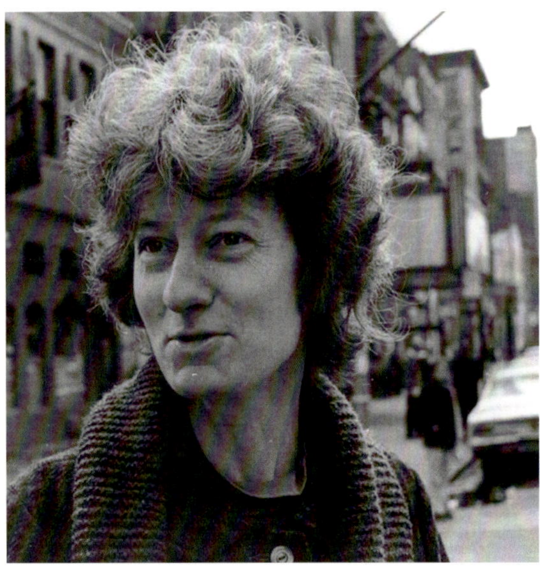

LOIS DODD

b. 1927, Montclair, NJ

Lois Dodd is known for her deceptively casual landscapes, figure studies, and floral studies, as well as for her interior and exterior scenes. She studied art and textile design at The Cooper Union in New York in the late 1940s under the aegis of Peter Busa and Byron Thomas. In the early 1950s, Dodd also lived in Italy with her then-husband, the sculptor William King. She was one of the five founding members of the Tanager Gallery in 1952, among the first of the artist-run cooperative galleries in downtown New York. From the 1970s to the 1990s, Dodd taught at both Brooklyn College and at the Skowhegan School of Painting and Sculpture in Madison, Maine, where she is a Governor Emerita.

Dodd paints her immediate everyday surroundings of the places where she has chosen to live and work—the Lower East Side, rural midcoast Maine, and the Delaware Water Gap. Her paintings are usually intimately scaled and are almost always completed in one plein-air sitting. Her subjects include New England outbuildings, lush summer gardens, dried leafless plants, moonlit skies, and exterior views from interior rooms. She often returns to familiar motifs at different times of the year with dramatically varied results. Windows, flowers, gardens, and clotheslines are of particular fascination for Dodd.

After discovering Maine and plein-air painting during a summer session at Skowhegan, along with her friend Alex Katz, Dodd began spending her summers in the midcoast region of Penobscot Bay, which a wave of New York modernists had begun to explore after the end of the Second World War, seeking companionship and an escape from city life. Dodd currently lives in New York and works in Maine and New Jersey. Among her many honors are an Italian Study grant; a Longview Foundation purchase; and an Ingram Merrill Foundation grant. Dodd's works are in private, corporate, and public permanent collections throughout the United States, including the Whitney Museum of American Art, the Museum of Modern Art, and The Cooper Union in New York City, as well as the Portland Museum of Art, Portland, Maine, and Colby College, Waterville, Maine. She is represented by Alexandre Gallery, New York City.

Selected Solo Exhibitions

2018–2019: *Lois Dodd: Flashings*, Alexandre Gallery, New York, NY

2016: *Lois Dodd: Day and Night*, Alexandre Gallery, New York, NY

2008: *Lois Dodd: Landscapes and Structures*, Alexandre Gallery, New York, NY

1999: *Lois Dodd: Flower Paintings*, Fischbach Gallery, New York, NY

1991: *The Artist in the Garden*, National Academy of Design, New York, NY

1969, 1970, 1971: Green Mountain Gallery, New York, NY

1954, 1957, 1958, 1961, 1962: Tanager Gallery, New York, NY

Selected Group Exhibitions

2020: *Figuration Never Died*, Brattleboro Museum & Art Center, Brattleboro, VT

1967: Ithaca College Museum of Art, Ithaca, NY

1965: *Drawings*, Purdue University, Lafayette, IN

1964: *Drawings and Watercolors*, Yale University, New Haven, CT

1962: *Out of Doors Landscape*, Kornblee Gallery, New York, NY

1960: *Artisti Americani Residenti a Roma*, Palazzo Venezia, Rome, Italy

1958: *Stable Annual*, Stable Gallery, New York, NY

1953: *Dodd-Katz*, Tanager Gallery, New York, NY

Collections

Brooklyn College, Brooklyn, NY

Bryn Mawr College, Bryn Mawr, PA

Colby College, Waterville, ME

The Cooper Union, New York, NY

Cooper Hewitt Art Museum, New York, NY

Dartmouth College Art Museum, Hanover, NH

Farnsworth Art Museum, Rockland, ME

Museum of Modern Art, New York, NY

National Academy of Design, New York, NY

Portland Museum of Art, Portland, ME

Whitney Museum of American Art, New York, NY

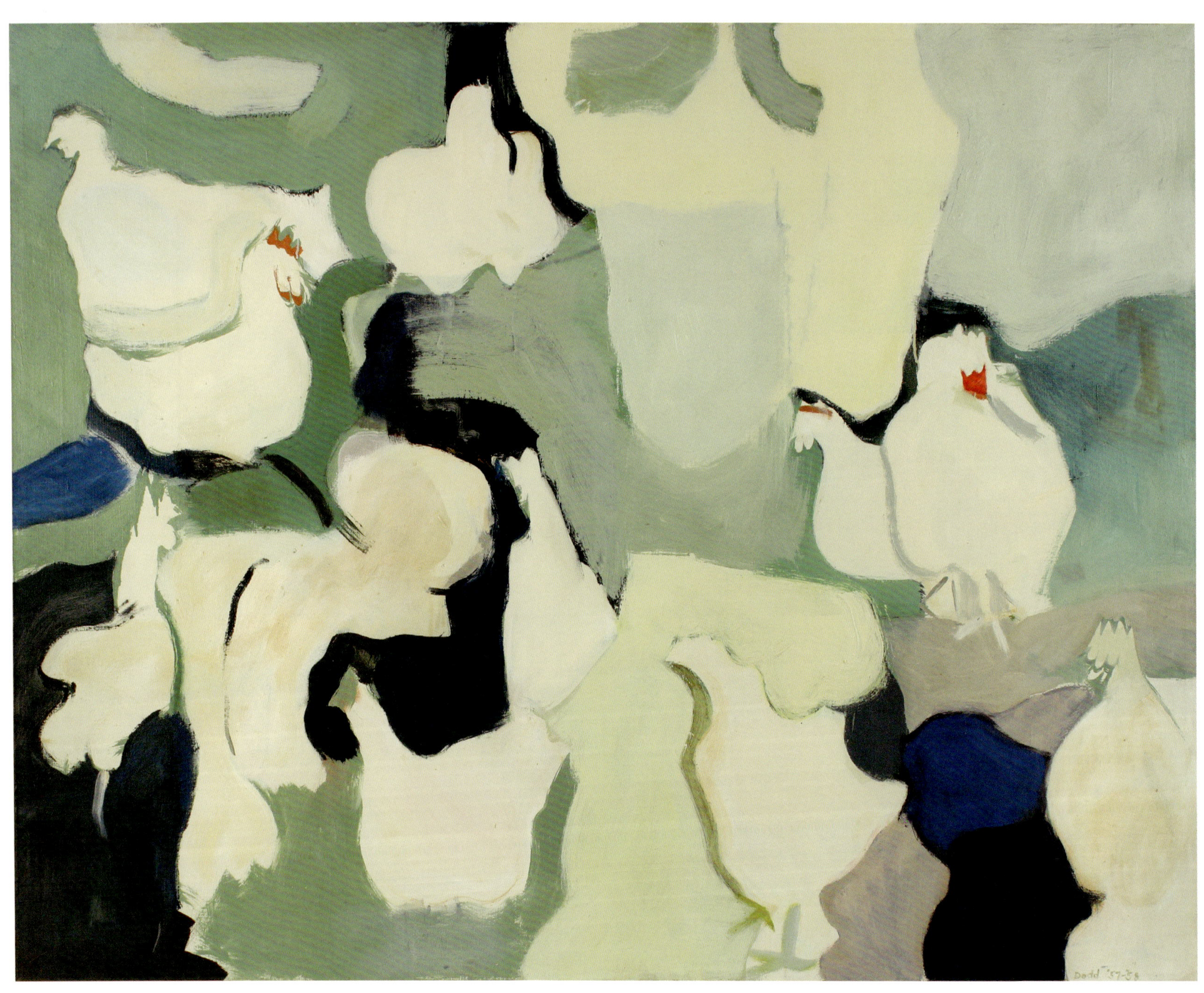

■ *Chickens*, 1957–1958.
Oil on linen, 42 x 54 in. (106.7 x 137.2 cm).
Alexandre Gallery, New York, NY.
© Lois Dodd, courtesy of Alexandre Gallery, New York, NY.
© 2020 Lois Dodd / Licensed by VAGA at Artists Rights
Society (ARS), New York, NY.

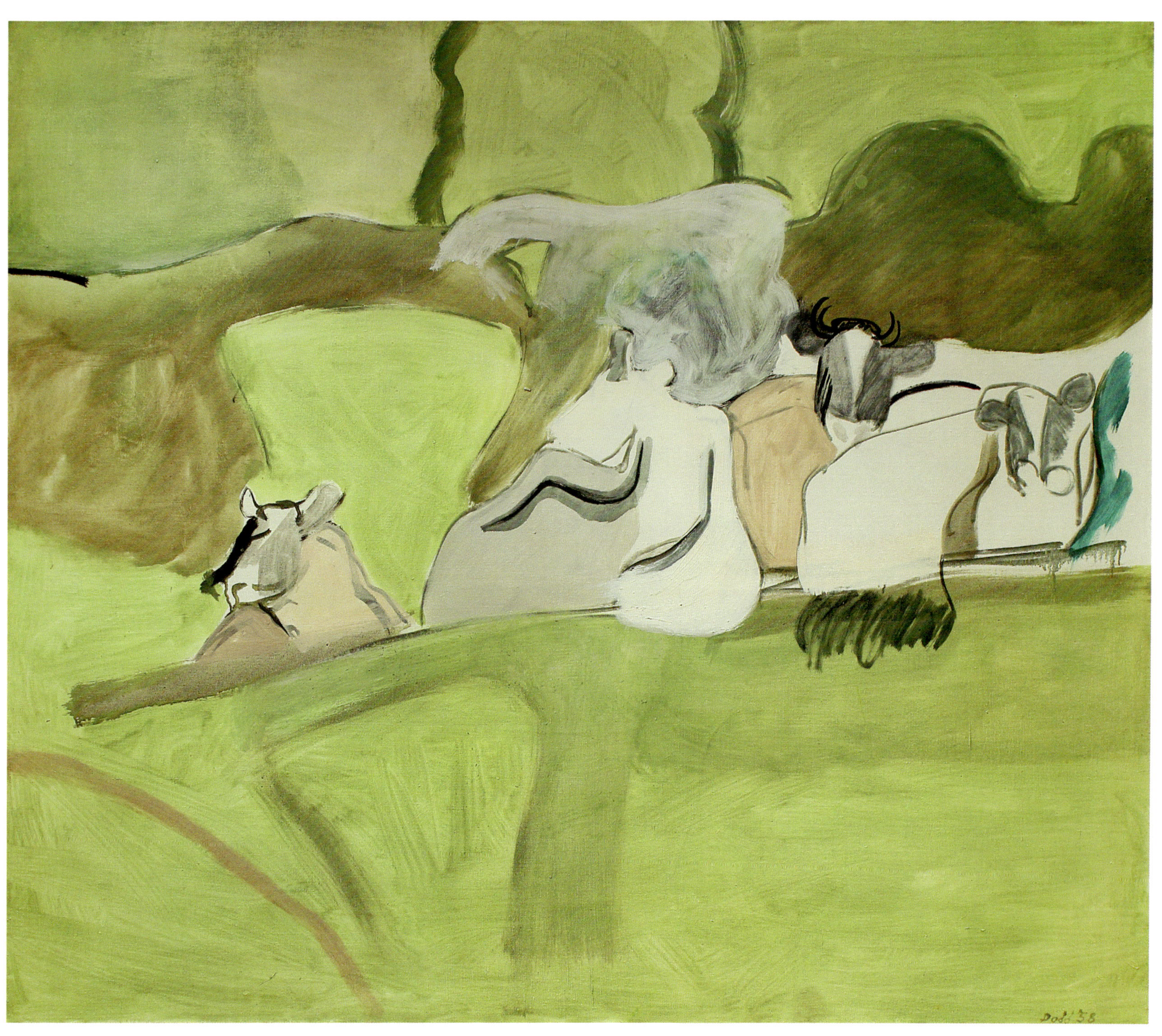

■ *Cows in Landscape*, 1958.
Oil on linen, 44 x 51 in. (111.8 x 129.5 cm).
Alexandre Gallery, New York, NY.
© Lois Dodd, courtesy of Alexandre Gallery, New York, NY.
© 2020 Lois Dodd / Licensed by VAGA at Artists Rights
Society (ARS), New York, NY.

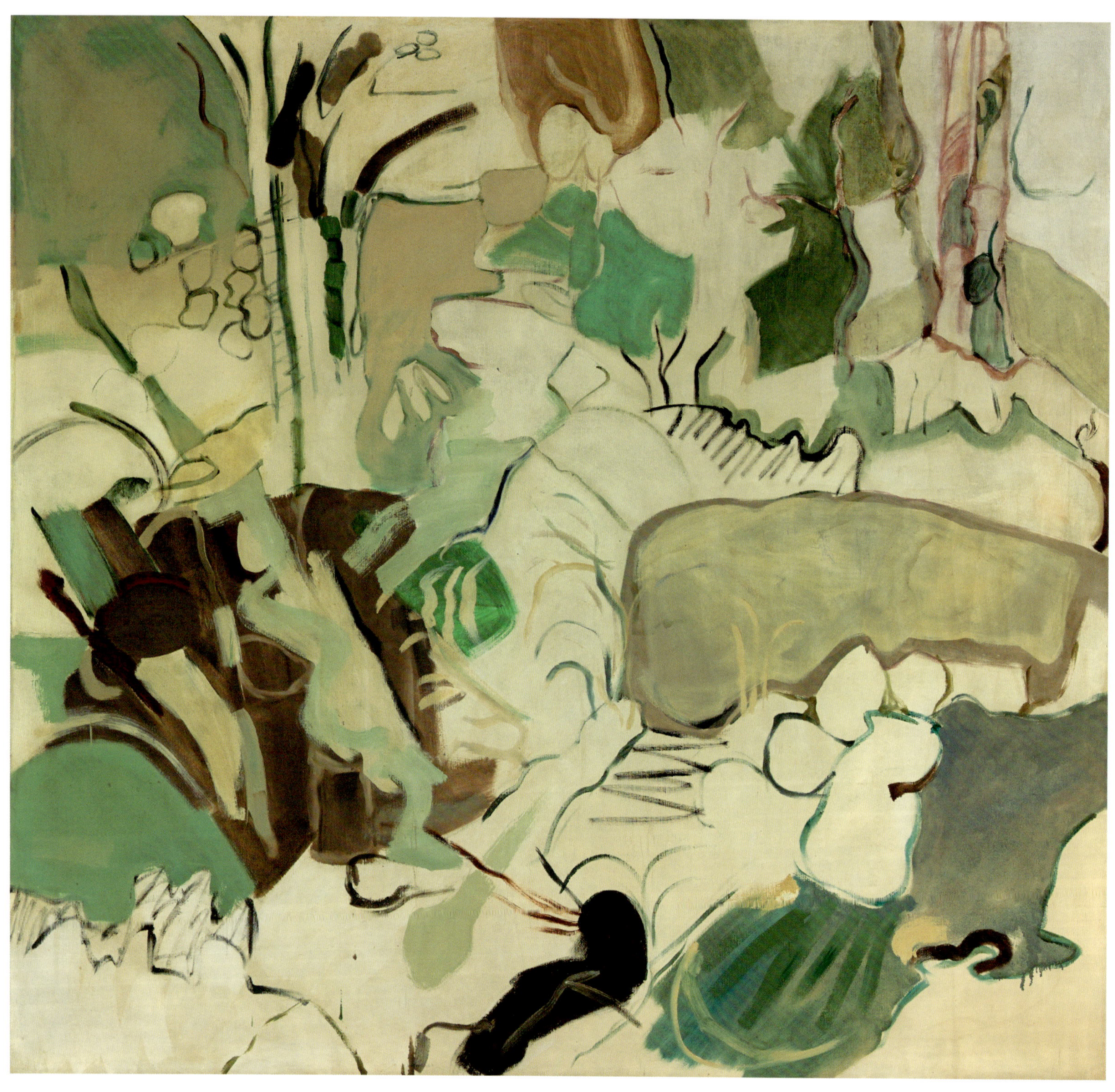

Brook, 1961.
Oil on linen, 72 x 76 in. (180.3 x 193 cm).
Portland Museum of Art, Portland, ME. Museum purchase with support
from the Peggy and Harold Osher Acquisition Fund and the Bernstein
Acquisition Fund, 2013.7.

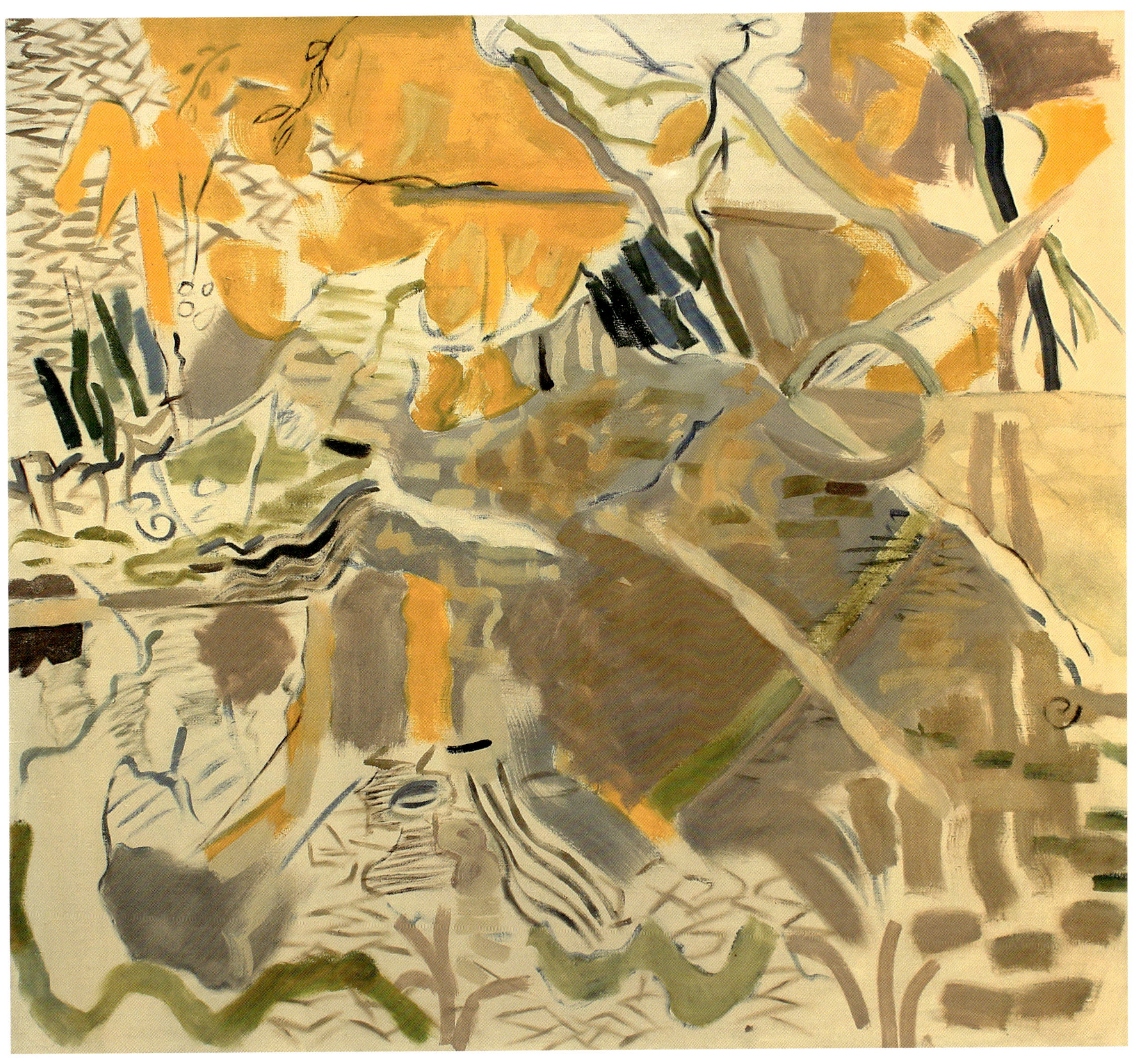

Pond, 1962.
Oil on linen, 58 x 65 in. (147.3 x 165.1 cm).
Alexandre Gallery, New York, NY.
© Lois Dodd, courtesy of Alexandre Gallery, New York, NY.
© 2020 Lois Dodd / Licensed by VAGA at Artists Rights Society
(ARS), New York, NY.

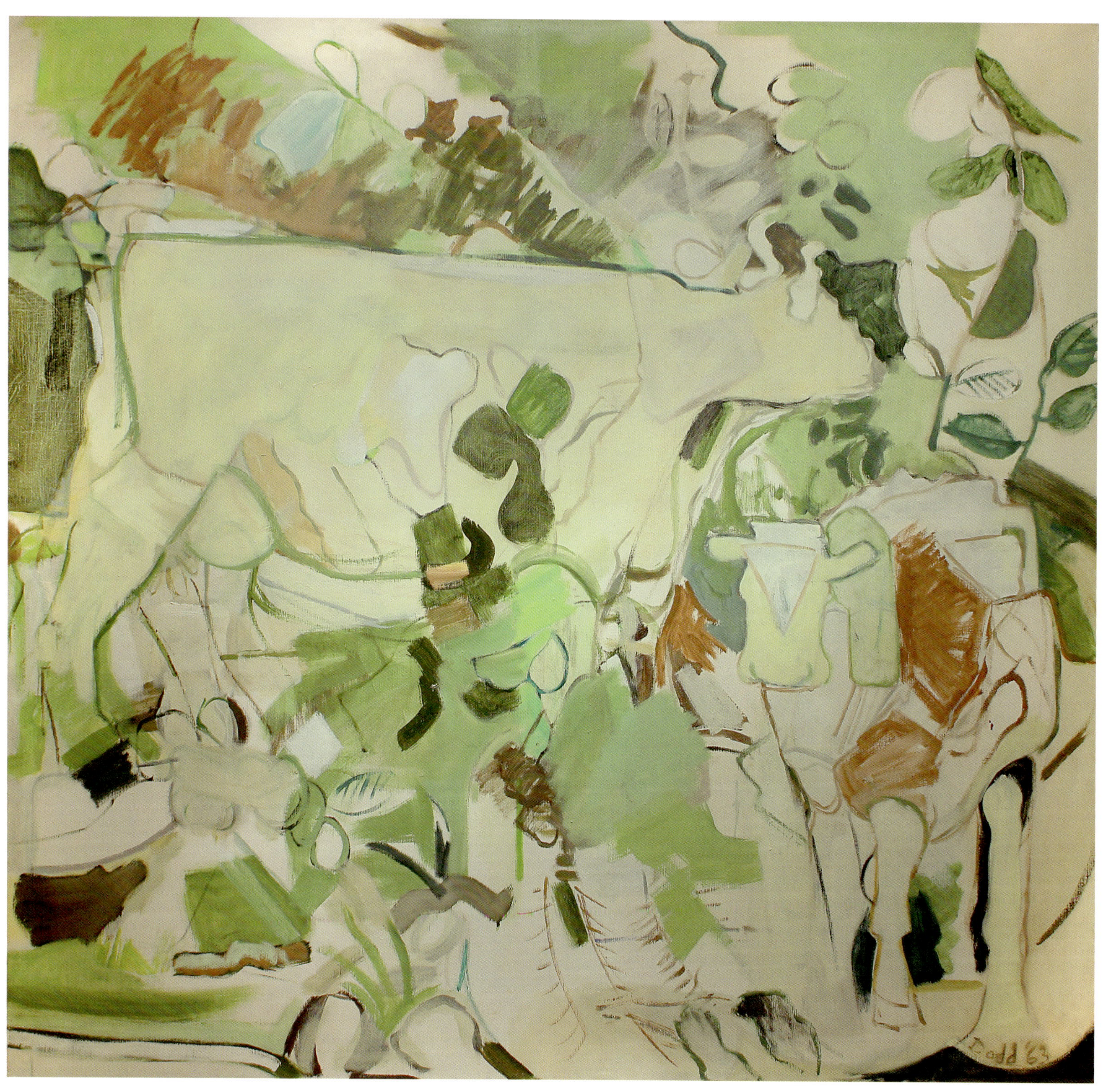

Cows, 1963.
Oil on linen, 72 x 76 in. (180.3 x 193 cm).
Private collection, Newport, RI.
© Lois Dodd, courtesy of Alexandre Gallery, New York, NY.
© 2020 Lois Dodd / Licensed by VAGA at Artists Rights Society
(ARS), New York, NY.

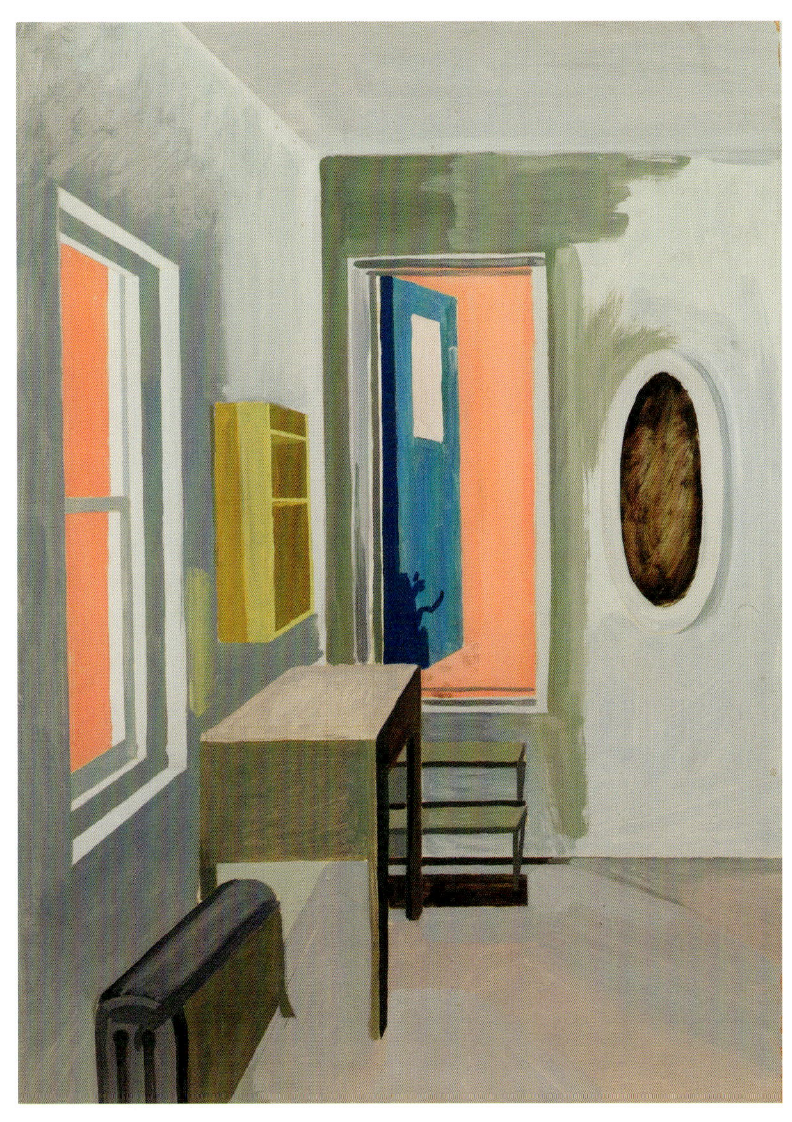

Loft Interior, 1968.
Oil on Masonite, 21 x 15¼ in. (53.3 x 38.7 cm).
Alexandre Gallery, New York, NY.
© Lois Dodd, courtesy of Alexandre Gallery, New York, NY.
© 2020 Lois Dodd / Licensed by VAGA at Artists Rights
Society (ARS), New York, NY.

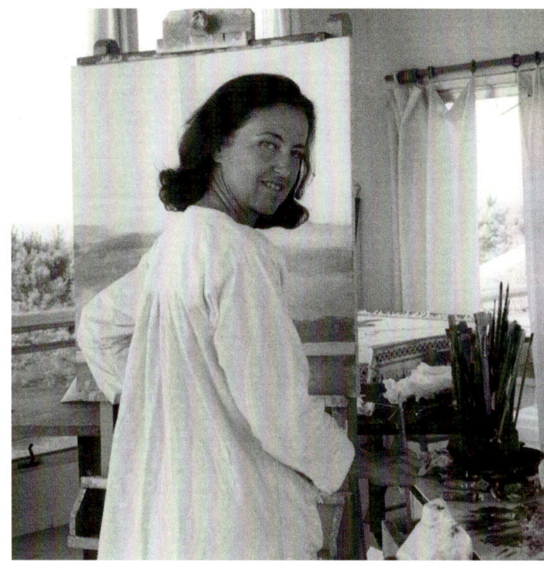

JANE FREILICHER

b.1924, Brooklyn, NY; d. 2014, New York, NY

Pursuing a distinctive painterly realism for over 60 years, Jane Freilicher has gained increasing recognition from critics, collectors, and generations of younger painters. Early in her career, she adopted the tenets of Abstract Expressionism, as well as painting from observation, but subsequently concentrated mainly on landscape and still lifes that typically feature flowers arranged on windowsills with a Manhattan view or a vista from her Water Mill, Long Island, studio in the background.

Freilicher came of age at the center of a group of influential artists and poets associated with Abstract Expressionism, including painters Willem de Kooning, Joan Mitchell, Larry Rivers, Fairfield Porter, and Alex Katz, as well as poets John Ashbery, Kenneth Koch, Frank O'Hara, and photographer and filmmaker Rudy Burckhardt.

A Brooklyn native, her parents, Martin Niederhoffer, a linguist, and Berthe, a pianist, were immigrants from Eastern Europe. Freilicher graduated from Brooklyn College and received a master's degree from Columbia University's Teachers College in 1948. She went on to study with Hans Hofmann, both in New York and in Provincetown, Massachusetts. In 1952, she had her first solo exhibition at the Tibor de Nagy Gallery.

Freilicher's work is widely collected and is represented in major museum collections throughout the United States, including the Whitney Museum of American Art, The Metropolitan Museum of Art, and the Museum of Modern Art, all in New York City. Her paintings were included in the 1995 Whitney Biennial.

Freilicher was a longtime member of the American Academy of Arts and Letters, and the National Academy of Design, both in New York City. Her many honors include the National Academy of Design Saltus Gold Medal, the Academy of the Arts Lifetime Achievement Award from the Guild Hall Museum, and the Gold Medal in Painting from the Academy of Arts and Letters, its highest honor. She is represented by Kasmin Gallery, New York City.

Selected Solo Exhibitions

2018: *50s New York*, Paul Kasmin Gallery, New York, NY

2015: *Theme and Variatio*n, Tibor de Nagy Gallery, New York, NY

1995: Fischbach Gallery, New York, NY

1989: Kornbluth Gallery, Fairlawn, NJ

1974: Benson Gallery, Bridgehampton, New York, NY

Selected Group Exhibitions

2020: *Figuration Never Died*, Brattleboro Museum & Art Center, Brattleboro, VT

2016: *Mira Dancy, Jane Freilicher, Daniel Heidkamp*, Derek Eller Gallery, New York, NY

2015: *Jane Freilicher & Jane Wilson: Seen and Unseen*, Parrish Art Museum, Water Mill, NY

2013: *John Ashbery Collects: Poet Among Things*, Loretta Howard Gallery, New York, NY

2010: *American Still Life: Treasures from the Parrish Art Museum*, Parrish Art Museum, Southampton, NY

2007: *182nd Annual Exhibition of Contemporary American Art*, National Academy Museum, New York, NY

Collections

The Metropolitan Museum of Art, New York, NY

Museum of Art, Rhode Island School of Design, Providence, RI

Museum of Modern Art, New York, NY

Parrish Art Museum, Water Mill, NY

Rahr–West Art Museum, Manitowoc, WI

Rose Art Museum, Brandeis University, Boston, MA

San Francisco Museum of Modern Art, San Francisco, CA

Whitney Museum of American Art, New York, NY

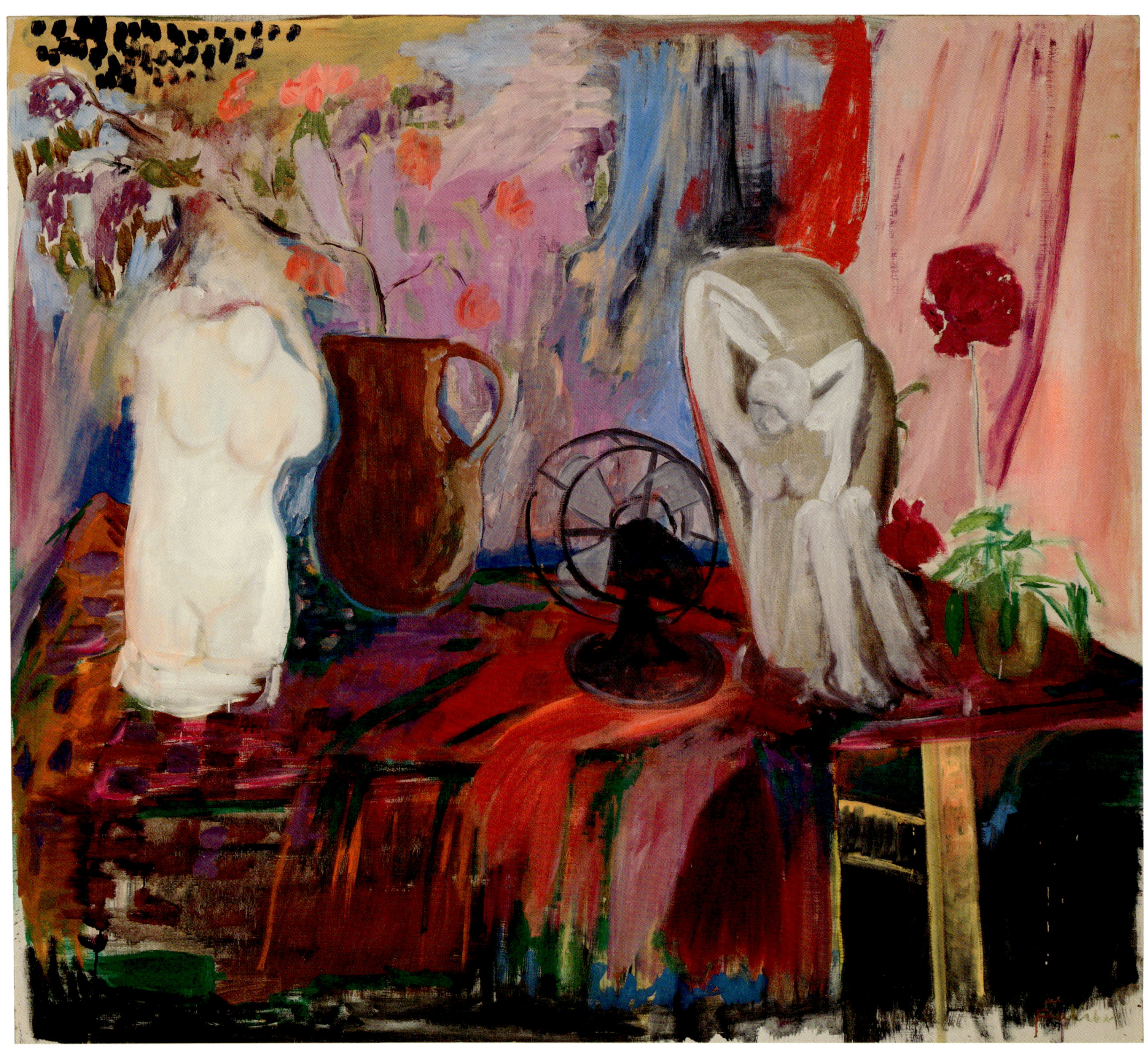

■ *The Electric Fan*, 1957.
Oil on canvas, 49⅝ x 56 in. (126 x 142.2 cm).
Christian Levett and Mougins Museum of Classical Art.

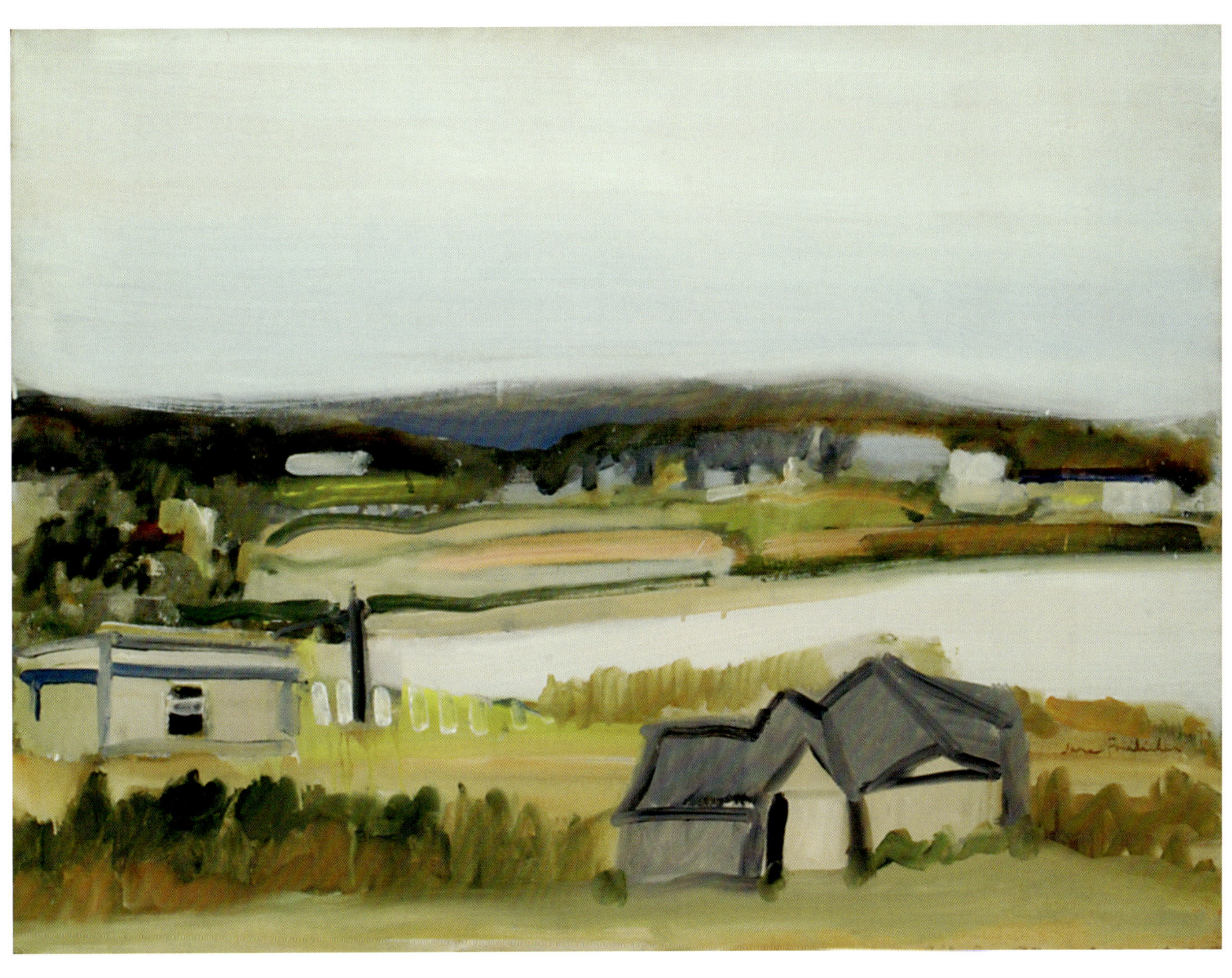

■ *Grey Day*, 1963.
Oil on canvas, 24 x 32 in. (61 x 81.3 cm).
Parrish Art Museum, Water Mill, NY. Gift of Larry Rivers.

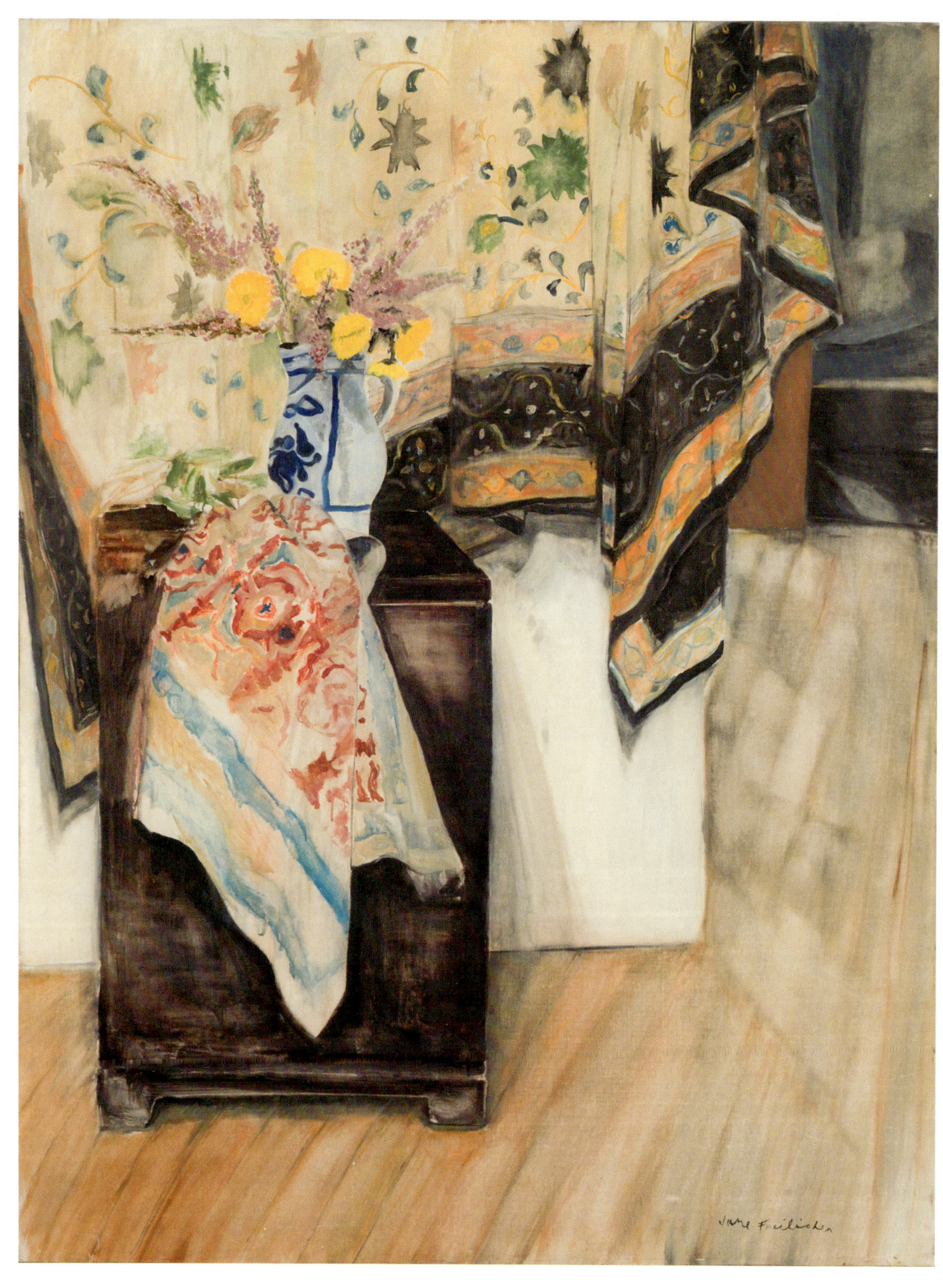

Still Life with Calendulas, 1955.
Oil on canvas, 65½ x 49½ in. (166.4 x 125.7 cm).
Eric Brown / Paul Kasmin Gallery, New York, NY.

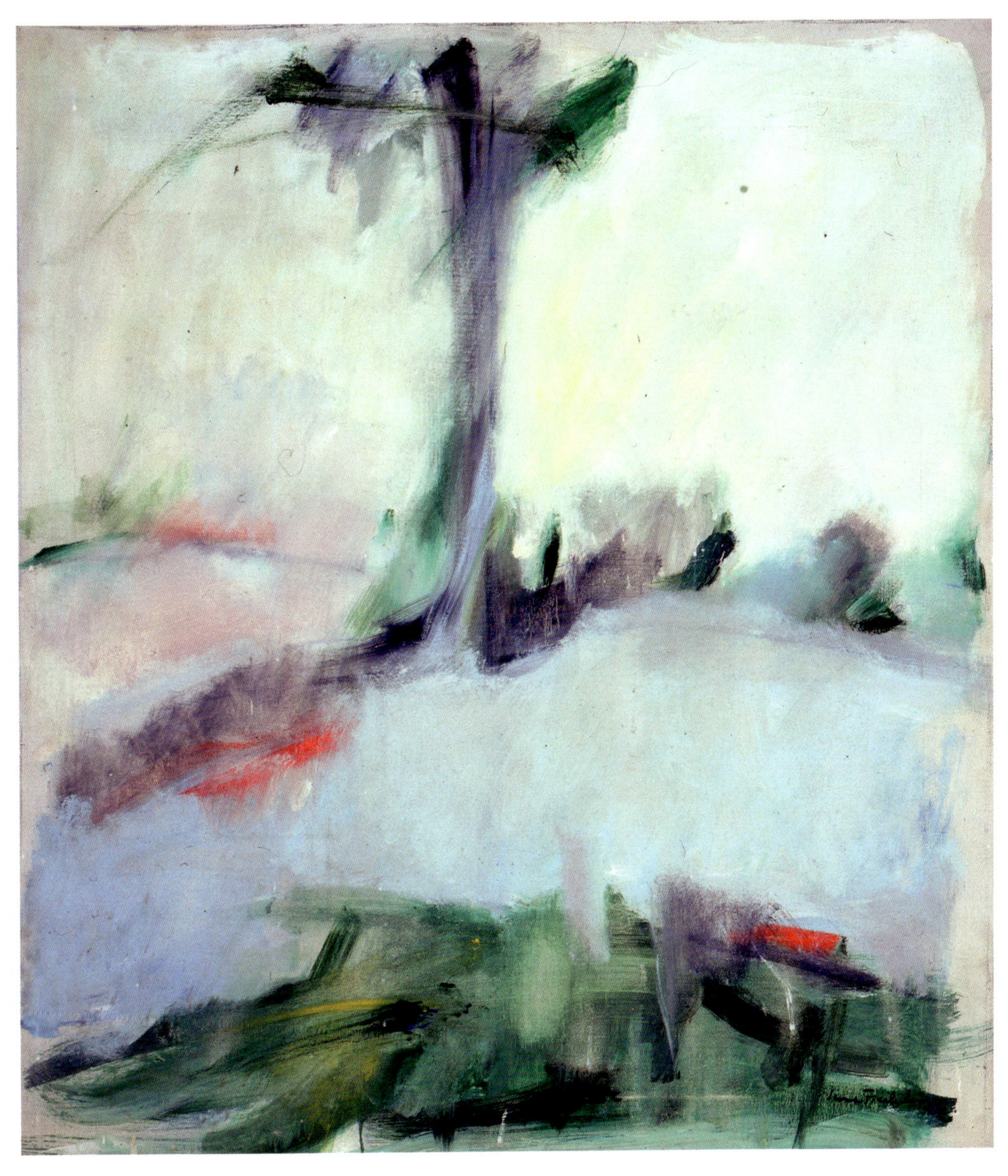

Flying Point Road, 1959.
Oil on linen, 31 x 50 in. (78.7 x 121.9 cm).
Estate of the artist.

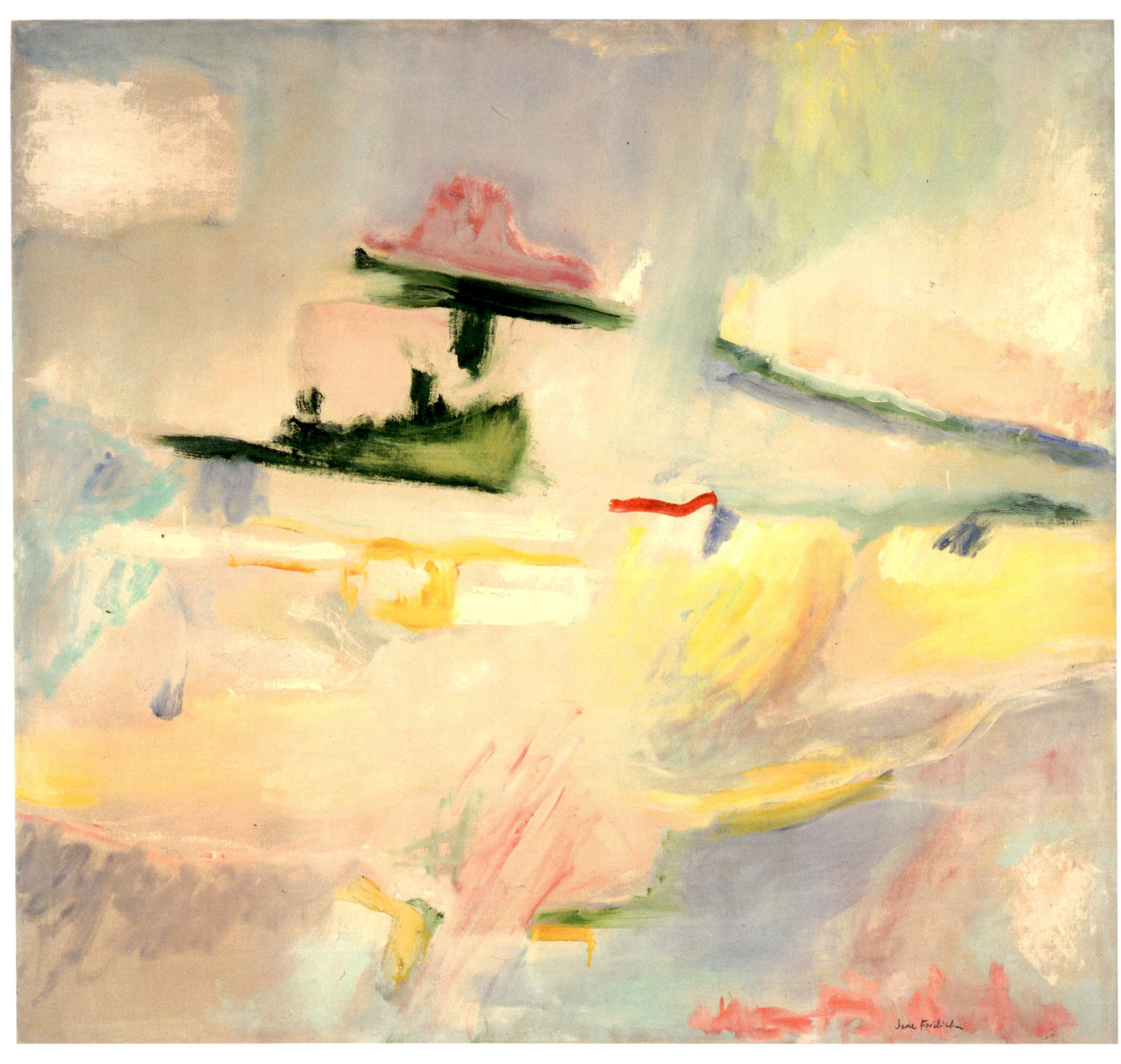

The Sky, 1960.
Oil on linen, 46 x 51 in. (116.8 x 129.5 cm).
Estate of the artist.

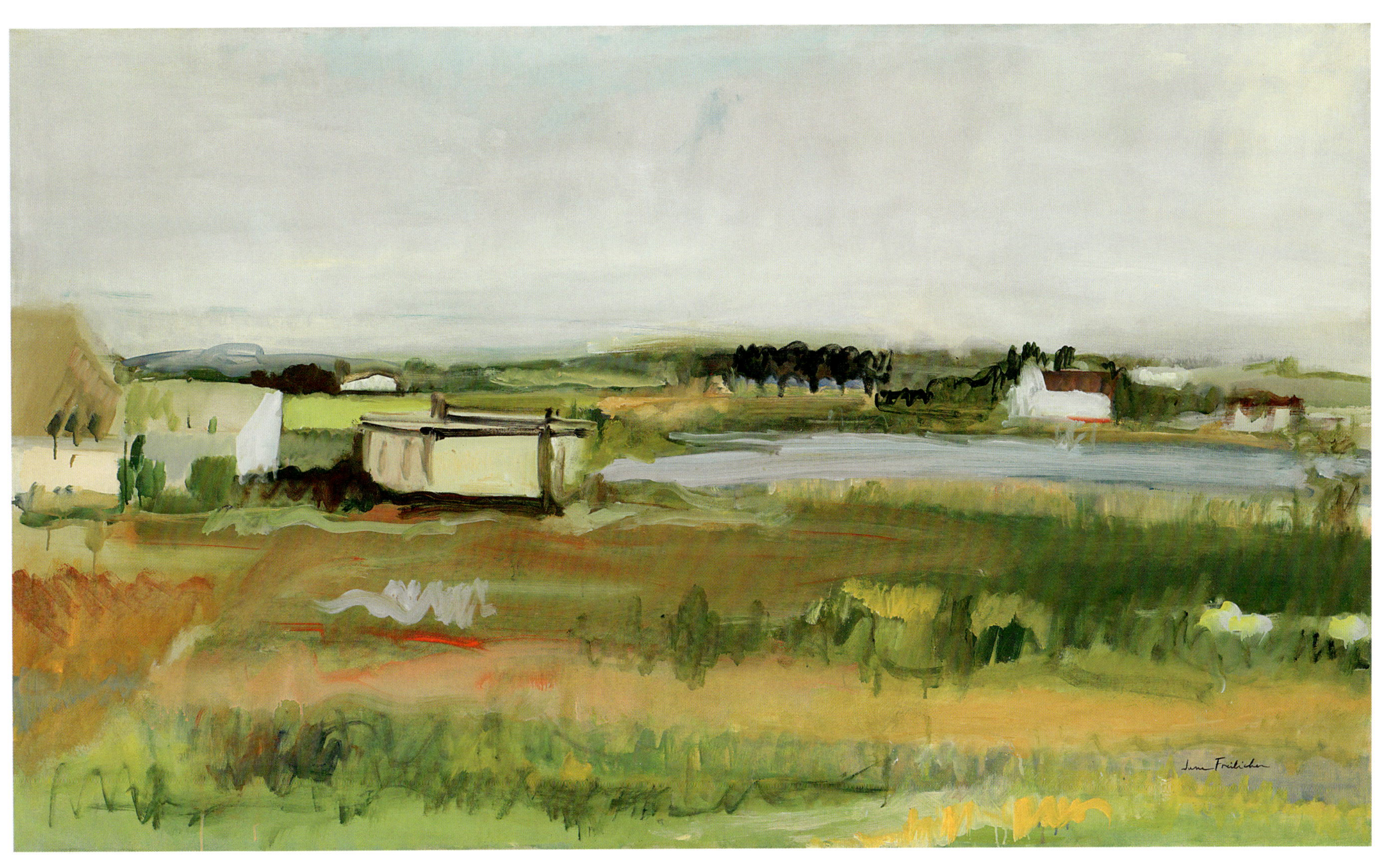

Wide Landscape, 1963.
Oil on canvas, 40 x 68⅛ in. (101.6 x 173 cm).
The Whitney Museum of American Art, New York, NY.
Gift of Donald M. Treiman in memory of Joyce Treiman, 99.118. Digital image
© Whitney Museum of American Art / Licensed by Scala / Art Resource, NY.

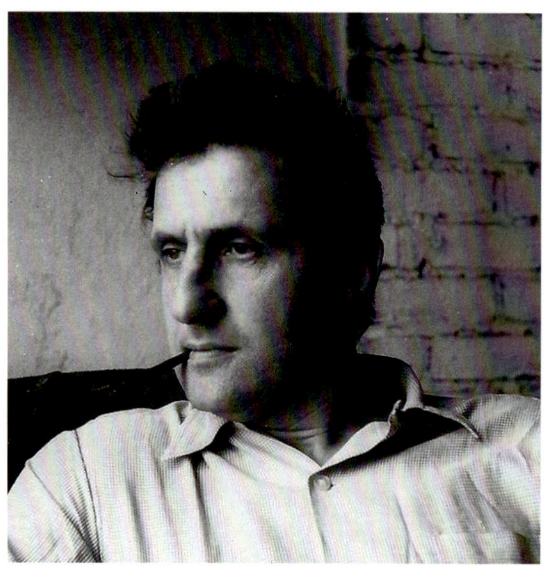

PAUL GEORGES

b. 1923, Portland, OR; d. 2002, Isigny-sur Mer, Normandy, France

Throughout his working life, Paul Georges explored figure painting, still life, landscape, self-portraiture, and group portraits with references to mythology, art history, and contemporary politics. He spent his career traveling between a farmhouse in Normandy, France, and downtown New York, and he was known to have shuttled his works-in-progress between both locations. A decorated World War II veteran, Georges studied, postwar, with Hans Hofmann in the United States. He also studied in Paris at the Académie de la Grande Chaumière and the Atelier Fernand Léger.

Georges' paintings combine painterly French Modernism, Rococo exuberance, and New York street attitude. In the 1960s, he felt compelled to respond to the decade's social and political turmoil, often in the form of large-scale history paintings. His first overtly political work was a modest study of JFK's 1963 Dallas motorcade, and he continued to paint responses to contemporary trends and events, including the AIDS epidemic, as well as denunciations of religious extremism and urban homelessness. His political paintings were often the target of critical attacks from conservative critics, as he also combined them with allegories teeming with beautiful women floating naked in Tiepolo skies.

Among his many awards are the Whitney Museum of American Art's 1966 Neysa McMein Purchase Award, and the National Academy Museum's 1983 Andrew Carnegie Prize for the 158th Annual Exhibition, and its 1991 Gladys Emerson Cook Prize for the 166th Annual Exhibition. His work can be found in the permanent collections of the Museum of Modern Art and the Whitney Museum of American Art in New York City; the Smithsonian American Art Museum, Washington, DC; and the J. Paul Getty Museum, Los Angeles, California.

2003: *My Posthumous Series*, Salander-O'Reilly Galleries, New York, NY

2000: *The Big Idea: A Retrospective*, Center for Figurative Painting, New York, NY

1996: *New Paintings*, Vered Gallery, East Hampton, NY

1885: William W. Crapo Gallery and Studio, Swain School of Design, New Bedford, MA

1983: College of the Mainland, Texas City, TX

Selected Group Exhibitions

2020: *Figuration Never Died*, Brattleboro Museum & Art Center, Brattleboro, VT

2016: *The Cat Show*, Worcester Art Museum, Worcester, MA

2001: *Les Voluptés*, Borusan Art Gallery, Istanbul, Turkey

1999: *American Academy Invitational Exhibition of Painting & Sculpture*, National Academy Museum and School of
Fine Art, New York, NY

1994: *Face to Face: Artists on Artists*, Gallery Swan, New York, NY

1990: *Regarding Art: Artworks about Art*, John Michael Kohler Arts Center, Sheboygan, WI

Collections

Guild Hall of East Hampton, East Hampton, NY

J. Paul Getty Museum. Los Angeles, CA

Museum of Modern Art, New York, NY

National Academy Museum, New York, NY

Parrish Museum, Water Mill, NY

Portland Art Museum, Portland, OR

Rose Art Museum, Brandeis University, Waltham, MA

Smart Museum, University of Chicago, Chicago, IL

Virginia Museum of Fine Arts, Richmond, VA

Weatherspoon Art Museum, University of North Carolina, Greensboro, NC

Whitney Museum of American Art, New York, NY

Smithsonian American Art Museum, Washington, DC

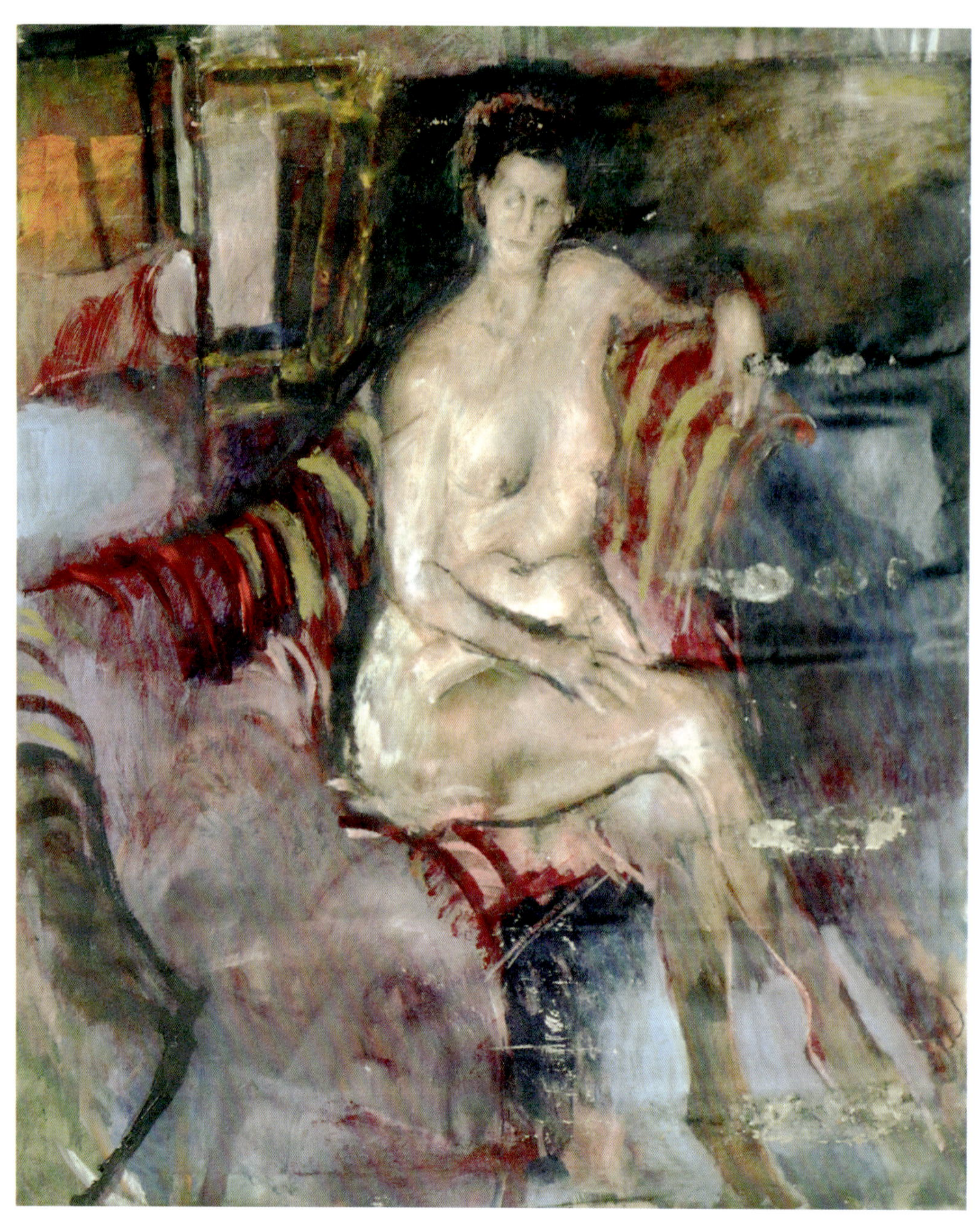

■ *Lisette*, 1958.
Oil on canvas, 61½ x 50½ in. (156.2 x 128.3 cm).
Estate of the artist. Courtesy © 2020 Paul Georges
Foundation Inc., 85 Walker Street, NYC 10013.

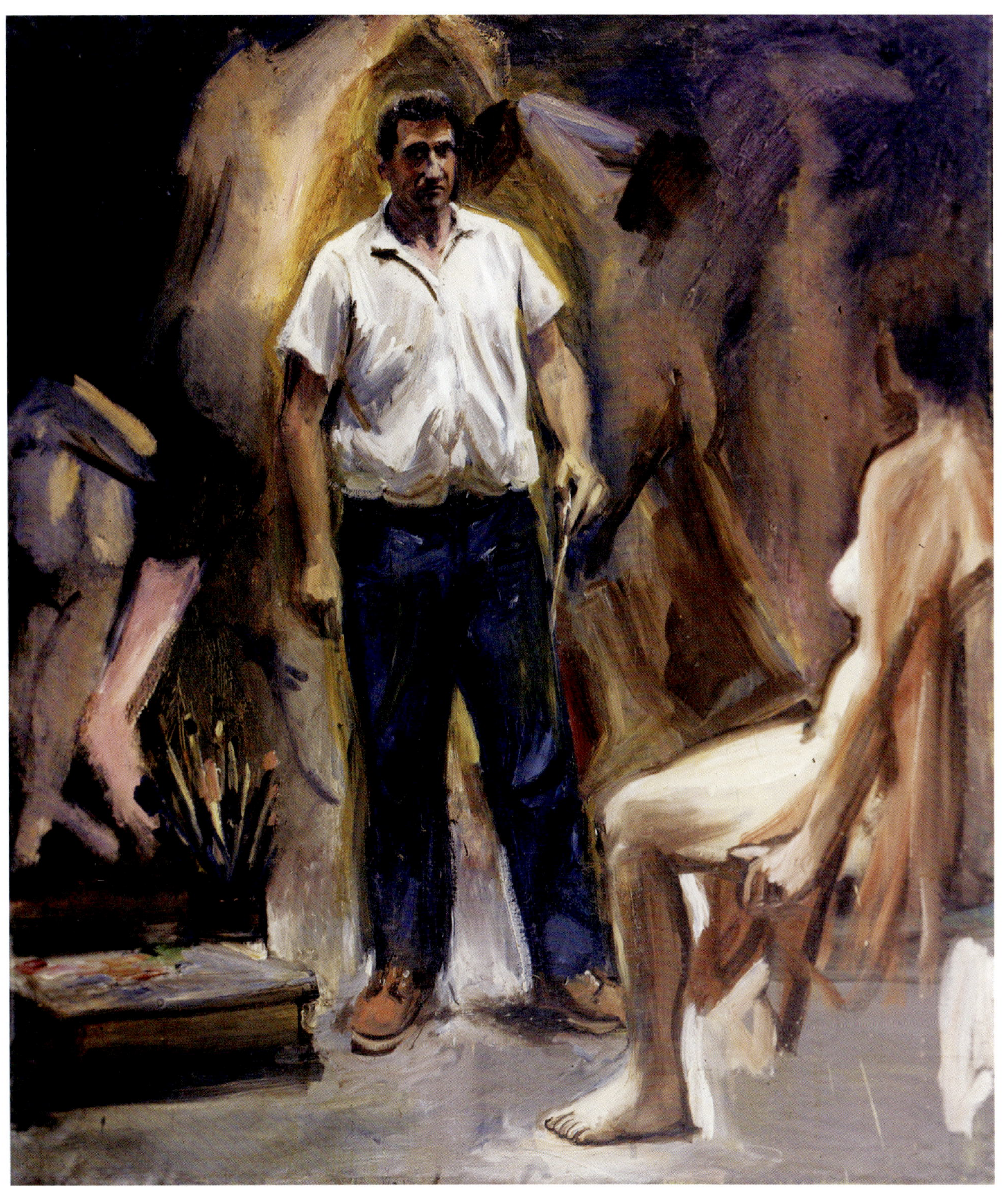

■ *Artist in Studio*, 1963.
Oil on linen, 80¼ x 70¼ in. (203.8 x 178.4 cm).
Center for Figurative Painting, New York, NY.

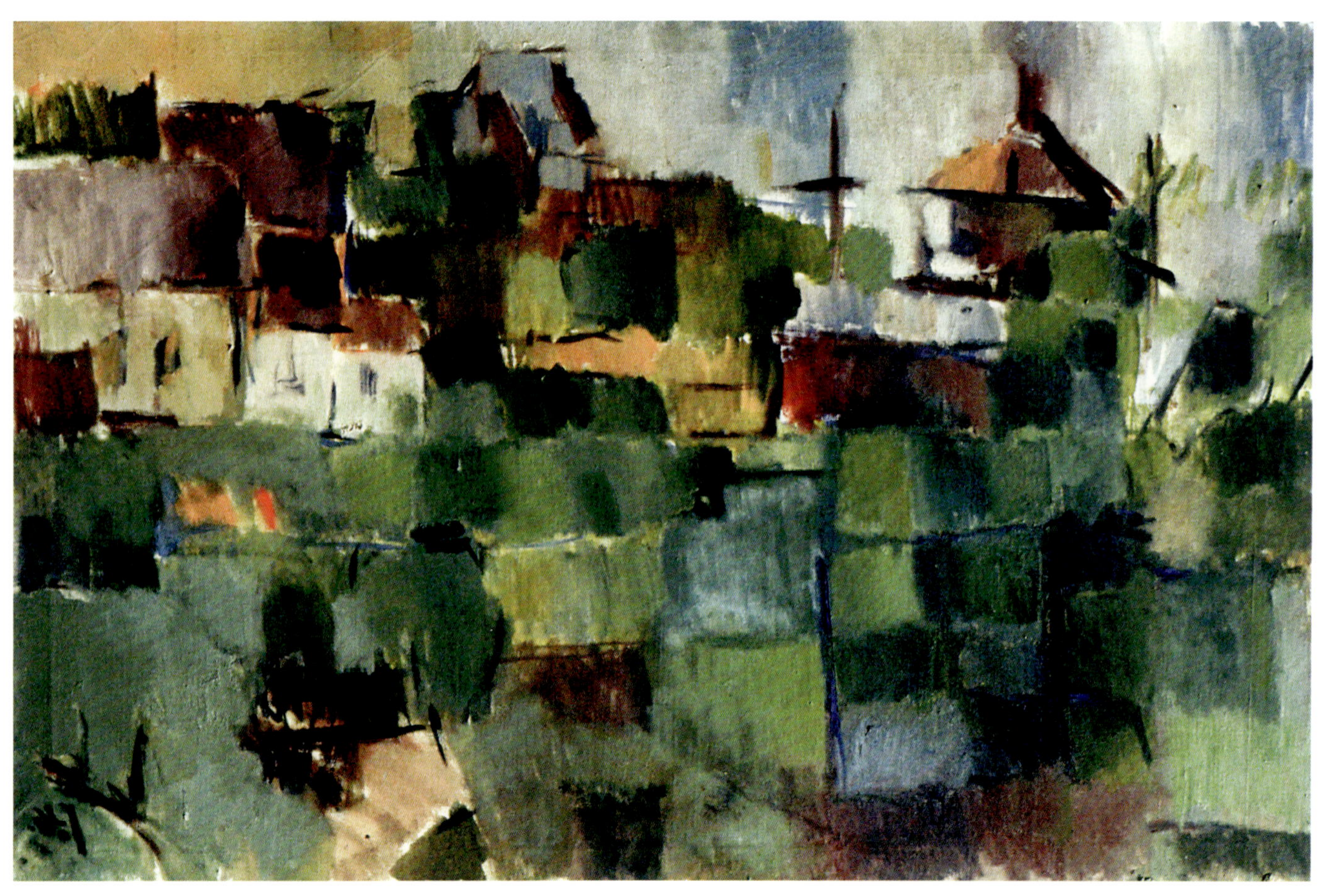

Hofmann School, Provincetown, June 4, 1947, 1947.
Oil on canvas, 30 x 46 in. (76.2 x 116.8 cm).
Estate of the artist. Courtesy © 2020 Paul Georges Foundation Inc.,
85 Walker Street, NYC 10013.

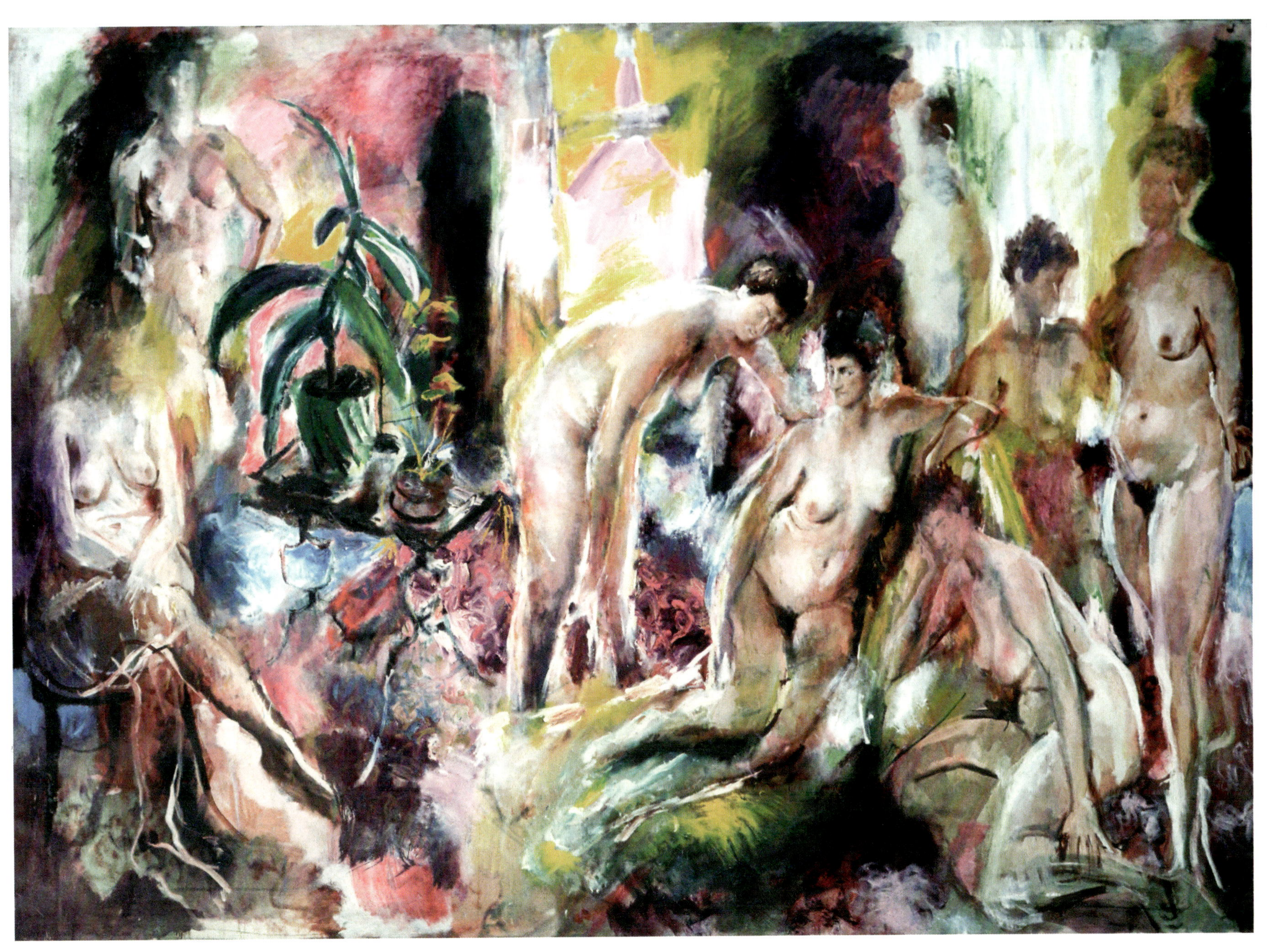

In My 11th Street Studio, 1953–1956.
Maroger on canvas, 78 x 113½ in. (198.1 x 288.1 cm).
Estate of the artist. Courtesy © 2020 Paul Georges Foundation Inc.,
85 Walker Street, NYC 10013.

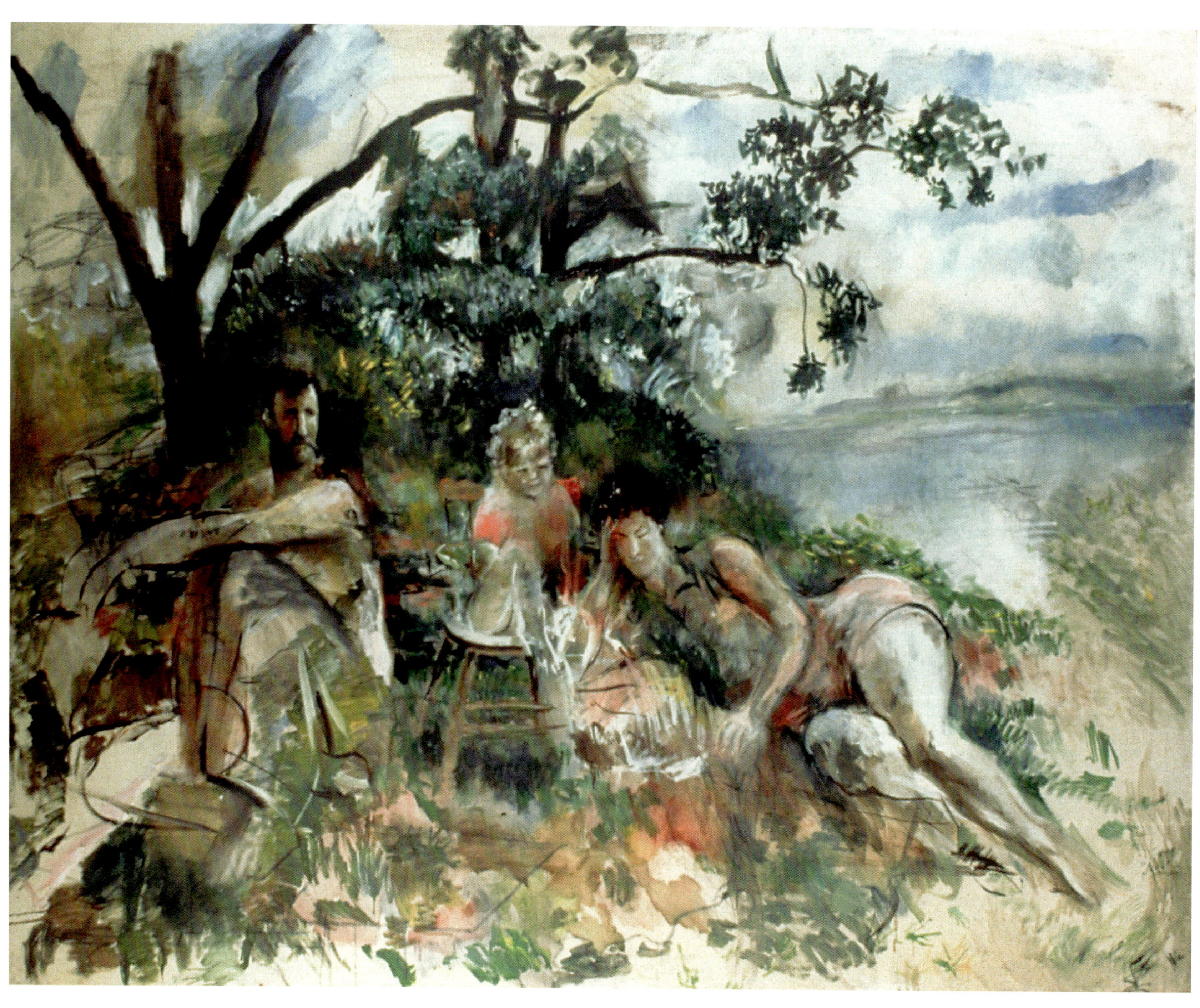

Family in East Hampton, 1956.
Oil on canvas, 80 x 101 in. (203.2 x 256.5 cm).
Estate of the artist. Courtesy © 2020 Paul Georges Foundation Inc.,
85 Walker Street, NYC 10013.

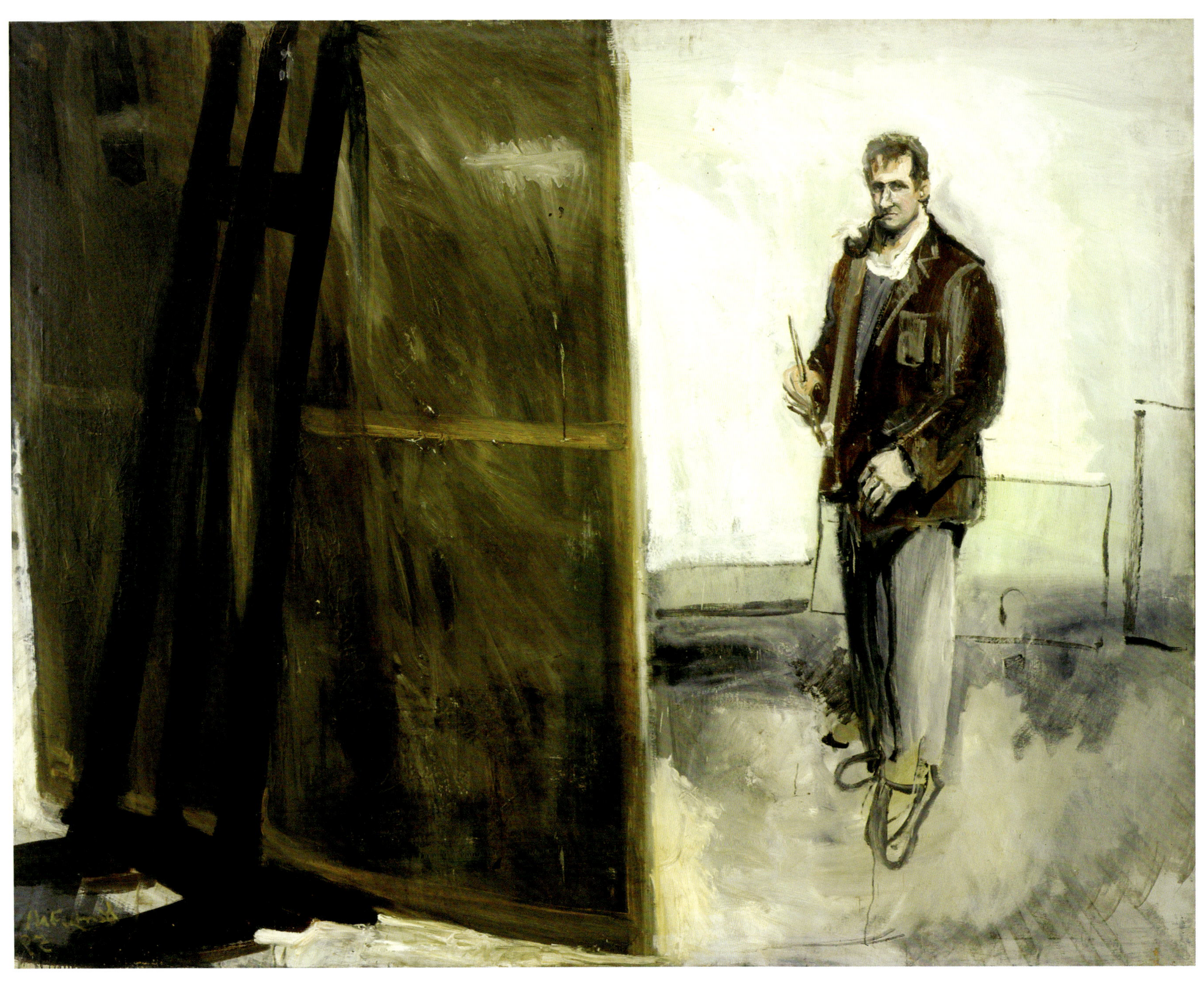

Self-Portrait in Studio, 1959.
Oil on linen, 81¼ x 101¾ in. (206.4 x 258.4 cm).
Center for Figurative Painting, New York, NY.

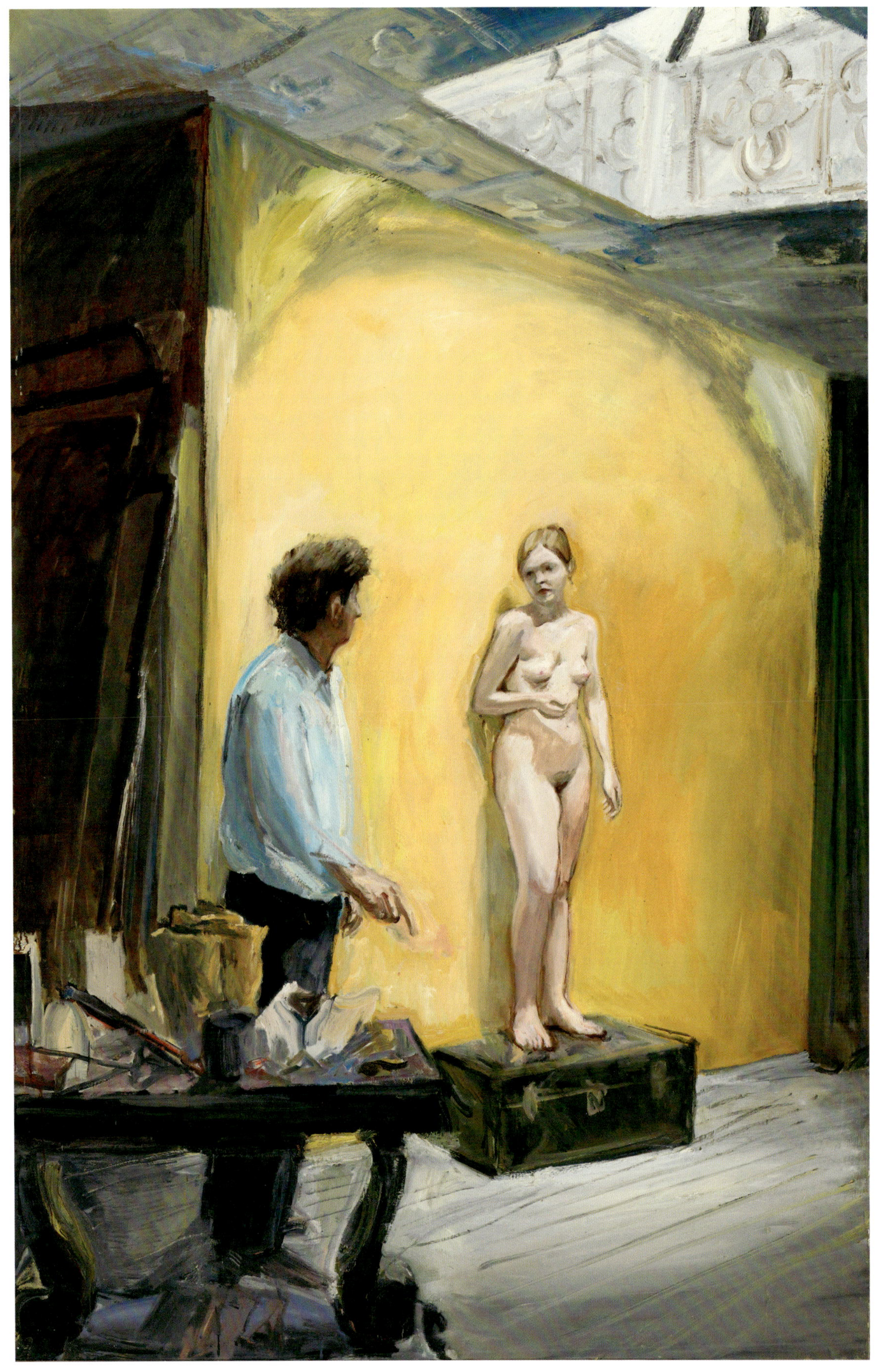

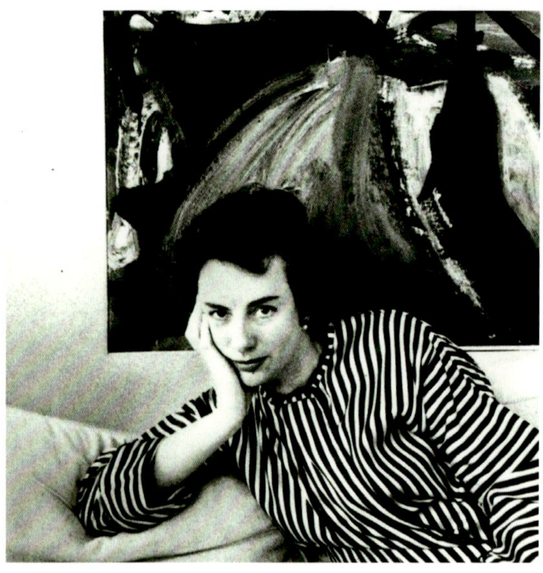

GRACE HARTIGAN

b.1922, Newark, NJ; d. 2008, Baltimore, MD

Grace Hartigan claimed she became an artist almost against her will. "I didn't choose painting. It chose me. I didn't have any talent. I just had genius,"[1] she said. At 19, she planned to move to Alaska with her husband, Robert Jachens, where they would live like pioneers. However, when her husband was drafted in 1942, Hartigan returned to New Jersey with her newborn and enrolled in the Newark College of Engineering, where she studied mechanical drafting and practiced it in an airplane factory to support her family while making watercolors on the side.

After graduation from Newark College, Hartigan took private painting lessons with Isaac Lane Muse. Through him, she was introduced to the work of Henri Matisse and to Kimon Nicolaïdes' *The Natural Way to Draw*.[2] After moving to New York with her teacher, she quickly joined the downtown artistic community. Hartigan became interested in Abstract Expressionism after seeing Jackson Pollock's drip paintings and later became close to the painter and his wife, Lee Krasner. Pollock and Willem de Kooning became her informal mentors.

In 1950, one of Hartigan's paintings was selected by Clement Greenberg and Meyer Schapiro for the *New Talent* show at the Kootz Gallery. She had her first solo show the following year at the newly founded Tibor de Nagy Gallery, which also exhibited Helen Frankenthaler, Larry Rivers, and Jane Freilicher, all of whom became part of her circle. In 1958, Hartigan was named "the most celebrated of the young American women painters" by *Life* magazine,[3] although during this time, she had briefly exhibited under the name George Hartigan in an attempt to achieve greater recognition for her work.[4]

From 1964 until the end of her life, Hartigan taught at what is now the Maryland Institute College of Art, while exhibiting widely. Though her early works were abstract, after 1952 she began incorporating recognizable motifs from sources ranging from Old Master images to shop windows. She continued to move between figuration and abstraction throughout her long career, concentrating on representation in her later paintings from the 1980s through the 2000s. Hartigan's work is in the collections of most major American museums, including the Neuberger Museum of Art, Purchase, New York, and the Museum of Modern Art and the Whitney Museum of American Art in New York City. She is represented by C. Grimaldis Gallery, Baltimore, Maryland.

1 William Grimes, "Grace Hartigan, 86, Abstract Painter, Dies," *New York Times*, November 11, 2018, https://www.nytimes.com/2008/11/18/arts/design/18hartigan.html (accessed 14th January 2020).
2 Delia Gaze, *Dictionary of Women Artists* (Chicago: Fitzroy Dearborn Publishers, 1997), 644.
3 Grimes, "Grace Hartigan, 86, Abstract Painter, Dies."
4 The Museum of Modern Art, https://www.moma.org/collection/works/78375 (accessed 14th January 2020).

2013: *Grace Hartigan (1922–2009): A Memorial Exhibition*, C. Grimaldis Gallery, Baltimore, MD

1997: *Hartigan's Women*, Paul Robeson Gallery, Newark, NJ

1993: *Grace Hartigan and the Poets: Paintings and Prints*, Schick Art Gallery, Skidmore College, Saratoga Springs, NY

1988: Gruenebaum Gallery, New York, NY

1975: William Zierler Gallery, New York, NY

1955: Vassar College Art Gallery, Poughkeepsie, NY

Selected Group Exhibitions

2020: *Figuration Never Died*, Brattleboro Museum & Art Center, Brattleboro, VT

2006–2007: *New York School: Another View*, Opalka Gallery, Albany, NY

1999: *American Century, Part II*, Whitney Museum of American Art, New York, NY

1995: *Artist's Choice—Modern Women*, Museum of Modern Art, New York, NY

1993–1998: *Hand-Painted Pop: American Art in Transition 1955–62*, The Museum of Contemporary Art, Los Angeles, CA

1987: *Color: Pure and Simple*, Stamford Museum and Nature Center, Stamford, CT

Collections

Museum of Modern Art, New York, NY

Neuberger Museum of Art, Purchase, NY

Rose Museum, Brandeis University, Boston, MA

St. Louis Art Museum, St. Louis, MO

Wadsworth Athenaeum, Hartford, CT

Walker Art Center, Minneapolis, MN

Whitney Museum of American Art, New York, NY

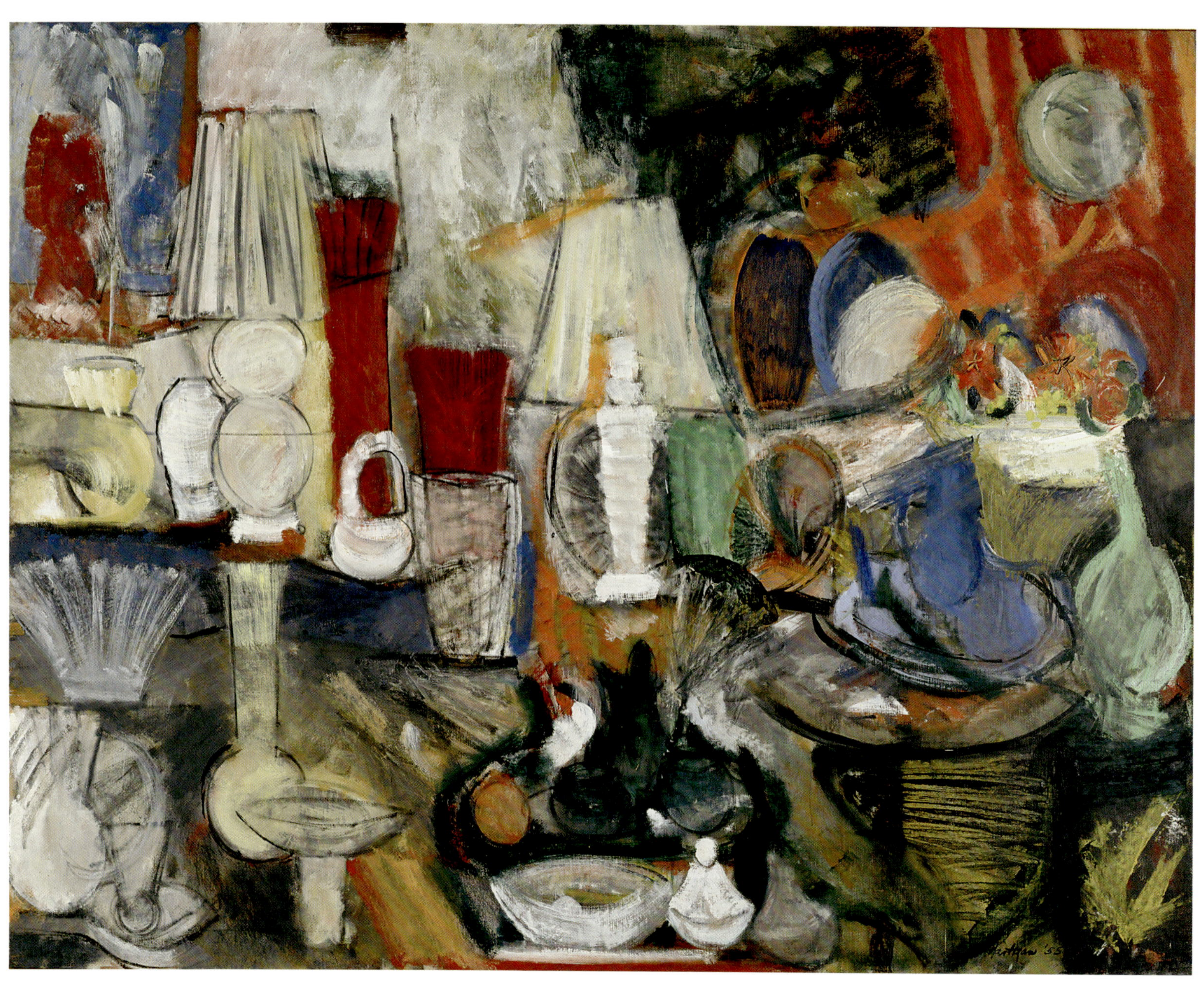

■ *Giftwares*, 1955.
Oil and charcoal on canvas, 63 x 81⅛ in. (160 x 206 cm).
Signed and dated lower right: "Hartigan '55."
Collection of Neuberger Museum of Art, Purchase College, State University of New York,
Purchase, NY. Gift of Roy R. Neuberger, 1975.15.16.

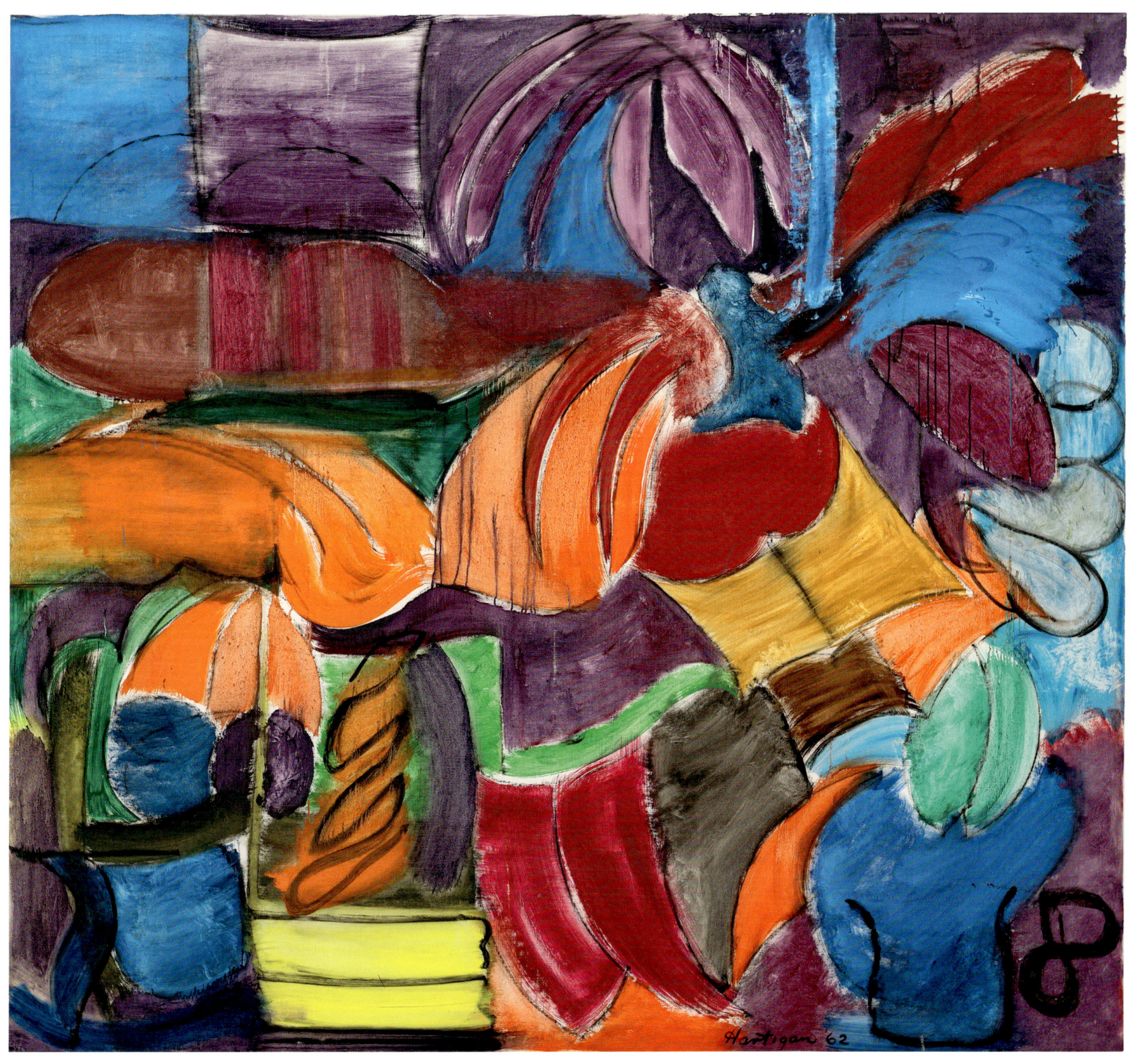

■ *Phoenix*, 1962.
Oil on canvas, 80 x 88 in. (203.2 x 223.5 cm).
Collection of Hart Perry.

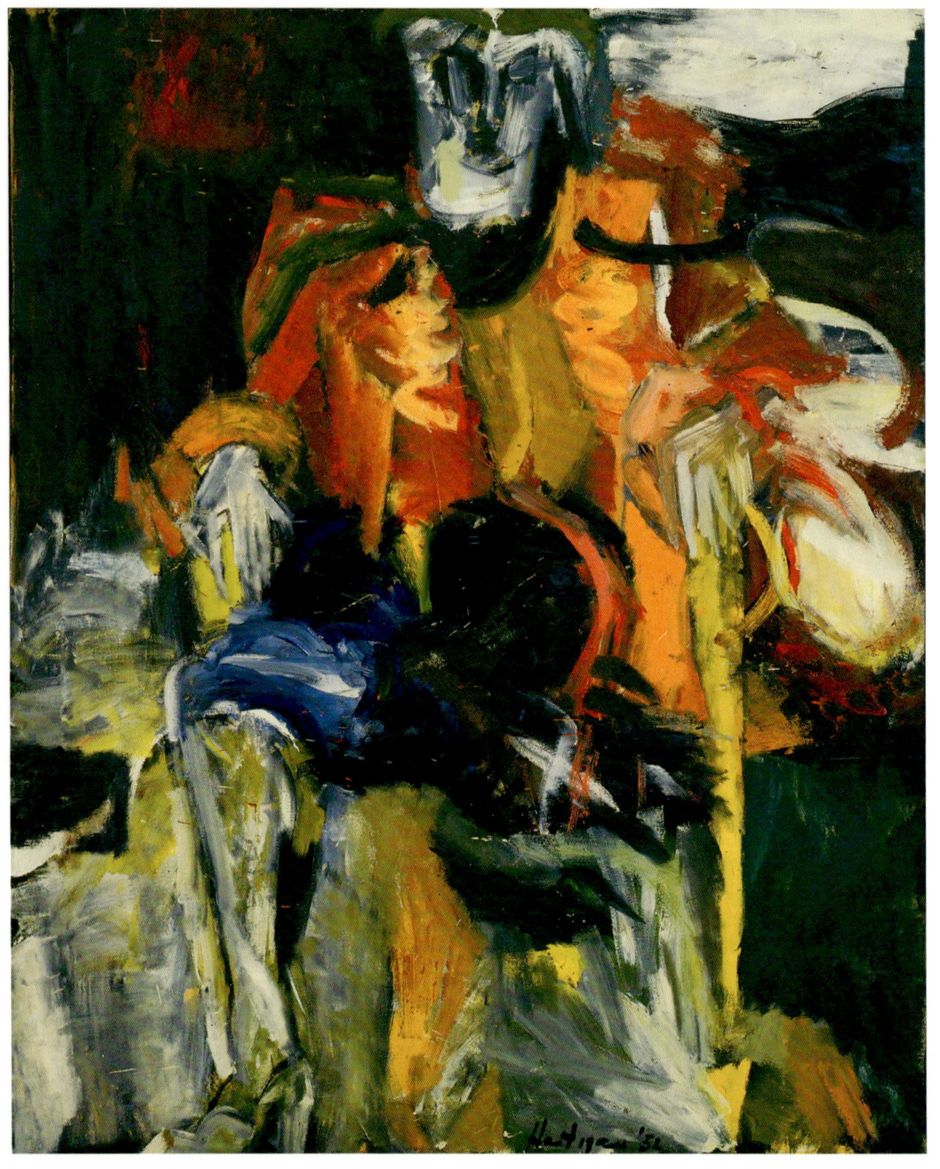

The Persian Jacket, 1952.
Oil on canvas, 52½ x 48 in. (146 x 121.9 cm).
The Museum of Modern Art, New York, NY.
Gift of George Poindexter, 413.1953.
Digital Image © The Museum of Modern Art /
Licensed by SCALA / Art Resource, NY.

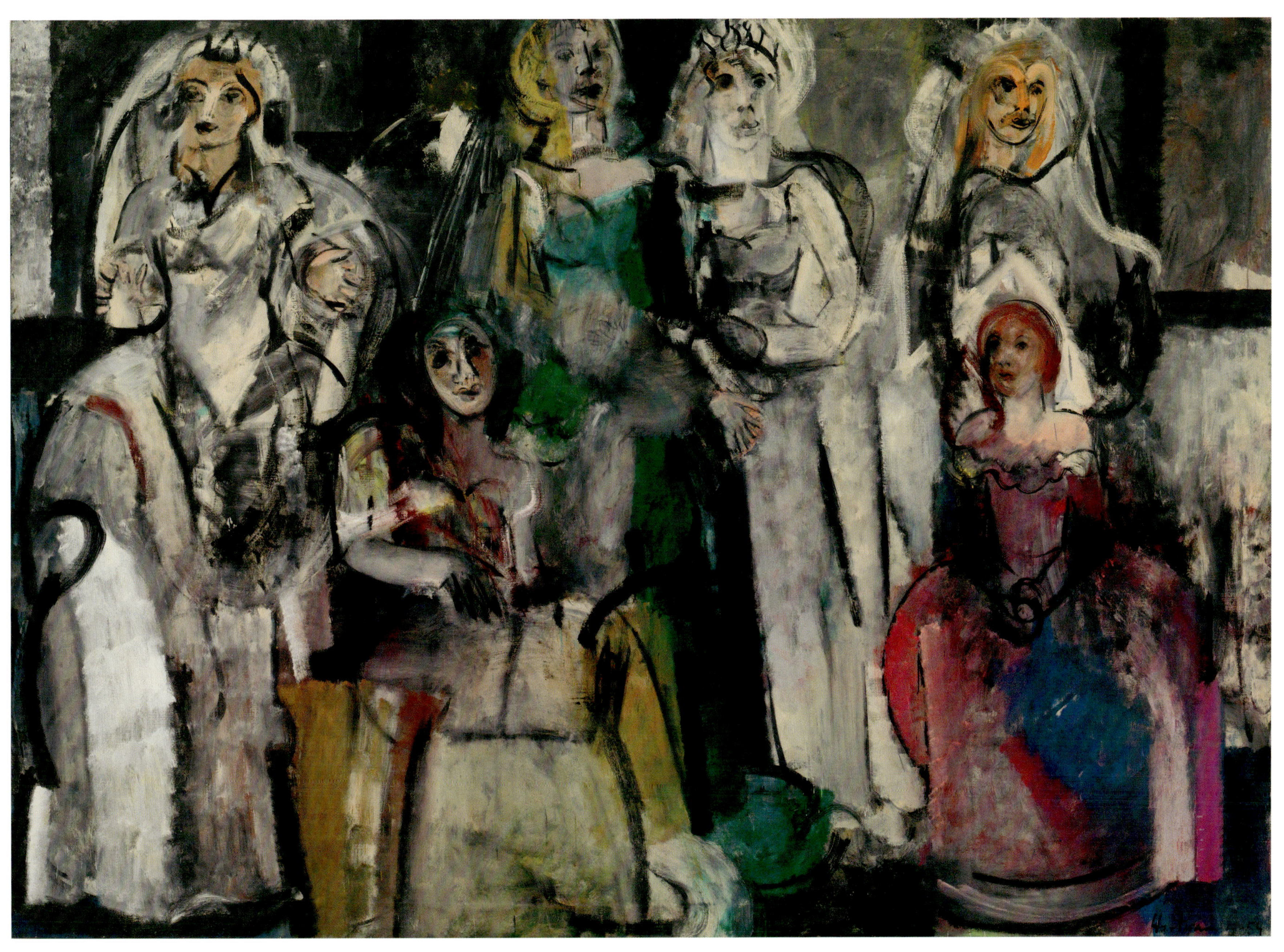

Grand Street Brides, 1954.
Oil on canvas, 72⁹/₁₆ x 102⁹/₁₆ in. (184.3 x 260 cm).
Whitney Museum of American Art, New York, NY. Purchase, with funds
from an anonymous donor, 55.27. Digital image © Whitney Museum of
American Art / Licensed by Scala / Art Resource, NY.

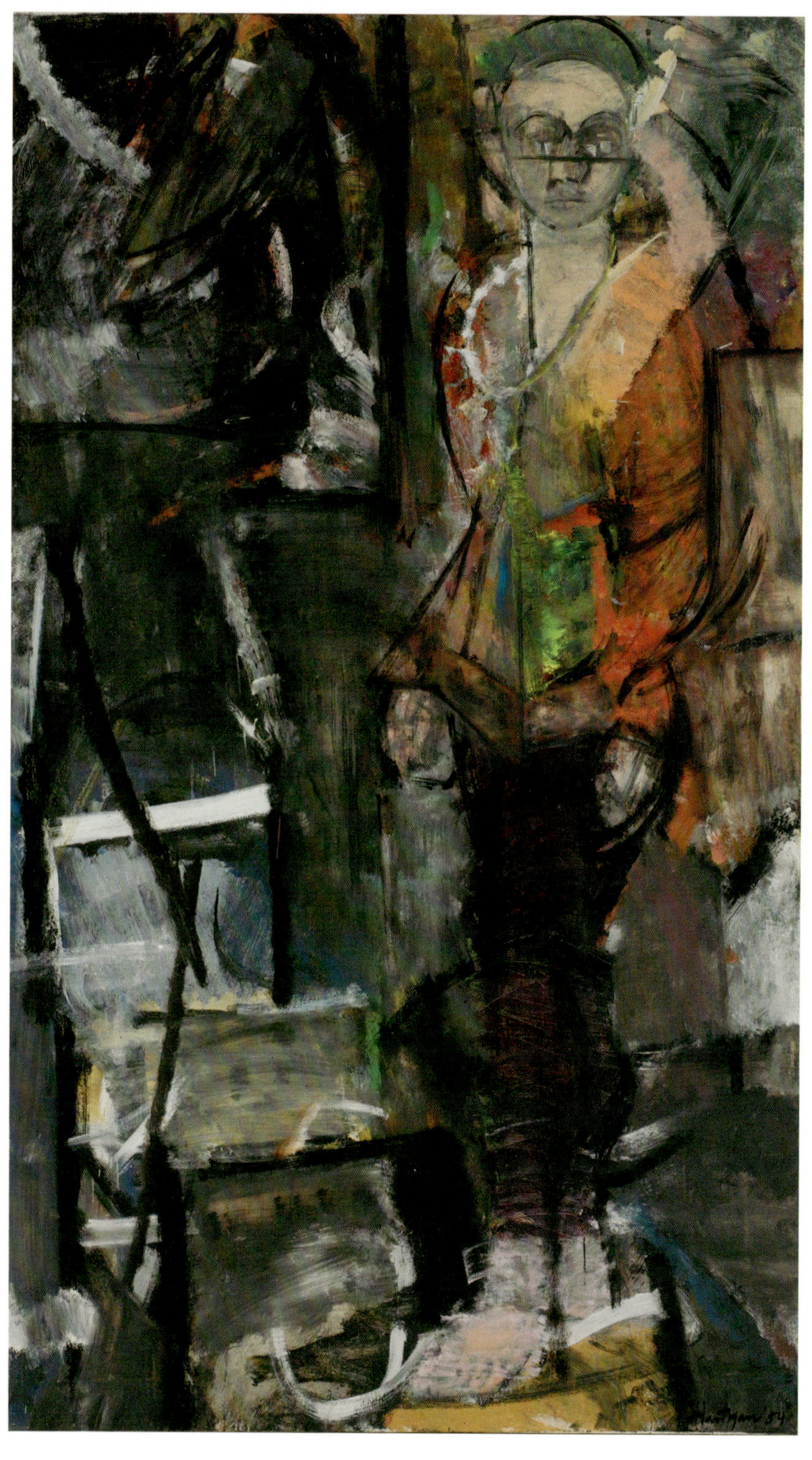

The Masker, 1954.
Oil on canvas, 72 x 41¾ in. (182.9 x 106 cm).
The Frances Lehman Loeb Art Center, Vassar College,
Poughkeepsie, NY. Museum purchase, 1954.9.

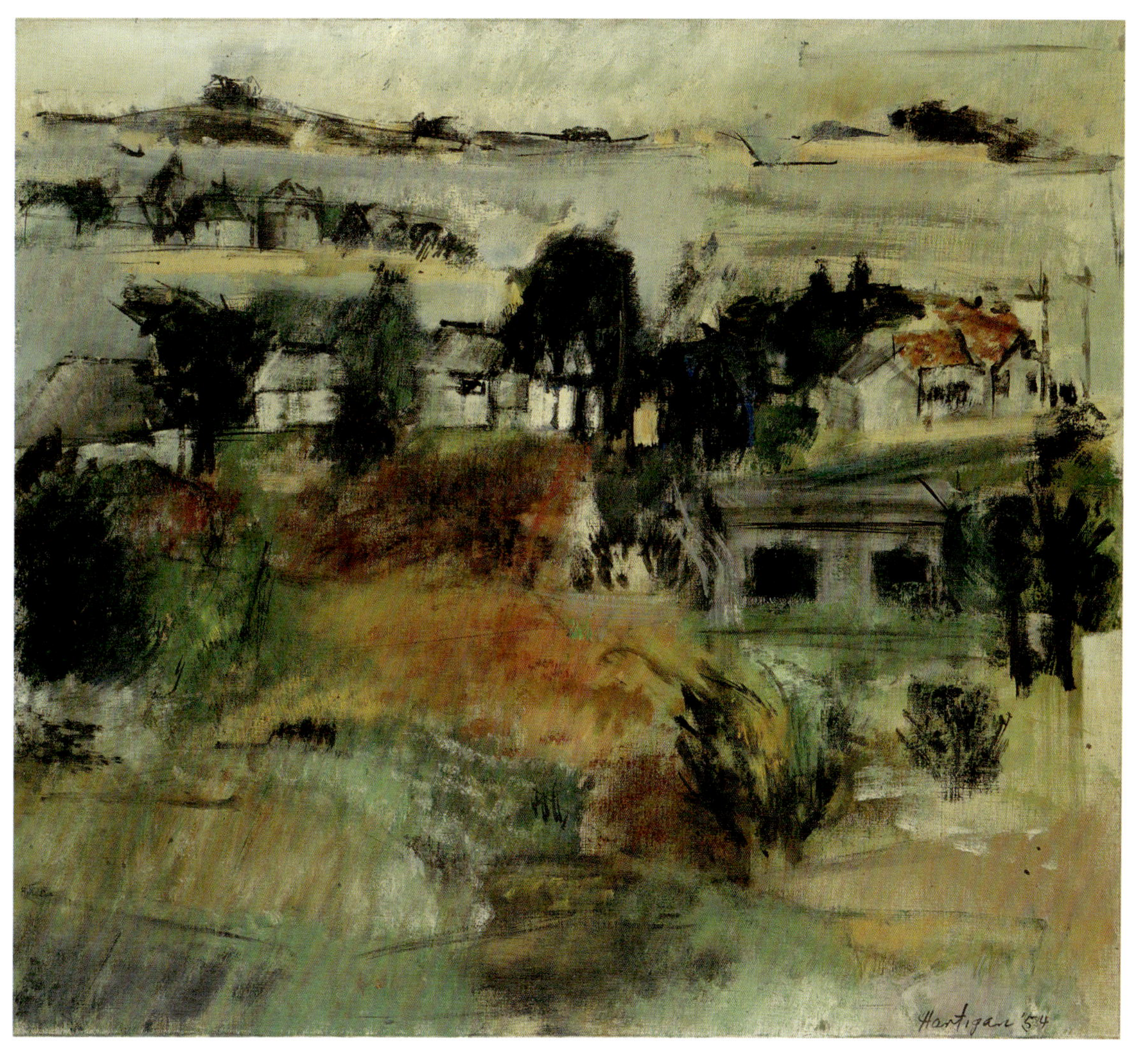

Southampton Fields, 1954.
Oil on canvas, 32 x 36 in. (81.3 x 91.4 cm).
The Metropolitan Museum of Art, New York, NY.
Gift of Edmund E. Levin, 1982, 1982.105.
© The Metropolitan Museum of Art.
Image source: Art Resource, New York, NY.

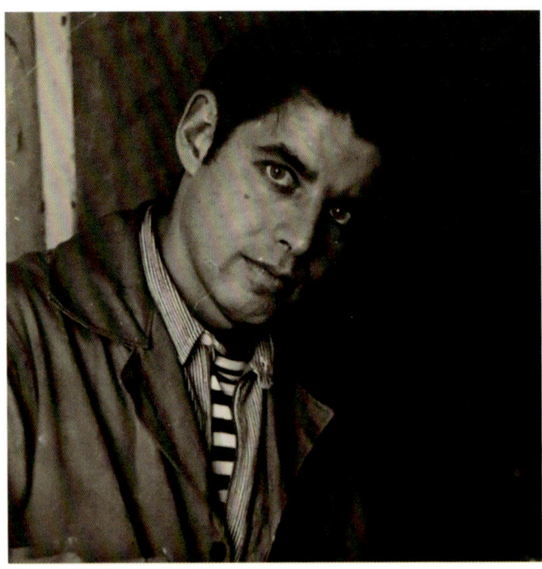

WOLF KAHN

b. 1927, Stuttgart, Germany; d. 2020, New York, NY

Born in Stuttgart, Germany, the son of a noted Jewish musician, in 1940 Kahn emigrated with his family, by way of England, to the United States. In 1945, he graduated from the High School of Music & Art in New York City, before serving in the Navy. Following his service, he returned to study with Hans Hofmann and ultimately became Hofmann's studio assistant. In 1950, he enrolled in the University of Chicago and graduated in 1951 with a bachelor of arts degree.

Kahn then traveled across America and worked as a lumberjack in Oregon before returning to New York to paint. He became part of the vanguard downtown scene, later saying that the best thing that came out of the Artists' Club was meeting his wife, the painter Emily Mason, there. Kahn and other former Hofmann students established the Hansa Gallery in the fall of 1952, a cooperative gallery where Kahn had his first solo exhibition in 1953.

In 1956, he joined the Grace Borgenicht Gallery, where he exhibited regularly until 1995.

Although he came of age in the era of Abstract Expressionism, Kahn turned to nature for stimulus. He traveled extensively, painting landscapes in Egypt, Greece, Hawaii, Italy, Kenya, Mexico, Maine, and New Mexico, eventually dividing his time between New York and a hillside farm in southeastern Vermont. The woods, fields, and geometric buildings of the farm and its environs have been reflected both directly and obliquely in Kahn's work for decades, most obviously in his use of color, but also in recurrent motifs.

Kahn has received numerous awards, including a Fulbright Scholarship, a John Simon Guggenheim Fellowship, and an Award in Art from the Academy of Arts and Letters. His work is in private and public collections throughout the United States, including The Metropolitan Museum of Art, the Whitney Museum of American Art, and the Museum of Modern Art in New York City; the Smithsonian American Art Museum, Washington, DC; the Museum of Fine Arts, Boston, Massachusetts; and the Los Angeles County Museum of Art, Los Angeles, California, among others. Kahn is represented by Miles McEnery Gallery, New York.

2018: *Wolf Kahn: A 50 Year Survey*, Jerald Melberg Gallery, Charlotte, NC

2010: *Wolf Kahn—Pastels*, Morris Museum of Art, Augusta, GA

2006: *Wolf Kahn's Barns*, Gibbes Museum of Art, Charleston, NC

1999: *Wolf Kahn: Southern Landscapes*, Morris Museum of Art, Augusta, GA

1984: *Wolf Kahn: Landscapes*, San Diego Museum of Art, San Diego, CA

Selected Group Exhibitions

2020: *Figuration Never Died*, Brattleboro Museum & Art Center, Brattleboro, VT

2016: *Spring Group Exhibition*, Cavalier Gallery, New York, NY

2014: *Annual Small Works Exhibition*, Cavalier Gallery, New York, NY

1998: *Centennial Exhibition*, Academy of Arts and Letters, New York, NY

1994: *Art 25*, Basel, Switzerland

1993: *Foire Internationale d'Art Contemporain*, Paris, France

1985: *The Janss Collection*, San Francisco Museum of Art, San Francisco, CA

1960: *Young America 1960: 30 Painters Under 36*, Whitney Museum of American Art, New York, NY

Collections

Hirshhorn Museum and Sculpture Garden, Washington, DC

Los Angeles County Museum of Art, Los Angeles, CA

The Metropolitan Museum of Art, New York, NY

Museum of Fine Arts, Boston, Boston, MA

Museum of Modern Art, New York, NY

Smithsonian American Art Museum, Washington, DC

Whitney Museum of American Art, New York, NY

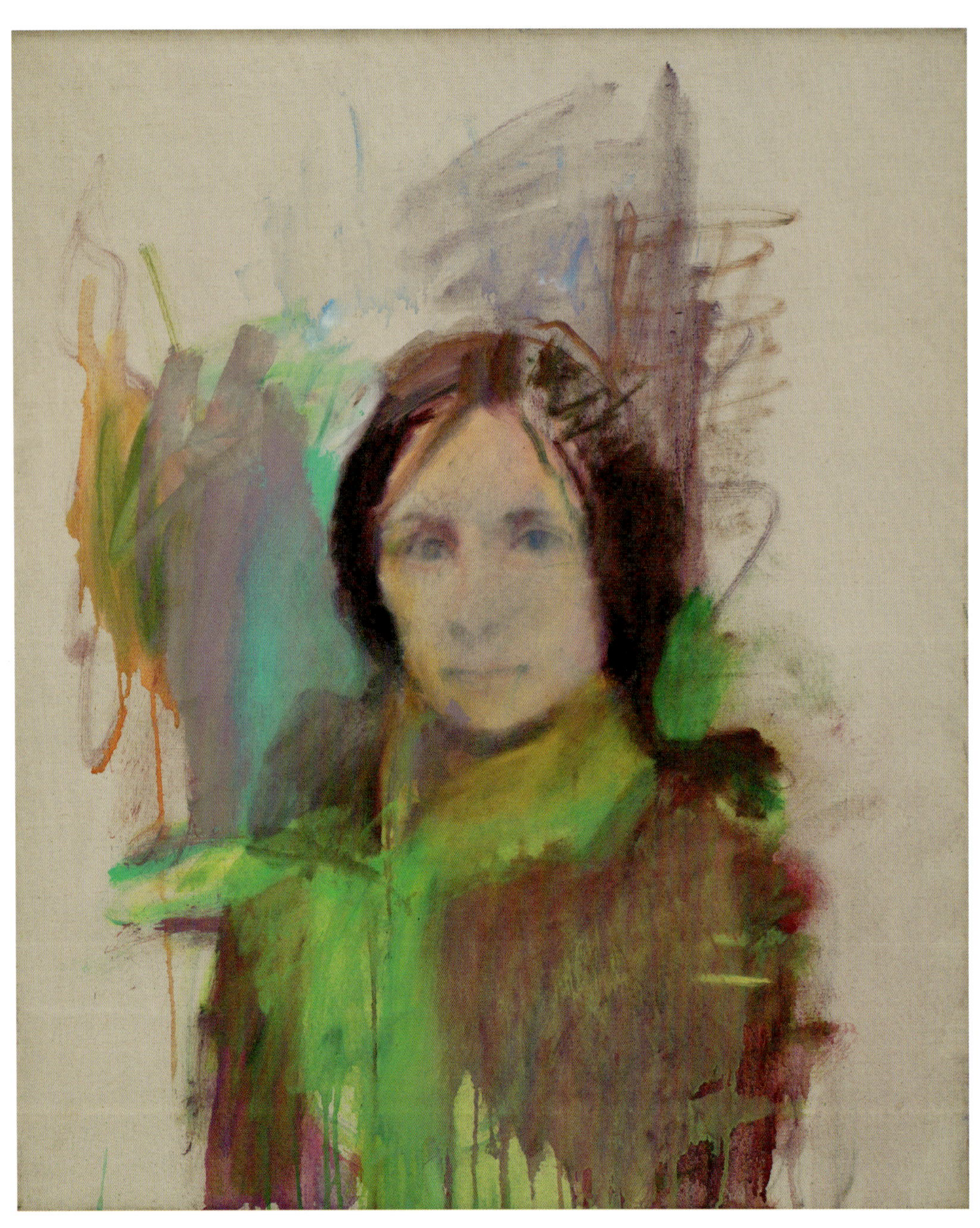

■ *Emily in 1958*, 1958.
Oil on canvas, 30 x 24 in. (76.2 x 61 cm).
Wolf Kahn and Emily Mason.

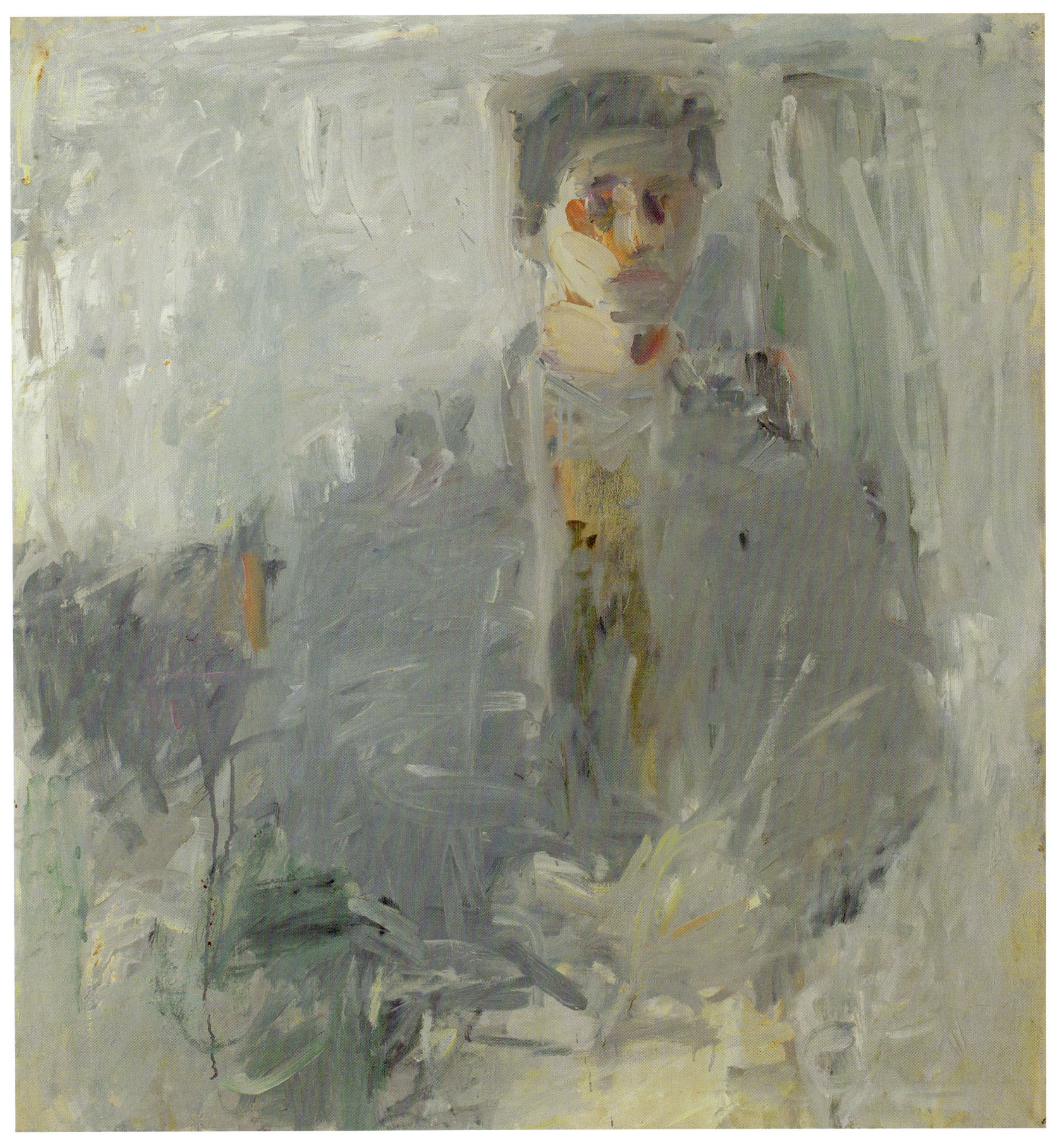

■ *Self-Portrait*, 1959.
Oil on canvas, 42 x 40 in. (106.7 x 101.6 cm).
Wolf Kahn and Emily Mason.

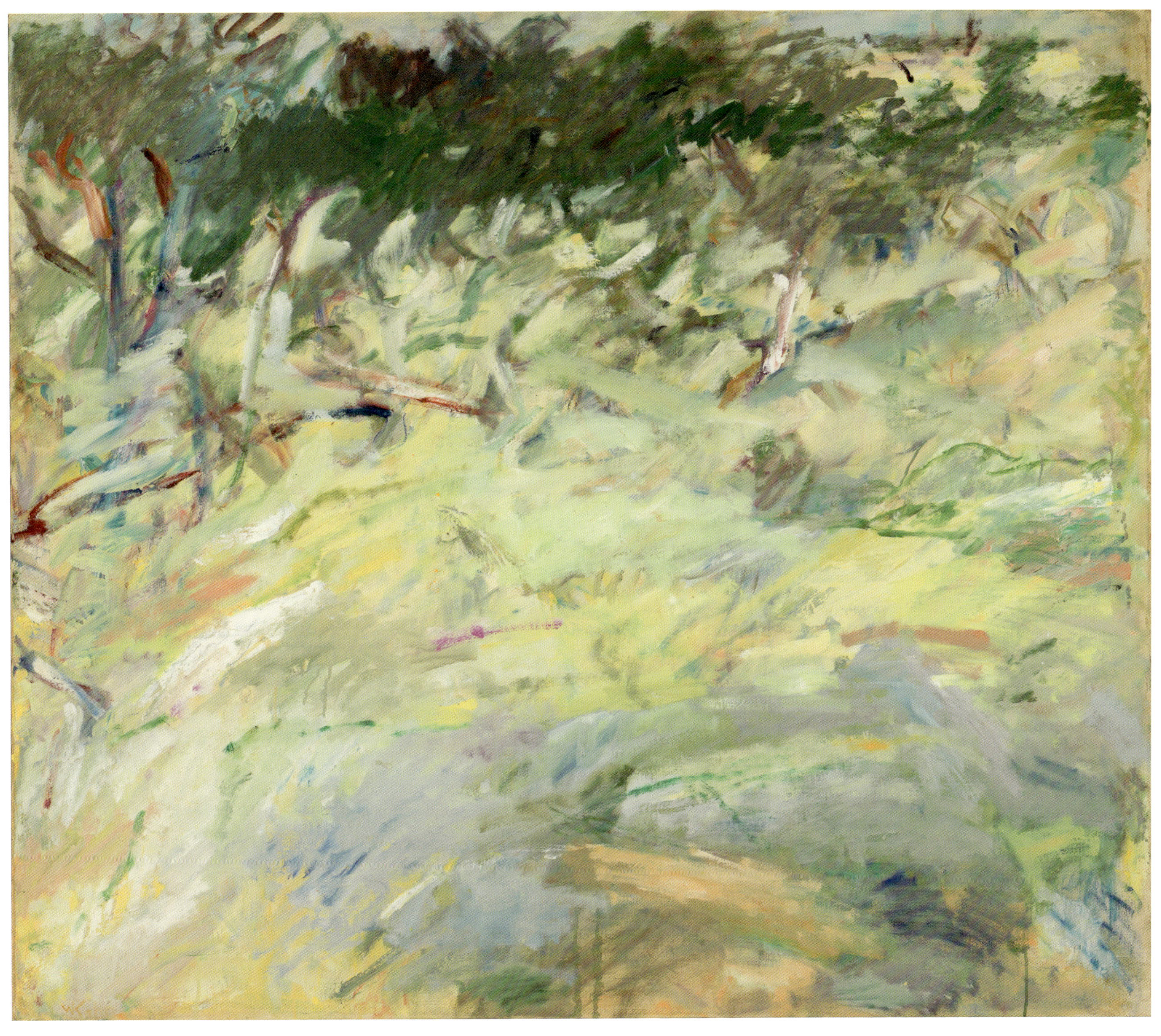

Silver Sea, 1959.
Oil on canvas, frame: 46⁷/₁₆ x 51⁵/₁₆ in. (106.7 x 101.6 cm).
Williams College Museum of Art, Williamstown, MA.
Bequest of Lawrence H. Bloedel, Class of 1923, 77.9.54. © 2020 Wolf
Kahn / Licensed by VAGA at Artists Rights Society (ARS), New York, NY.

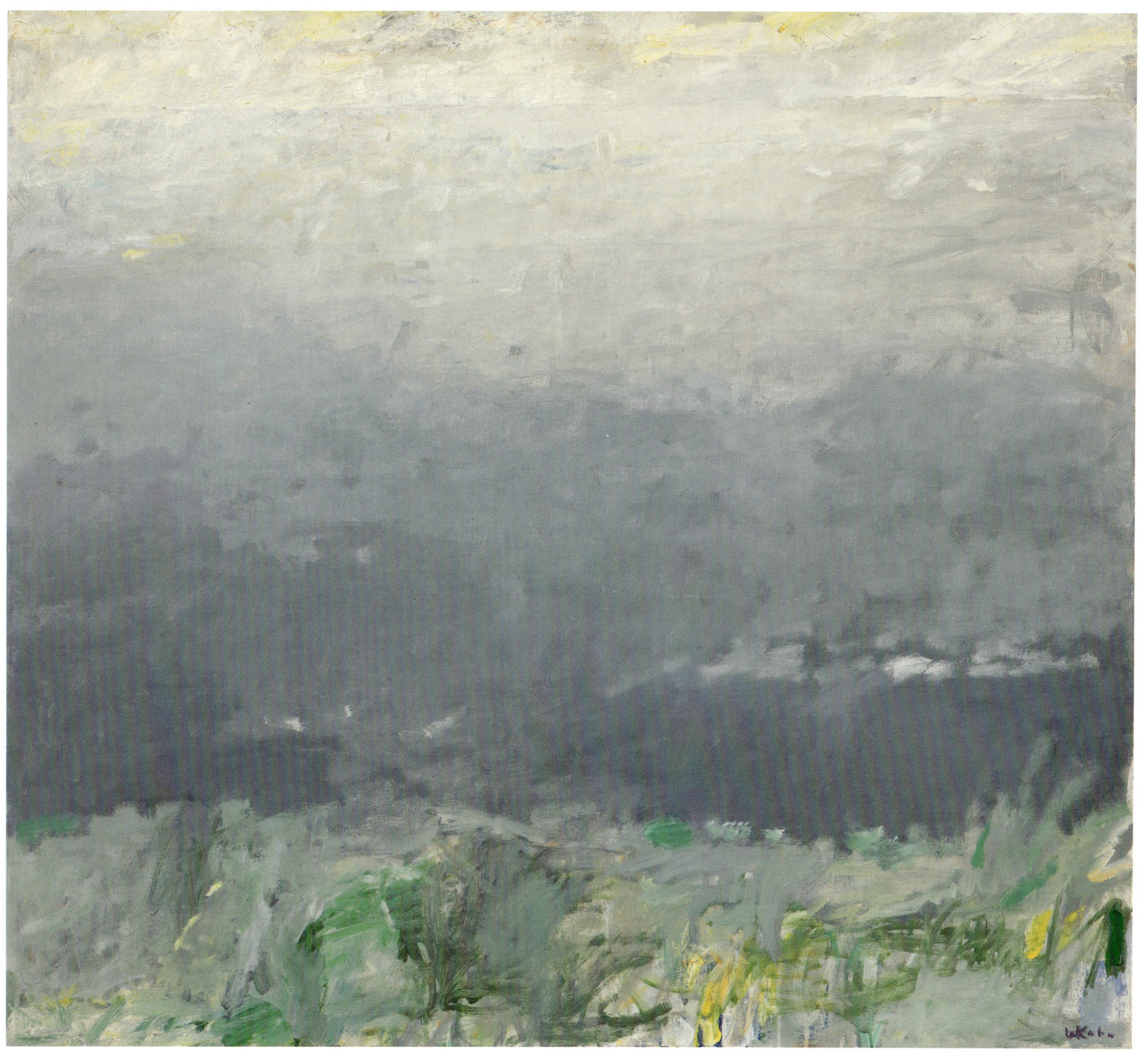

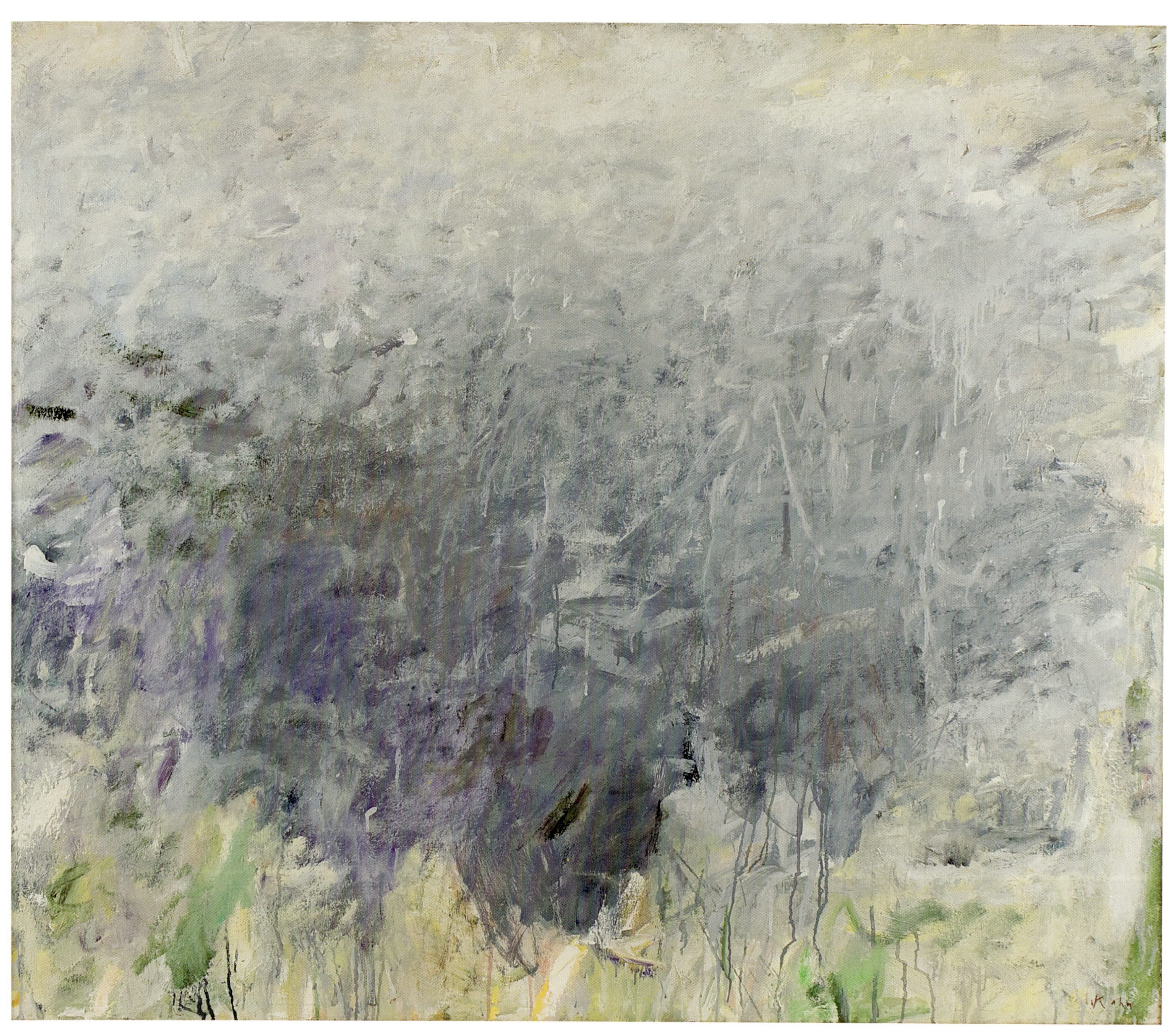

Atlantic Highlands, 1960.
Oil on canvas, 44⅛ x 53 in. (112.1 x 134.6 cm).
St. Louis Art Museum, St. Louis, MO. Gift of the Ford Foundation, 54:1962.
© Wolf Kahn / Artist Rights Society (ARS) New York, NY. © 2020 Wolf Kahn /
Licensed by VAGA at Artists Rights Society (ARS), New York, NY.

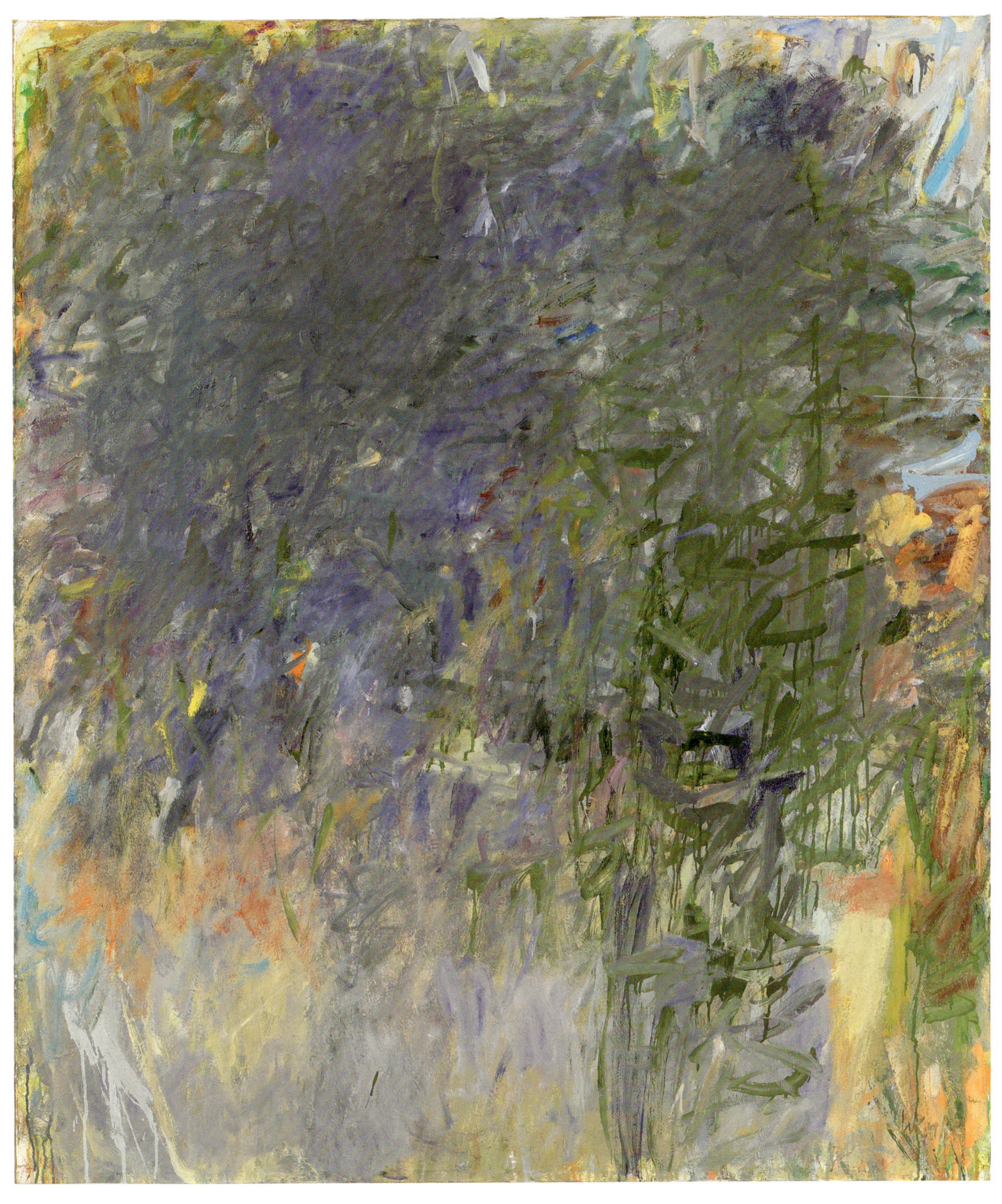

Into a Clearing, 1960.
Oil on canvas, 40 x 50 in. (101.6 x 127 cm).
Private collection.

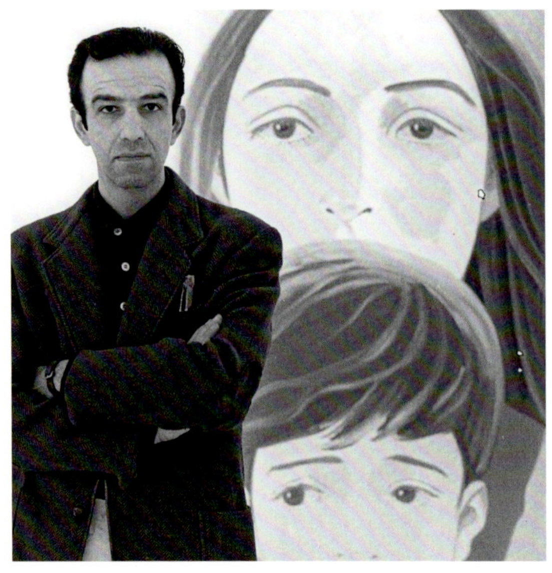

ALEX KATZ

b. 1927, Brooklyn, NY

Alex Katz's reputation was established by his deadpan portraits of friends, family, and members of the New York art world. More recently, he has produced ambitious landscapes of Maine, where he spends the summer, and evocative, sometimes nocturnal New York cityscapes.

Katz studied art at The Cooper Union from 1945 to 1949. His first solo show was held at the Roko Gallery in 1954. Later, he showed at such downtown institutions as Tanager Gallery and the Stable Gallery, before moving to prestigious uptown venues including Fischbach and Marlborough galleries. In the late 1950s, he found himself among a growing number of artists dissatisfied with the then-dominant genre of Abstract Expressionism and, triggered by a summer session of plein-air painting with his friend and colleague Lois Dodd at Maine's Skowhegan School of Painting and Sculpture, Katz began working more naturalistically. He became increasingly interested in

portraiture and painted his friends, and in particular, his wife and muse, Ada. In 1959, he made his first cutout, which would ultimately develop into a series of flat "sculptures": freestanding, two-sided portraits that exist in actual space. In the early 1960s, influenced by films, television, and billboard advertising, Katz began creating large-scale paintings of figures and heads, often dramatically cropped. In 1977, he was commissioned to produce an enormous frieze of 23 multiracial women's heads, each 20 feet high, wrapped around the RKO General Building at the corner of 42 Street and Seventh Avenue in New York City's Times Square. The mural, no longer extant, returned Katz's billboard-inspired imagery to its origins.

In 1968, Katz moved to an artists' cooperative building in SoHo, where he has lived and worked ever since. He continues to spend his summers in Lincolnville, Maine. His work has been the subject of more than 200 solo exhibitions and nearly 500 group exhibitions internationally. He has received numerous awards and his works can be found in private and public collections worldwide, including The Metropolitan Museum of Art, the Museum of Modern Art, and the Whitney Museum of American Art in New York City; the National Gallery of Art and the National Portrait Gallery in Washington, DC; the Detroit Institute of Arts; and the Museum of Fine Arts, Boston, Massachusetts. Katz is represented by Gavin Brown's Enterprise, New York City.

Katz has been a generous supporter of younger artists, buying their work and donating it to such institutions as the Colby College Museum, Waterville, Maine, and the Portland Museum of Art, Portland, Maine, among others.

2019: *Alex Katz*, Daegu Art Museum, Daegu, South Korea

Contemporary Counterpoint / Alex Katz Water Lilies–Homage to Monet Series, 2009–2010, Musée de l'Orangerie, Paris, France

2017: *Alex Katz: Black and White*, Tampa Museum of Art, Tampa, FL

2016: *Present Tense: Sixty Years of Master Drawings*, Richard Gray Gallery, New York, NY

2015: *Brand New and Terrific: Alex Katz in the 1950s*, Colby College Museum of Art, Waterville, ME

2010: *Alex Katz*, Philadelphia Museum of Art, Philadelphia, PA

2004: *Behind Closed Doors*, Katonah Museum of Art, Katonah, New York, NY

2000: *Regarding Alex Katz*, Carnegie Museum of Art, Pittsburgh, PA

Selected Group Exhibition

2020: *Figuration Never Died*, Brattleboro Museum & Art Center, Brattleboro, VT

2019: *The Collection of the Fondation*, Louis Vuitton Foundation, Paris, France

2014–2015: *Face Value*, The National Portrait Gallery, Washington, DC

2014: *Irving Sandler: Out of Tenth Street and into the 1960s*, Loretta Howard Gallery, New York, NY

2013: *Regarding Warhol: Sixty Artists, Fifty Years*, The Metropolitan Museum of Art, New York, NY

2001: *Alex Katz*, Ed Rusha, American Academy in Rome, Rome, Italy

1979: *1979 Biennial Exhibition*, Whitney Museum of American Art, New York, NY

Collections

Detroit Institute of Arts, Detroit, MI

Essl Museum, Vienna, Austria

The Metropolitan Museum of Art, New York, NY

Musée National d'Art Moderne, Centre Georges Pompidou, Paris, France

Museum of Art, Rhode Island School of Design, Providence, RI

Museum of Fine Arts, Boston, Boston, MA

Museum of Modern Art, New York, NY

National Museum of Art, Washington, DC

National Gallery of Art, Washington, DC

National Portrait Gallery, Washington, DC

Tate Gallery, London, UK

Staatliche Museen Preussischer Kulturbesitz Nationalgalerie, Berlin, Germany

Whitney Museum of American Art, New York, NY

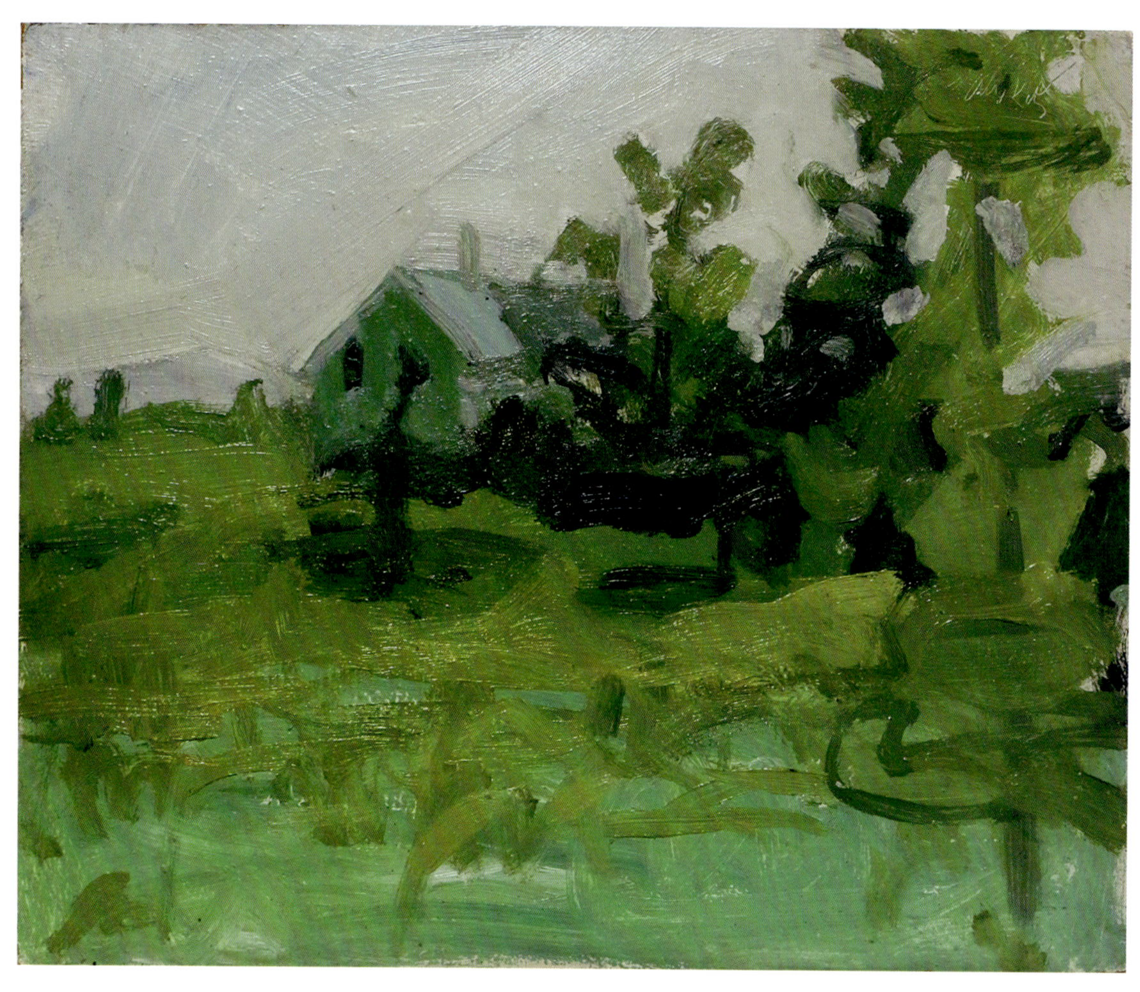

■ *Landscape with House,* 1955.
Oil on Masonite, 10 x 11¾ in. (25.4 x 30cm).
Collection of James Barron.

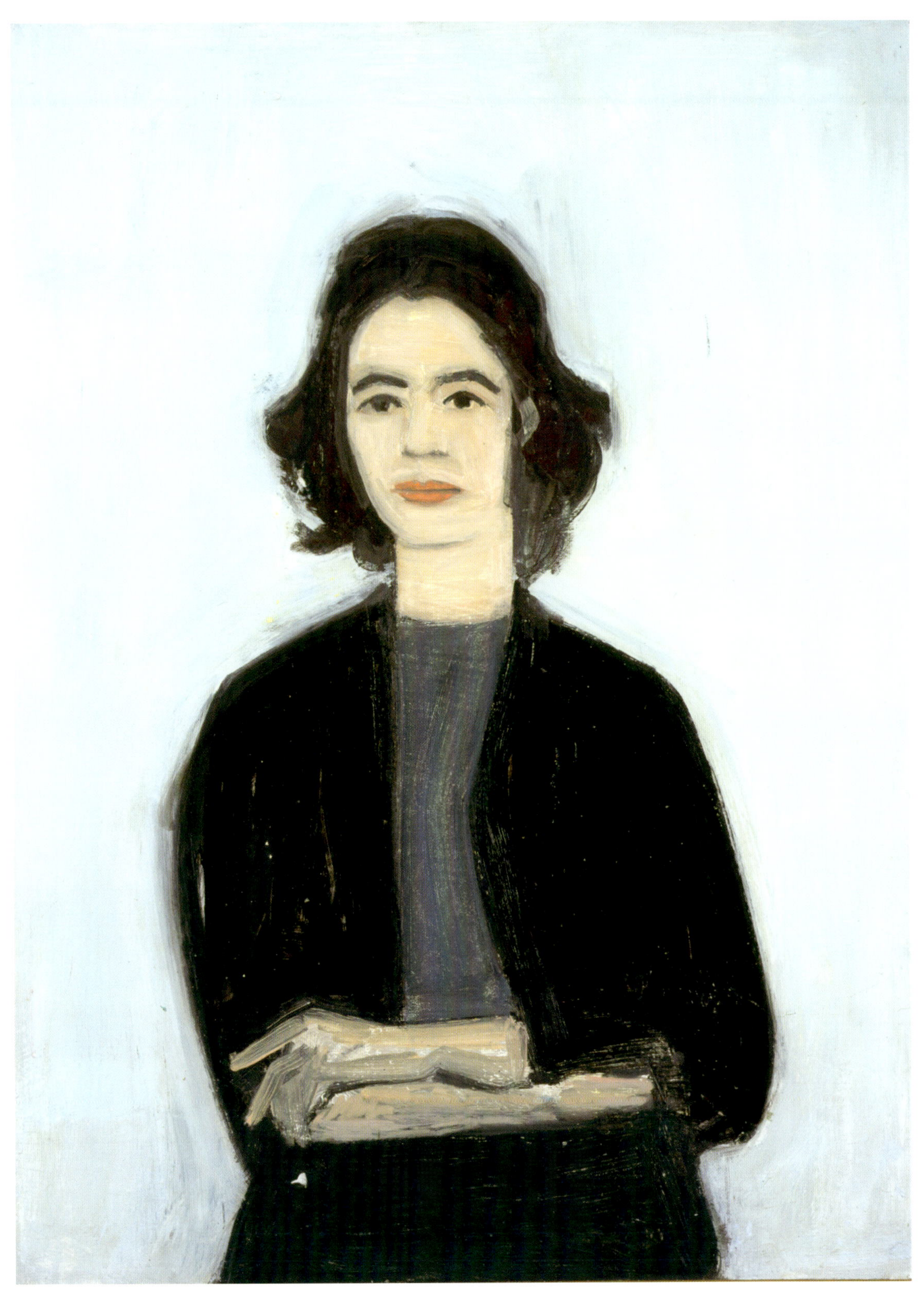

■ *Ada in Black Sweater*, 1957.
Oil on Masonite, 24 x 18 in. (61 x 45.7 cm).
Colby College Museum of Art, Waterville, ME.
Gift of the artist, 1995.063. © 2020 Alex Katz / Licensed by
VAGA at Artist Rights Society (ARS), New York, NY.

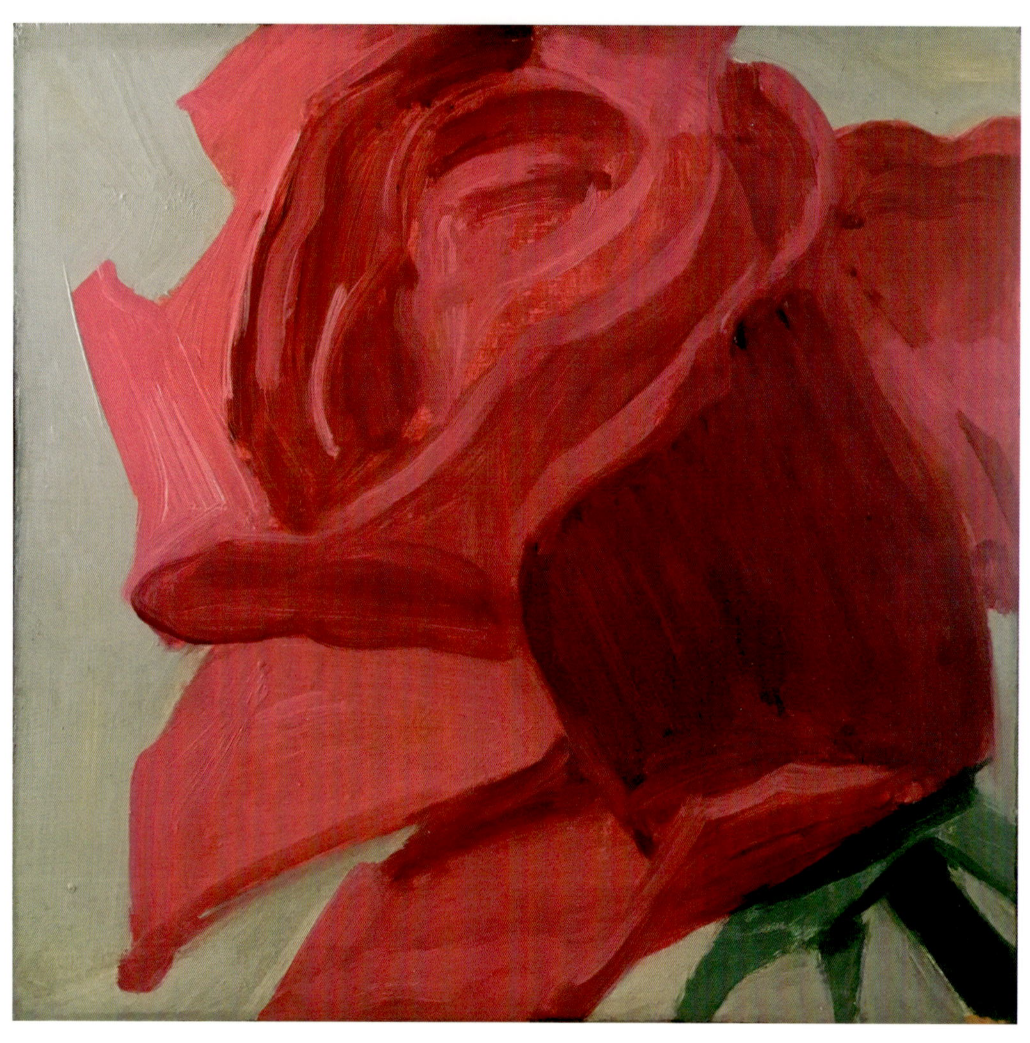

■ *Red Rose*, 1966–1967.
Oil on board, 8⅞ x 8½ in. (22.5 x 21.6 cm).
Private collection, USA.

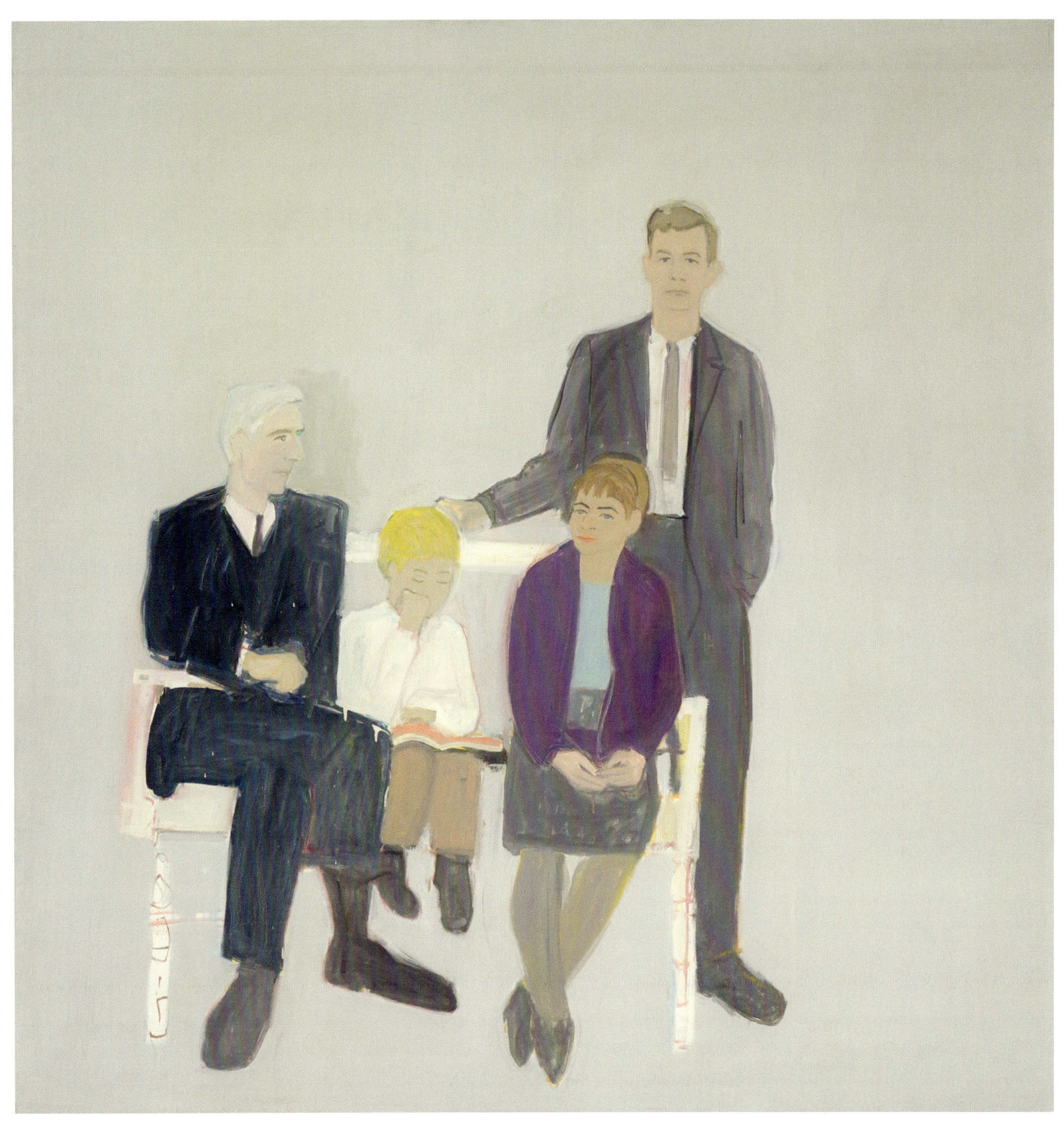

Family Album, 1958.
Oil on canvas, 73⅝ x 72¼ in. (189.2 x 185.4 cm).
North Carolina Museum of Art, Raleigh, NC.
Gift of Vincent Katz, 91.18. © 2020 Alex Katz /
Licensed by VAGA at Artist Rights Society (ARS),
New York, NY.

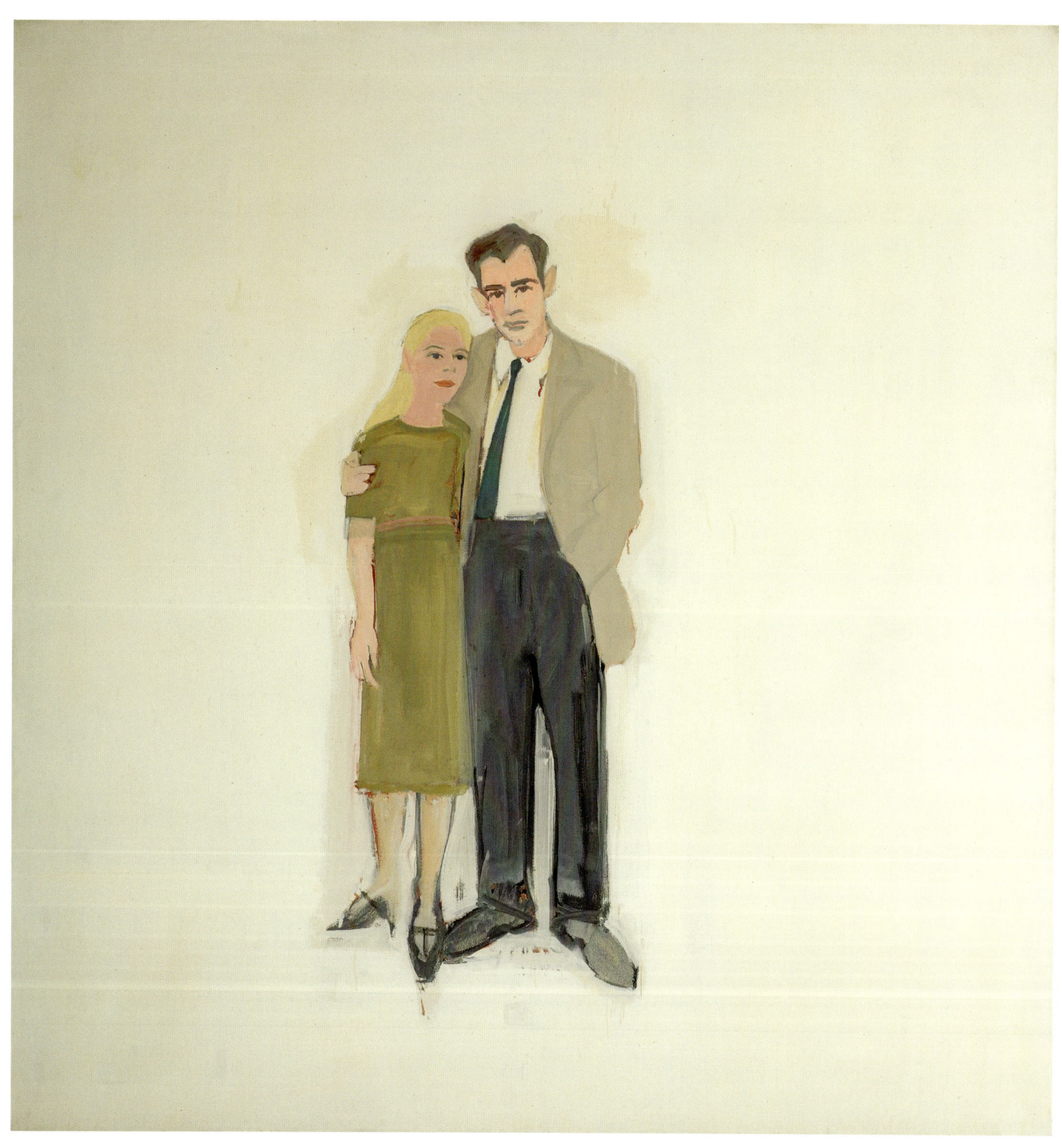

Irving and Lucy, 1958.
Oil on canvas, 60 x 90 in. (152.4 x 228.6 cm).
Collection of Lucy Sandler, NY.
Image courtesy of Colby College Museum of Art,
Waterville, ME. © 2020 Alex Katz / Licensed by
VAGA at Artist Rights Society (ARS), New York, NY.

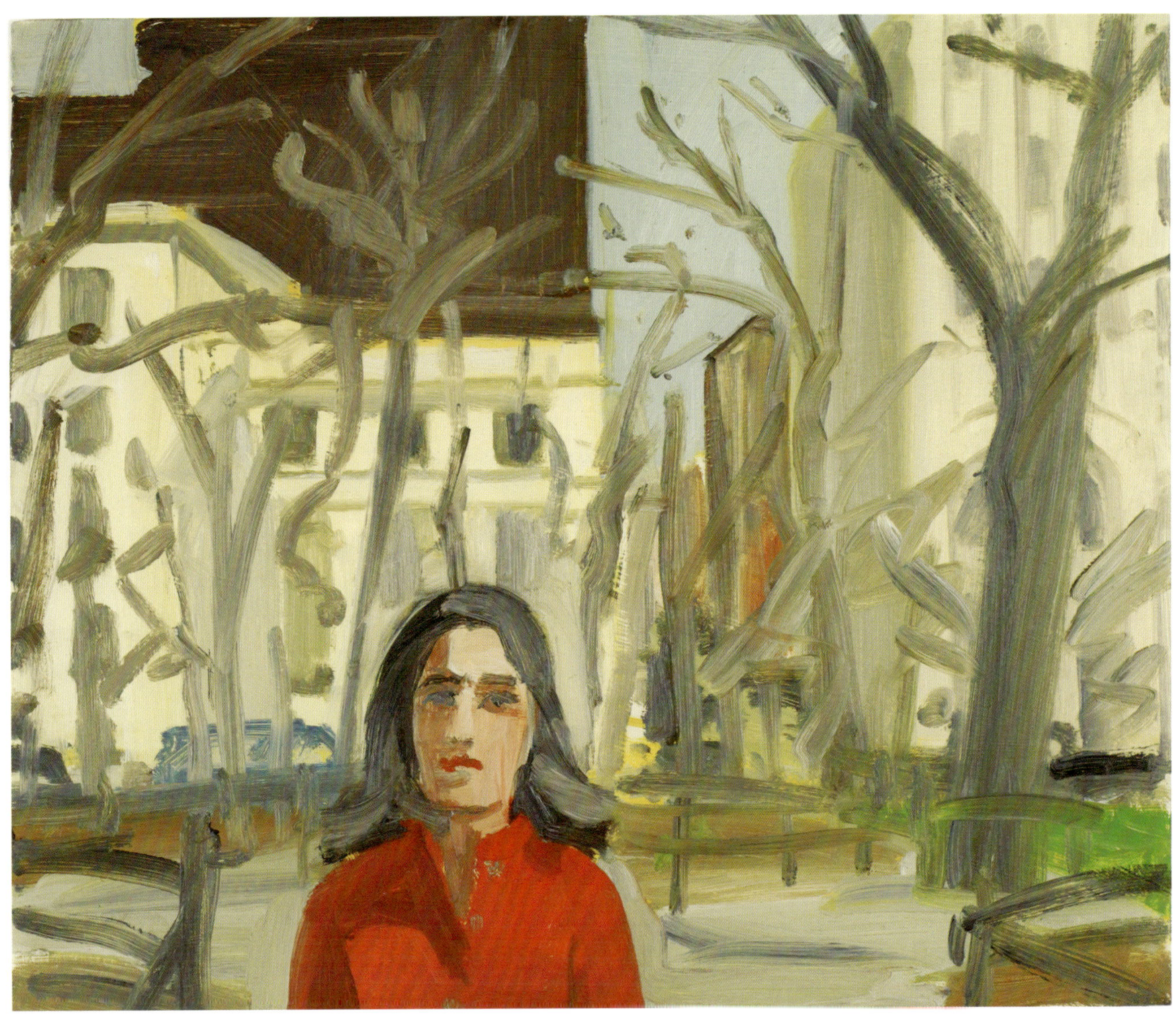

Ada in Red in Park, 1964.
Oil on Masonite, 17 x 20 in. (43.1 cm x 50.8 cm).
Colby College Museum of Art, Waterville, ME.
Gift of the artist, 1995.049. © 2020 Alex Katz / Licensed
by VAGA at Artist Rights Society (ARS), New York, NY.

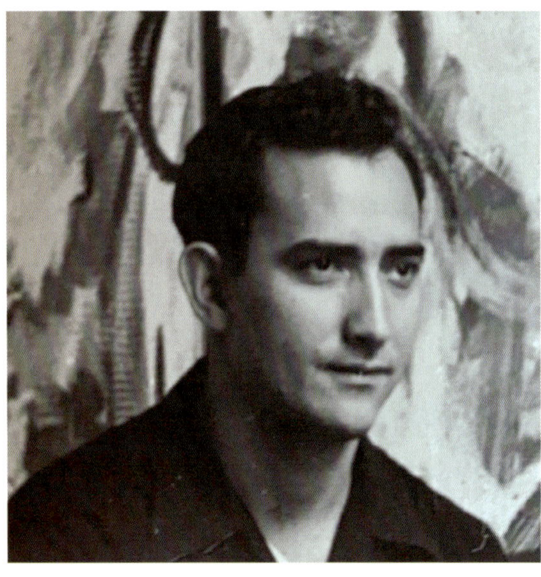

ALBERT KRESCH

b. 1922, Scranton, PA

At nine, Albert Kresch moved with his family from Scranton, Pennsylvania to Brooklyn, New York, his primary residence since the 1930s. Now almost 98, he paints daily in his Brooklyn studio. Kresch studied figure drawing informally at the Brooklyn Museum but soon embarked on more serious training at the Hans Hofmann School. Among his peers were Paul Resika, Leland Bell, Louisa Mattiasdottir, Nell Blaine, Judith Rothschild, and Robert De Niro, Sr. Kresch was one of the original members of the Jane Street Gallery (1943–1949), New York's first cooperative gallery. Like him, most of his fellow members were former Hofmann students. Kresch's first two shows with the Jane Street group included abstract works influenced by Piet Mondrian and Jean Arp, animated by his understanding of Hofmann's "push and pull" method. However, during the late 1940s, Kresch, inspired by the French figurative painter Jean Hélion, returned to representation. Other friendships, such as those with the poets Denise Levertov, and Frank O'Hara, reinforced his interest in working from perceptions of the everyday world around him.

Kresch came to regard abstraction not as an end in itself, but as an armature to support representational form. The structure that abstraction gives him underlies the dynamism of his landscapes, which are striking for their highly saturated color and dry-brushed scumble at the edges of strongly contrasting hues.

Kresch has been included in many group shows focusing on Hofmann students, particularly on the Jane Street group, and more broadly on his generation of vanguard New York artists. In his later years, his small, intimate works have been exhibited at the Center for Figurative Painting, Lohin Geduld Gallery, Tibor de Nagy Gallery, and Salander-O'Reilly Galleries, all in New York City, among other venues. Kresch is represented in the collections of the National Academy of Design, New York City; the Weatherspoon Art Museum, Greensboro, North Carolina; the Everhart Museum, Scranton, Pennsylvania; and Wright State University Galleries, Dayton, Ohio.

2010: *Paintings by Albert Kresch*, Lohin Geduld Gallery, New York, NY

2006–2007: *Albert Kresch: Paintings*, Wright State University, Dayton, OH

2002: *Albert Kresch: Paintings*, Salander-O'Reilly Galleries, New York, NY

Selected Group Exhibitions

2020: *Figuration Never Died*, Brattleboro Museum & Art Center, Brattleboro, VT

    Masterworks of American Painting, Center for Figurative Painting, New York, NY

    Showcase JPEGS, BCK Fine Arts Gallery at Montauk, Montauk, NY

    Special Holiday Gifts, BCK Fine Arts Gallery at Montauk, Montauk, NY

2019: *Colorscapes*, BCK Fine Arts Gallery at Montauk, Montauk, NY

2019: *For America: Paintings from the National Academy of Design*, National Academy Museum and
    School of Fine Arts, New York, NY

2018: *Sound & Image*, Federation of Modern Painters and Sculptors, Westbeth Gallery, Greenwich Village, NY

2016: *Looking at the Overlooked*, Westbeth Gallery, New York, NY

2013–2014: *See It Loud: Seven Post-War American Painters*, National Academy Museum, Washington, DC

Collections

The Everhart Museum, Scranton, PA

National Academy of Design, New York, NY

Wright State University Galleries, Dayton, OH

Weatherspoon Art Museum, University of North Carolina–Greensboro, Greensboro, NC

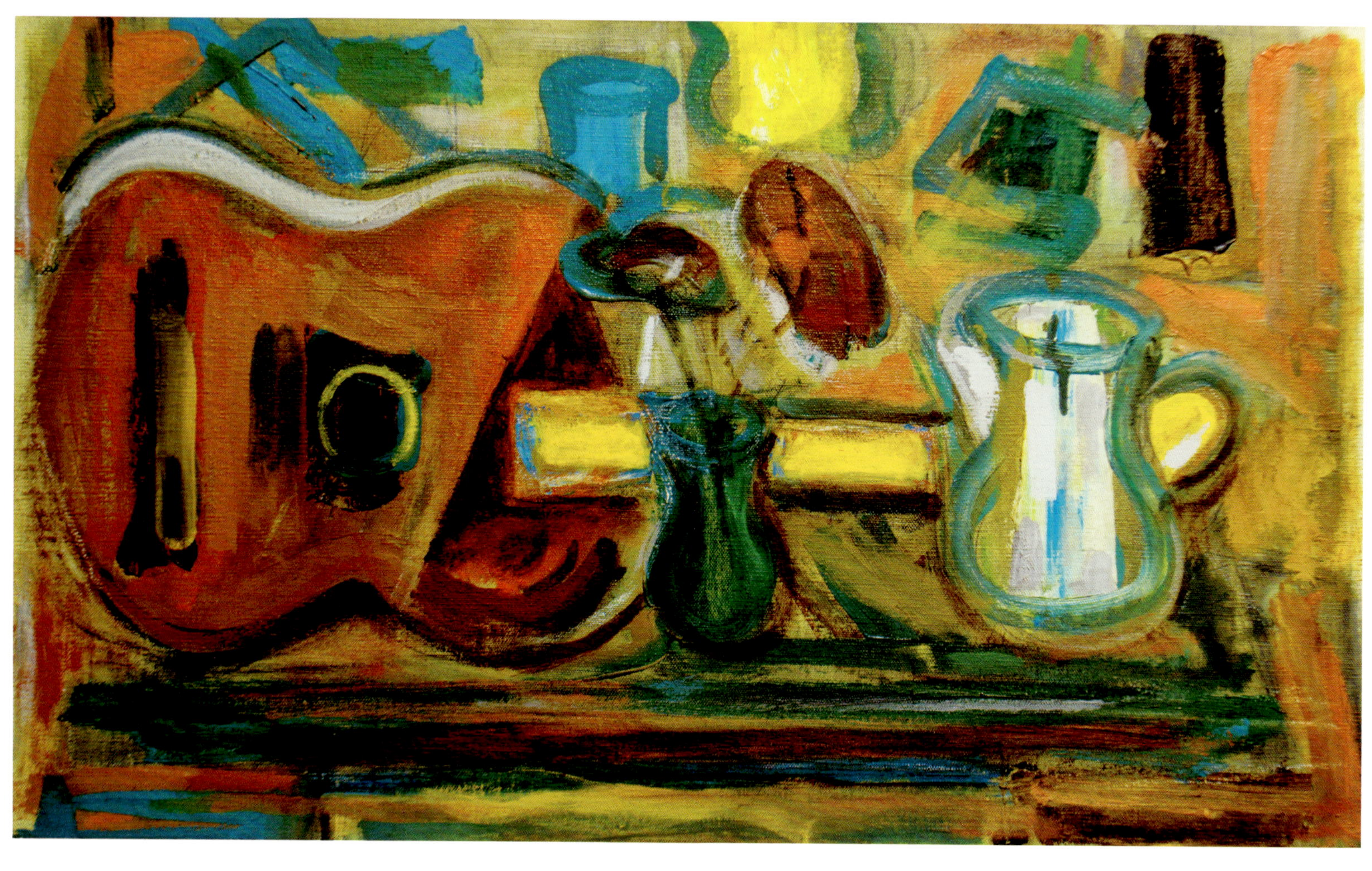

■ *Brown Still Life*, c. 1958–1959.
Oil on canvas, 15 x 24 in. (38.1 x 61 cm).
Collection of the artist.

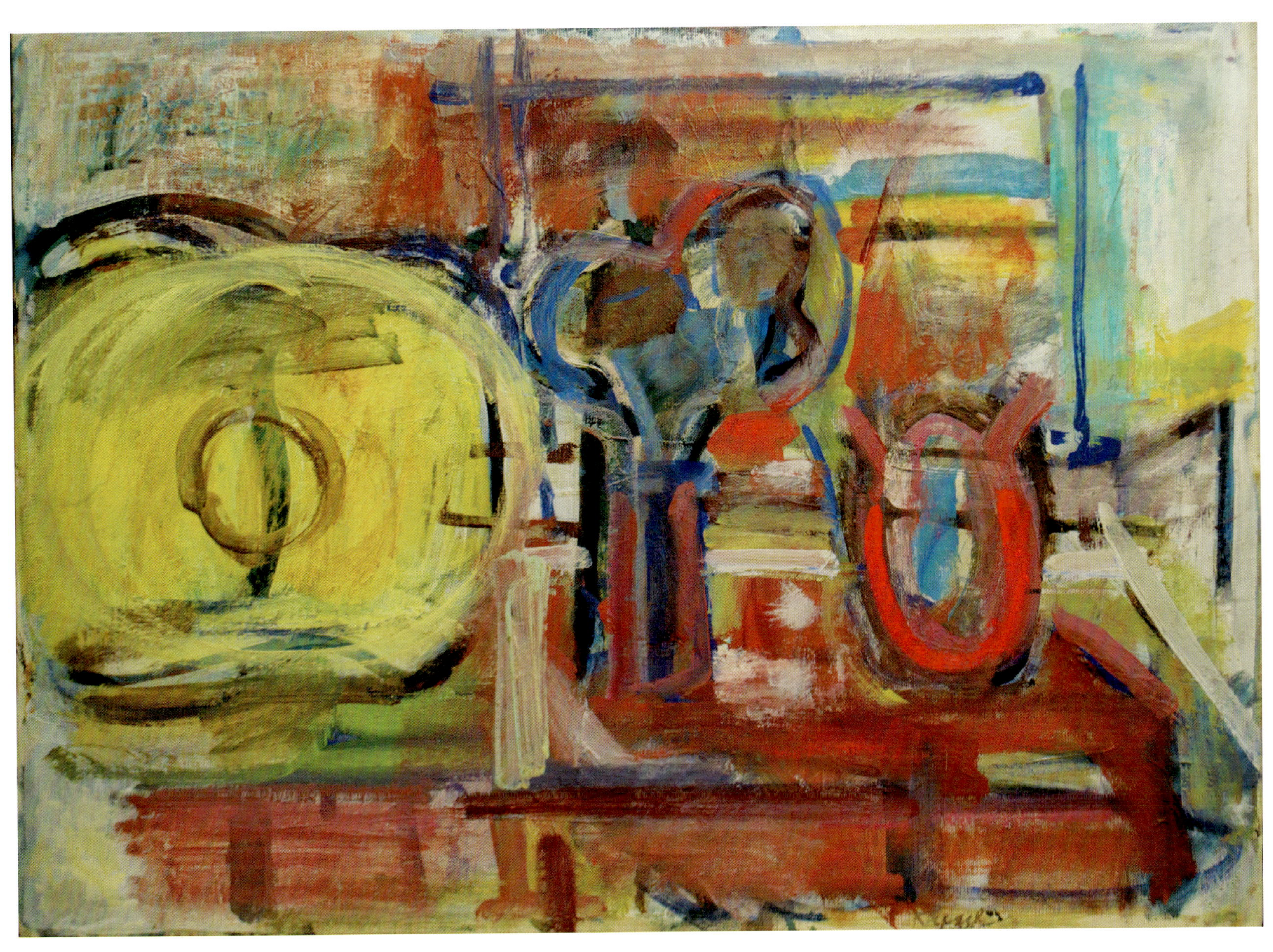

■ *Red Still Life*, c. 1958–1959.
Oil on canvas, 18 x 25 in. (45.7 x 63.5 cm).
Collection of the artist.

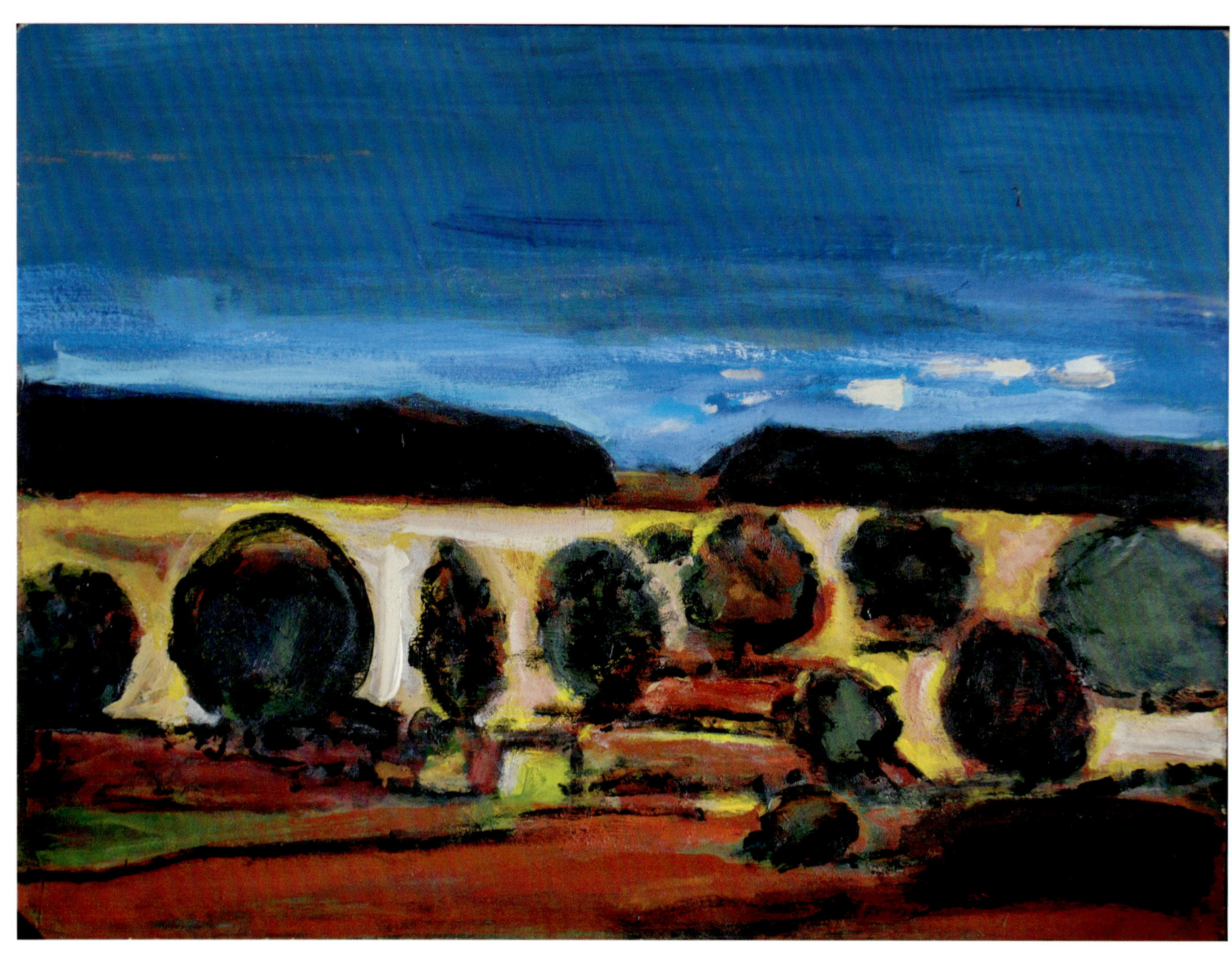

■ *Ten Trees in a Landscape*, c. 1970.
Oil on canvas, 18 x 23 in. (45.7 x 58.4 cm).
Estate of the artist.

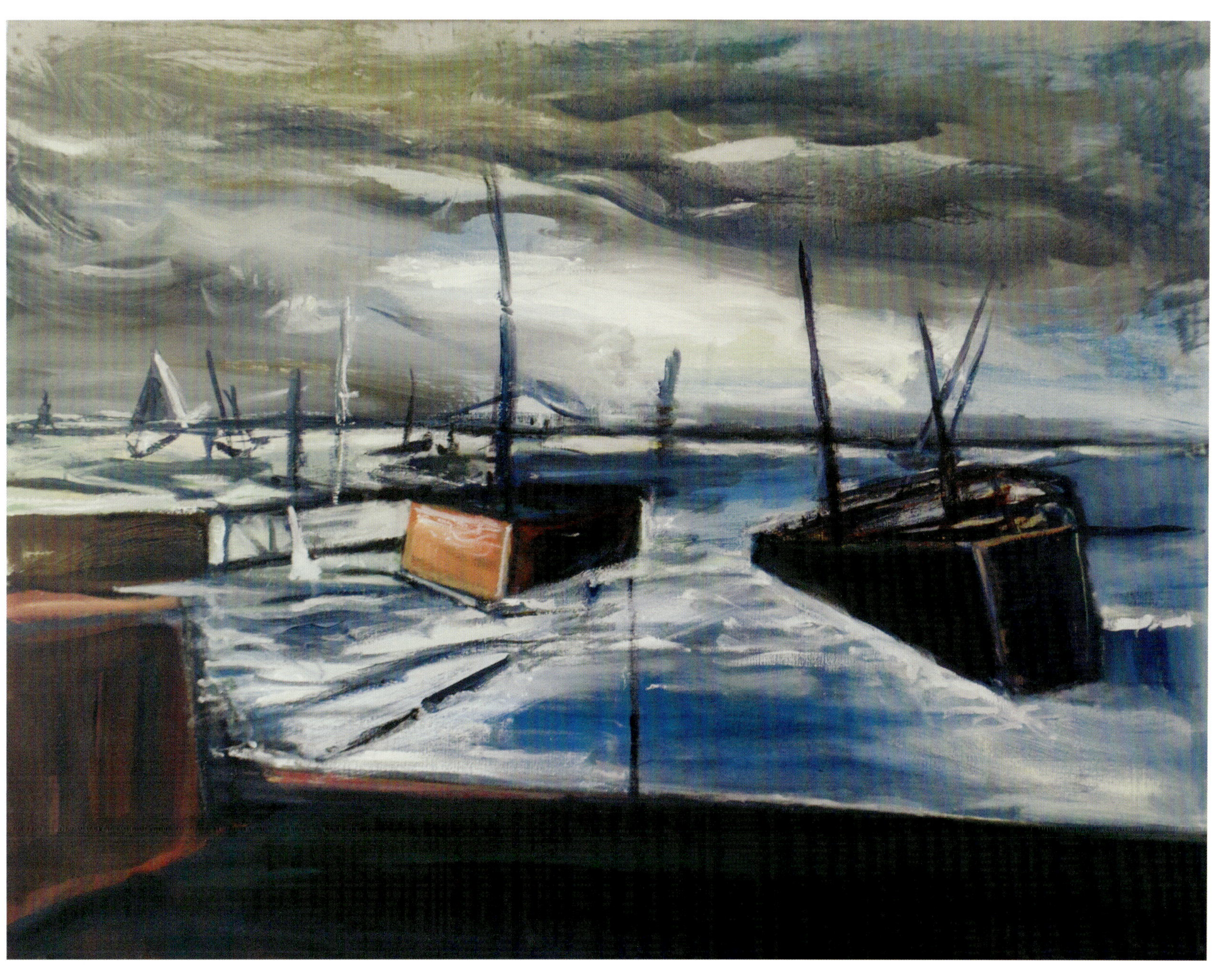

Provincetown (After the Storm), c. 1957.
Oil on canvas, 25 x 33 in. (63.5 x 83.2 cm).
Collection of the artist.

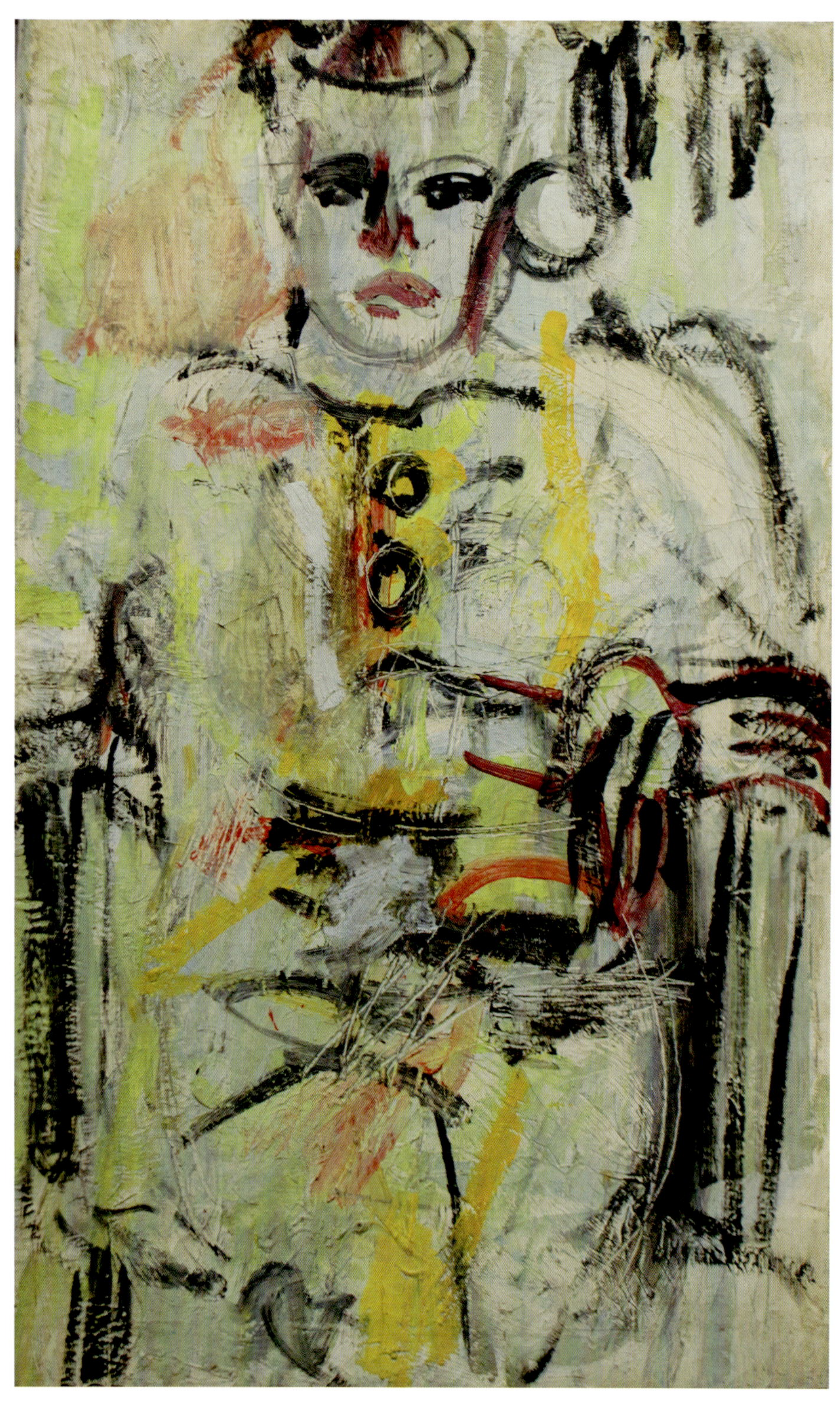

Woman, 1958–1959.
Oil on canvas, 36 x 22 in. (91.4 x 55.9 cm).
Collection of the artist.

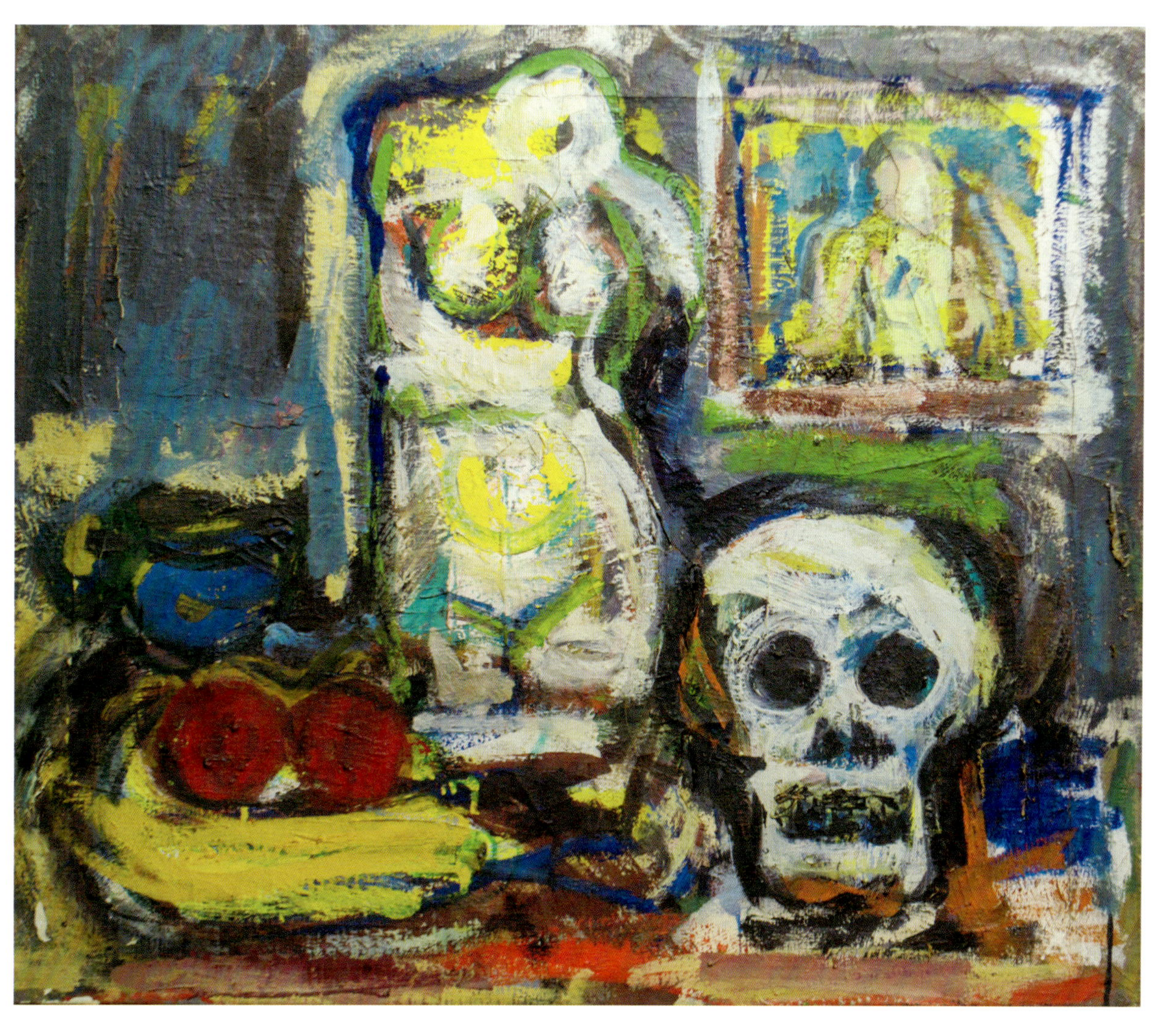

Skull, 1950s.
Oil on canvas, 21 x 25 in. (53.3 x 63.5 cm).
Collection of the artist.

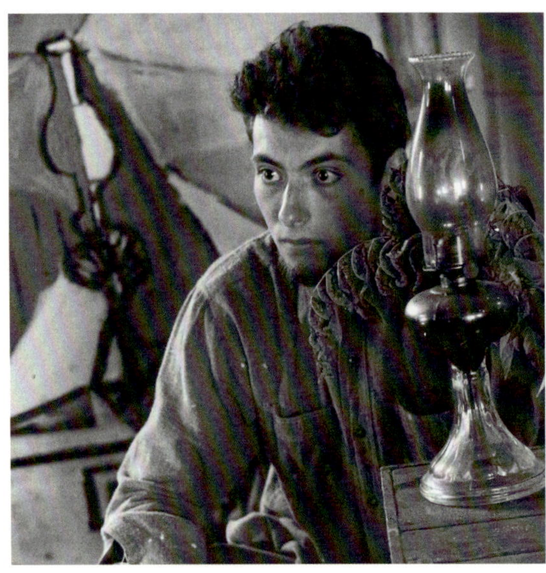

PAUL RESIKA

b. 1928, New York, NY

When he was 9, Paul Resika began taking painting lessons, encouraged by his Russian-immigrant mother; he studied with Sol Wilson when he was 12 and, from 1947 to 1950, he studied in Provincetown, Massachusetts, with Hans Hofmann, eventually becoming Hofmann's studio assistant. At 19, Resika had his first solo exhibition of paintings at the George Dix Gallery on Madison Avenue in New York City.

Resika traveled to Europe, settling in Venice for two years and studying independently, a self-imposed apprenticeship to the Old Masters that enriched, without cancelling out, the approach to form and structure that he absorbed from Hofmann. He returned to the United States in 1954. In 1958, he began to paint from observation outdoors, and this remains the foundation of his work, even though memory also plays a role. Since 1964, Resika has spent winters in New York and summers on Cape Cod in Massachusetts. Over the years, he has also spent time in France, Mexico, Jamaica, and Maine, focusing on particular motifs such as the waterfront buildings of Provincetown or a family home in Provence, and responding to the specifics of place in his work.

Resika was a founding member of Provincetown's Long Point Gallery. He credits Berta Walker for contributing greatly to his success, since she first began exhibiting and selling his work in 1984 as Founding Director of the Graham Modern Gallery in New York. Resika's work can be found in the collections of The Metropolitan Museum of Art and the Museum of Modern Art, New York City, and the National Museum of American Art, Washington, DC, as well as in numerous private collections. The recipient of many awards, he is represented by Bookstein Projects, New York.

2019: *Flowers*, Bookstein Projects, New York, NY

2018: *Geometry and the Sea*, Bookstein Projects, New York, NY

2016: *Boats and Sails*, Lawrence Fine Art, East Hampton, NY

2015: *Provincetown in New York*, Bookstein Projects, New York, NY

2013: *1947–48*, Bookstein Projects, New York, NY

Selected Group Exhibitions

2020: *Figuration Never Died*, Brattleboro Museum & Art Center, Brattleboro, VT

2019: *Landscapes, Skyscapes and Waterscapes*, Alpha 137 Gallery, New York, NY

2017: *Summer Fun: On-line Only*, Lawrence Fine Art, East Hampton, NY

2016: *Works in Progress: Artists in Their 80s and 90s*, Lawrence Fine Art, East Hampton, NY

1992: *Color As a Subject*, The Artist's Museum, New York, NY

Collections

American Academy of Arts and Letters, New York, NY

Colby College Museum of Art, Waterville, ME

Hood Museum of Art, Dartmouth College, Hanover, NH

Memorial Art Gallery, University of Rochester, Rochester, NY

The Metropolitan Museum of Art, New York, NY

Museum of Modern Art, New York, NY

National Academy Museum, New York, NY

National Museum of American Art, Washington, DC

Neuberger Museum of Art, State University of New York–Purchase, Purchase, NY

Sheldon Memorial Art Gallery, University of Nebraska, Lincoln, NE

Whitney Museum of American Art, New York, NY

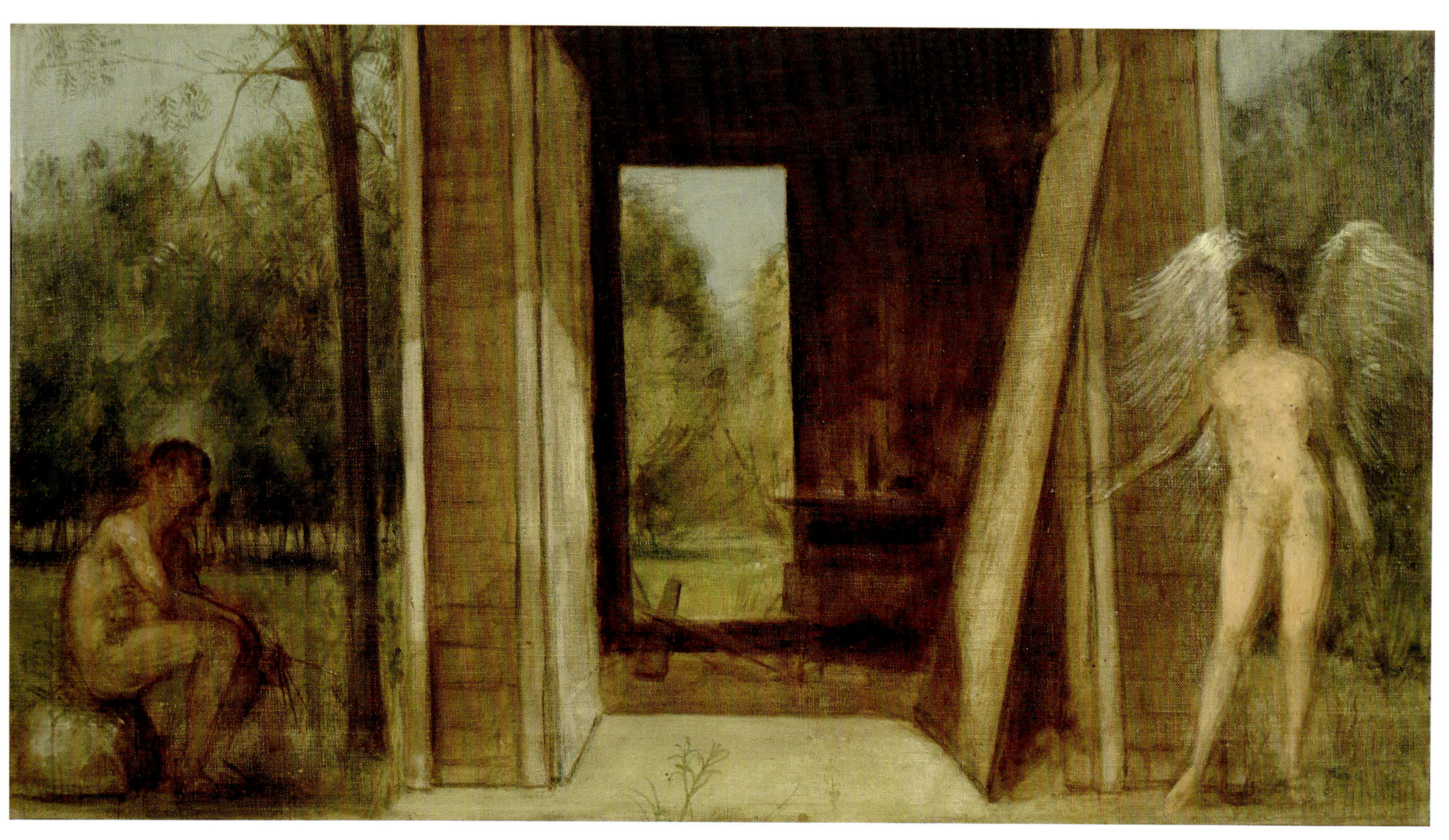

■ *The Visitation (An Angel and a Painter in a Landscape on Long Island)*, 1958.
Oil on canvas, 14 x 28 in. (35.6 x 66 cm).
Collection of the artist.

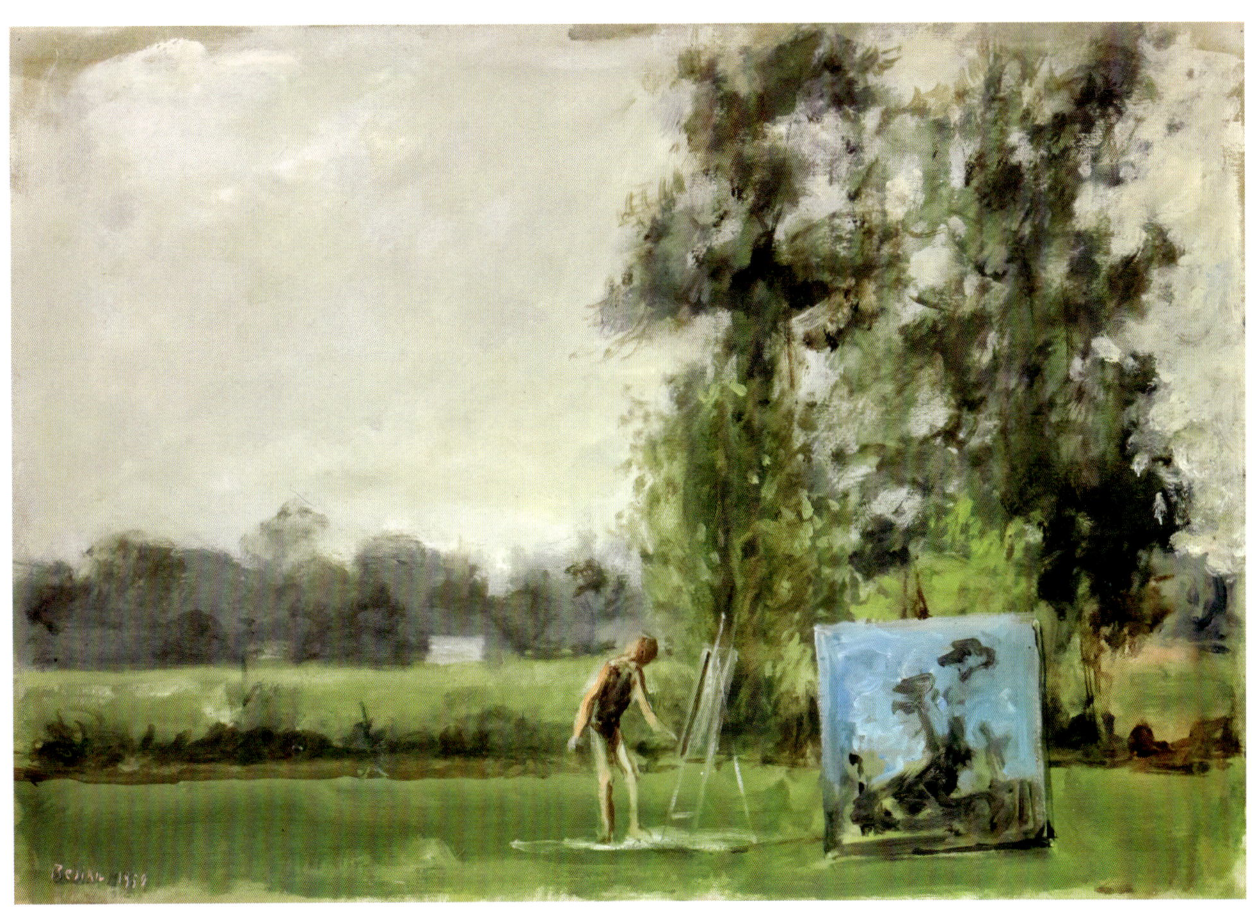

■ *Fairfield Porter Painting in Bridgehampton*, 1959.
Oil on canvas, 16 x 12 in. (40.6 x 30.5 cm).
Collection of the artist.

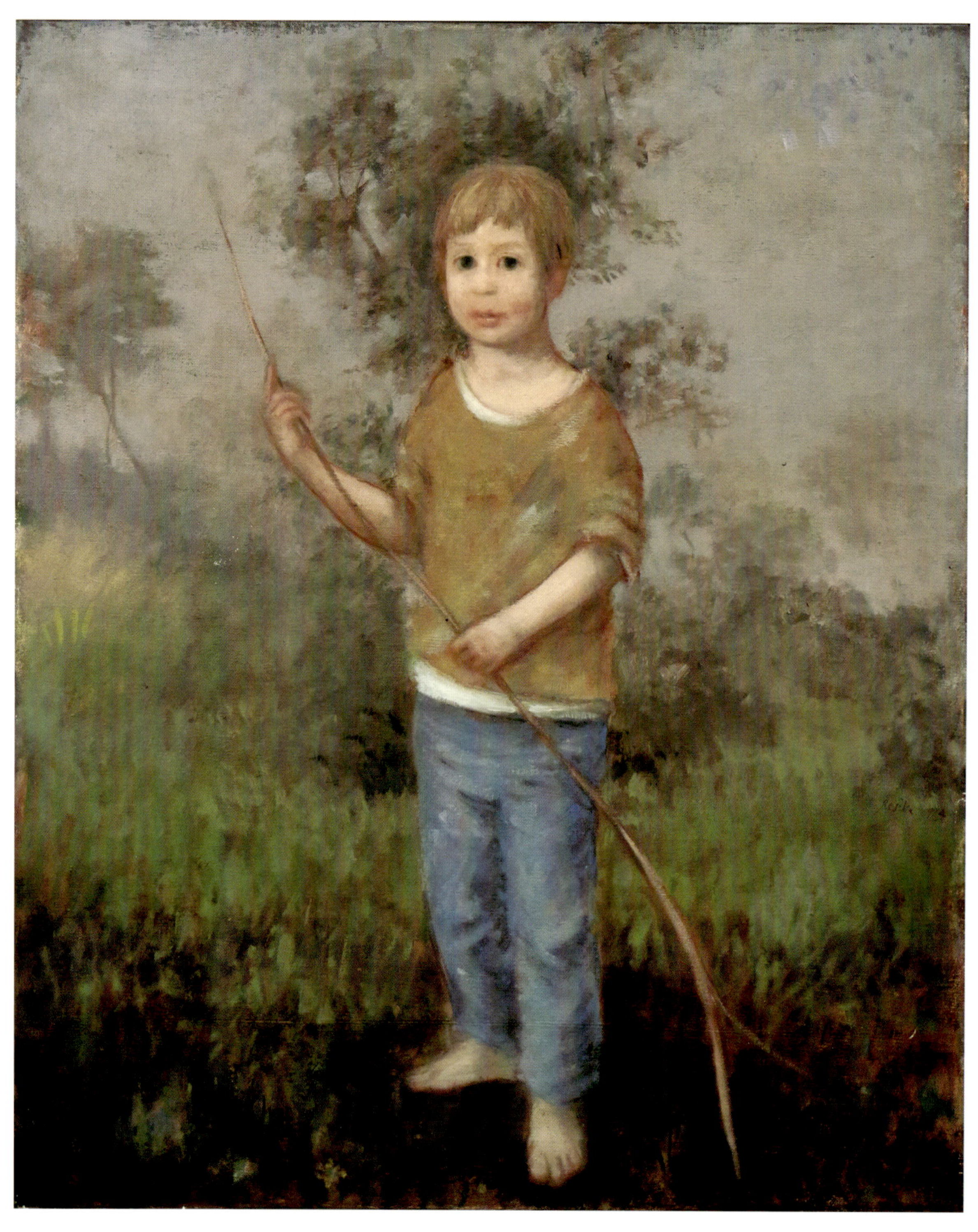

■ *Boy with a Stick (Nathan)*, 1963–1964.
Oil on canvas, 40 x 34 in. (101.6 x 86.4 cm).
Nathan Resika, Valhalla, NY.

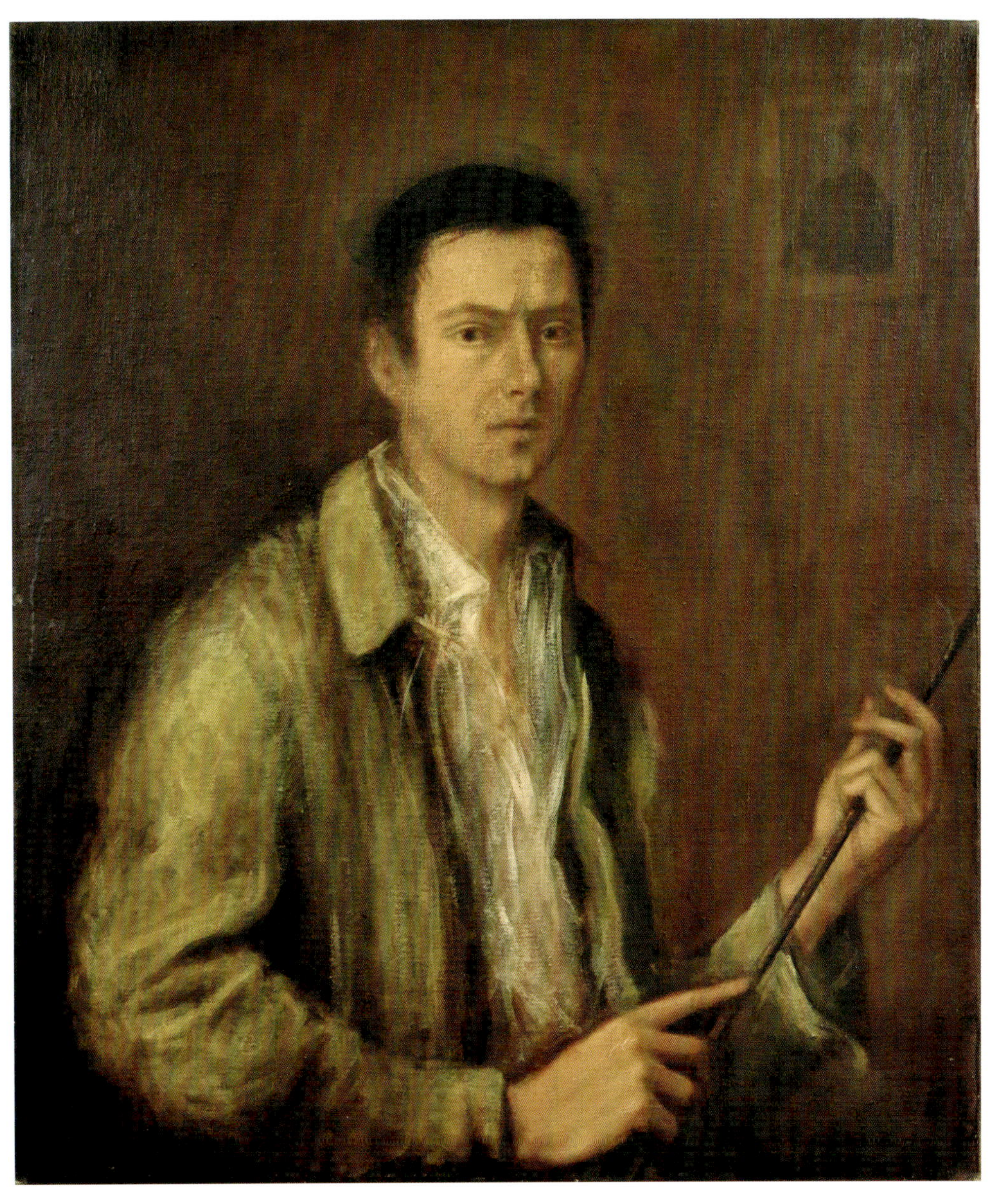

Self-Portrait with Stick, 1958.
Oil and tempera on canvas, 34 x 29 in. (86.4 x 73.7 cm).
Collection of the artist.

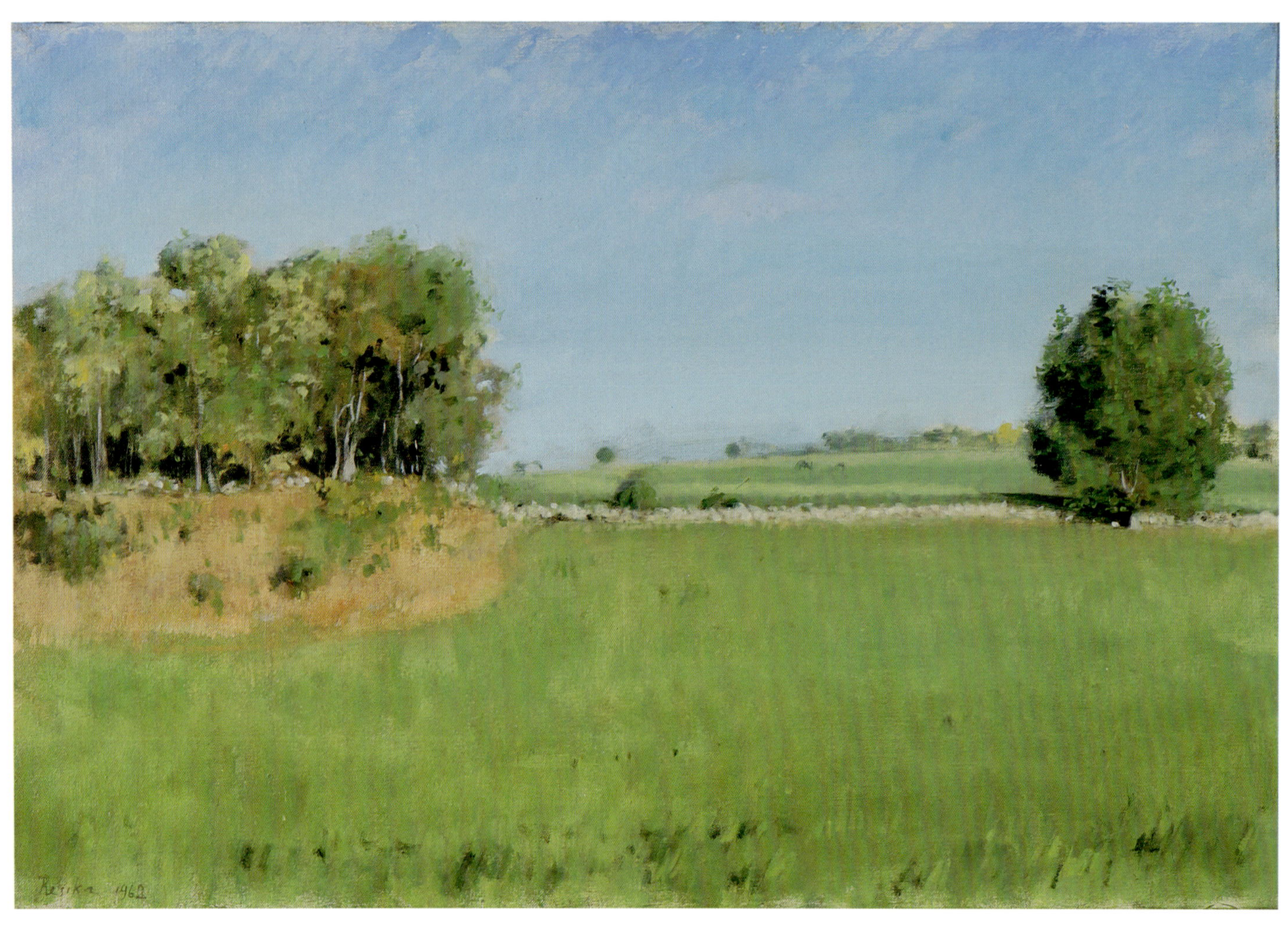

The Copse, 1962.
Oil on canvas, 20³/₁₆ x 30³/₁₆ in. (51.3 x 76.7cm).
The Sheldon Museum of Art, Nebraska Art Association, Lincoln, NE.
In memory of Alice Edmiston, N-154.1964. Photo © Sheldon Museum of Art.

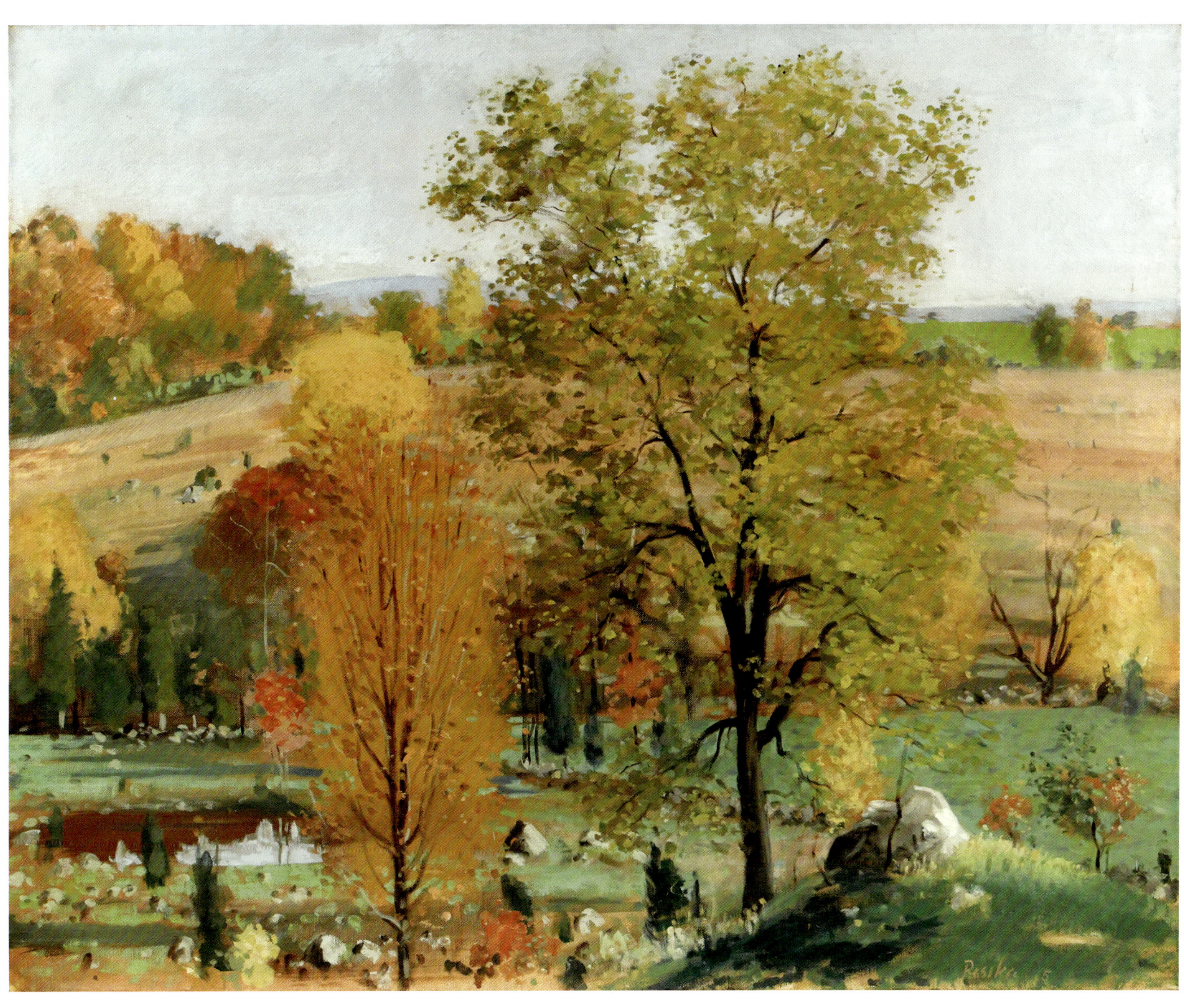

The Hill at Amity, 1968.
Oil on canvas, 48 x 60 in. (121.9 x 152.4 cm).
Collection of Caroline and Stephen Chinlund.

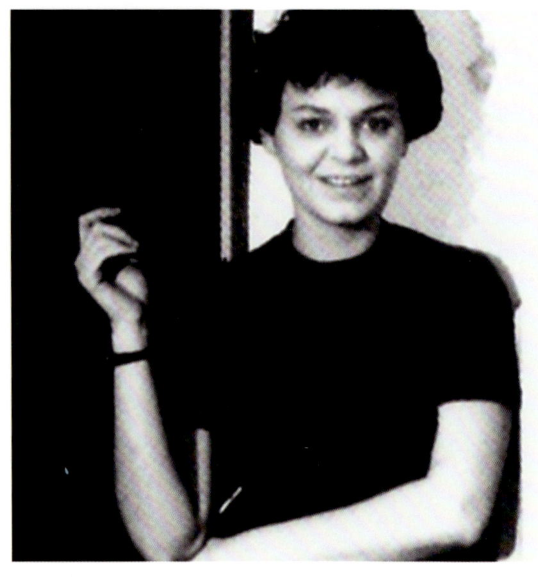

ANNE TABACHNICK

b. 1927, Derby, CT; d. 1995, Greenwich Village,
New York, NY

Anne Tabachnick had a lifelong admiration for what she called "the Grand Tradition," with her enthusiasms ranging from the Old Masters to the European Modernists. She was particularly interested in Henri Matisse, El Greco, Arshile Gorky, and the altarpieces of Renaissance painters such as Matthias Grunewald, Raphael, and Titian.

Tabachnick's father was a highly regarded Yiddish poet who had been a Russian revolutionary before emigrating to America. She attended Hunter College, earning a BA in anthropology and art, and then attended graduate school for art at the University of California–Berkley in 1951. After studying briefly with painter Nell Blaine, she was awarded a scholarship from Hans Hofmann and attended his schools in both New York City and Provincetown. Tabachnick also studied briefly with William Baziotes. Her first New York show was in 1951 at the Circle in

the Square Gallery, and she was later represented by the Ingber Gallery, and currently by Bookstein Projects.

Tabachnick created mixed-media abstract interpretations of landscapes and still lifes. Her work is characterized by the use of diluted acrylic paint in a light wash, overlaid with sharp contours of forms rendered in charcoal. Allusions to the history of art sometimes appear in her work. Tabachnick's interest in Old Master art led her to investigate traditional techniques, such as glazing, and she learned from her peers: Blaine introduced her to Leland Bell, his wife Louisa Matthiasdottir, and Robert De Niro, Sr. She was also significantly influenced by a seventeenth-century Chinese treatise on painting, *Mustard Seed Garden Manual of Painting (The Tao of Painting: Its Ideas and Technique)*, by Sze Mai-Mai. Like the Chinese masters, Tabachnick worked fast and spontaneously, and the influence of Chinese landscapes, with elements rendered in just a few brushstrokes, is evident in her work.

Her many honors and awards include the Long View Foundation award (its first woman recipient) in 1960; Radcliffe College's Bunting Institute grant (its first out-of-state recipient) in 1967 and 1969; and a CAPS grant sponsored by the New York City Council on the Arts in 1975 and 1978. Tabachnick received an Adolph and Esther Gottlieb fellowship in 1982 and, a year later, a John Solomon Guggenheim fellowship. Her work can be found in public collections that include The Metropolitan Museum of Art and the Museum of Modern Art, New York City, The Hyde Collection in Glen Falls, New York, and the Dayton Art Institute in Dayton, Ohio.

Selected Solo Exhibitions

2015: *Anne Tabachnick: Object as Muse*, Bookstein Projects, New York, NY

2008: *Anne Tabachnick Works from the Sixties and Seventies*, Bookstein Projects, New York, NY

1998: *The Late Paintings of Anne Tabachnick*, Lori Bookstein Fine Art, New York, NY

1971: Westbeth Galleries, New York, NY

1968: Colby Junior college, New London, NH

1962: Waverly Gallery, New York, NY

Selected Group Exhibitions

2020: *Figuration Never Died*, Brattleboro Museum & Art Center, Brattleboro, VT

2013: *Pioneers from Provincetown: The Roots of Figurative Expressionism*, Provincetown Art Association and Museum, Provincetown, MA

2007: *The Other Half: Women Artists in the Collection*, Boca Raton Museum of Art, Boca Raton, FL

Ten Years of Gallery Art and Artists, Lori Bookstein Fine Art, New York, NY

2006: *Gallery Selections*, Lori Bookstein Fine Art, New York, NY

2005: *In Black and White*, Lori Bookstein Fine Art, New York, NY

1999: *The Legacy of Hans Hofmann*, Lori Bookstein Fine Art, New York, NY

Collections

Dayton Art Institute, Dayton, OH

The Hyde Collection, Glens Falls, NY

The Metropolitan Museum of Art, New York, NY

Museum of Modern Art, New York, NY

The University Art Museum, University of California–Berkeley, Berkeley, CA.

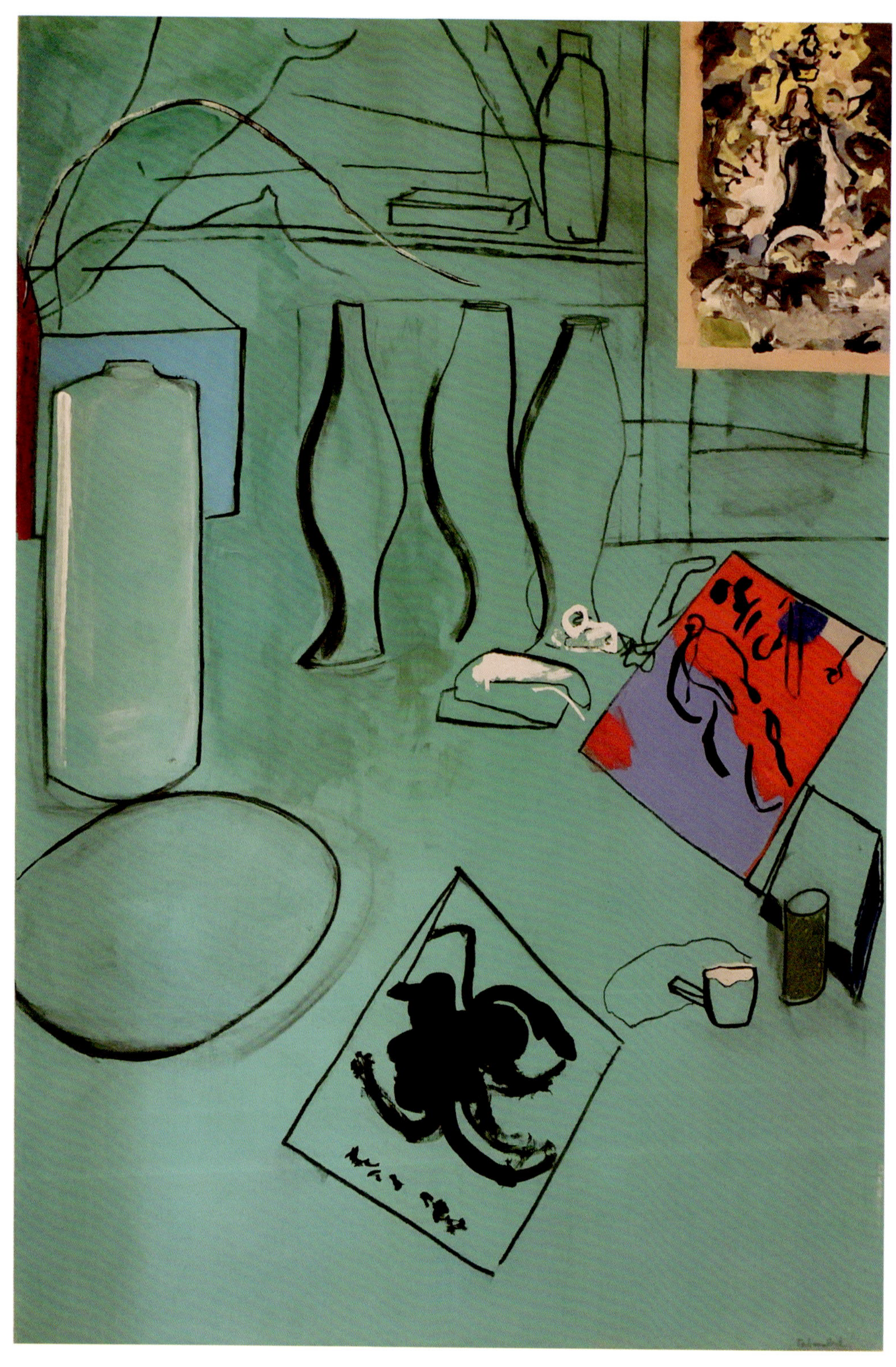

■ *Green Still Life*, c. 1960–1962.
Acrylic and charcoal on canvas, 48 x 33 in. (121.9 x 83.8 cm).
Private collection.

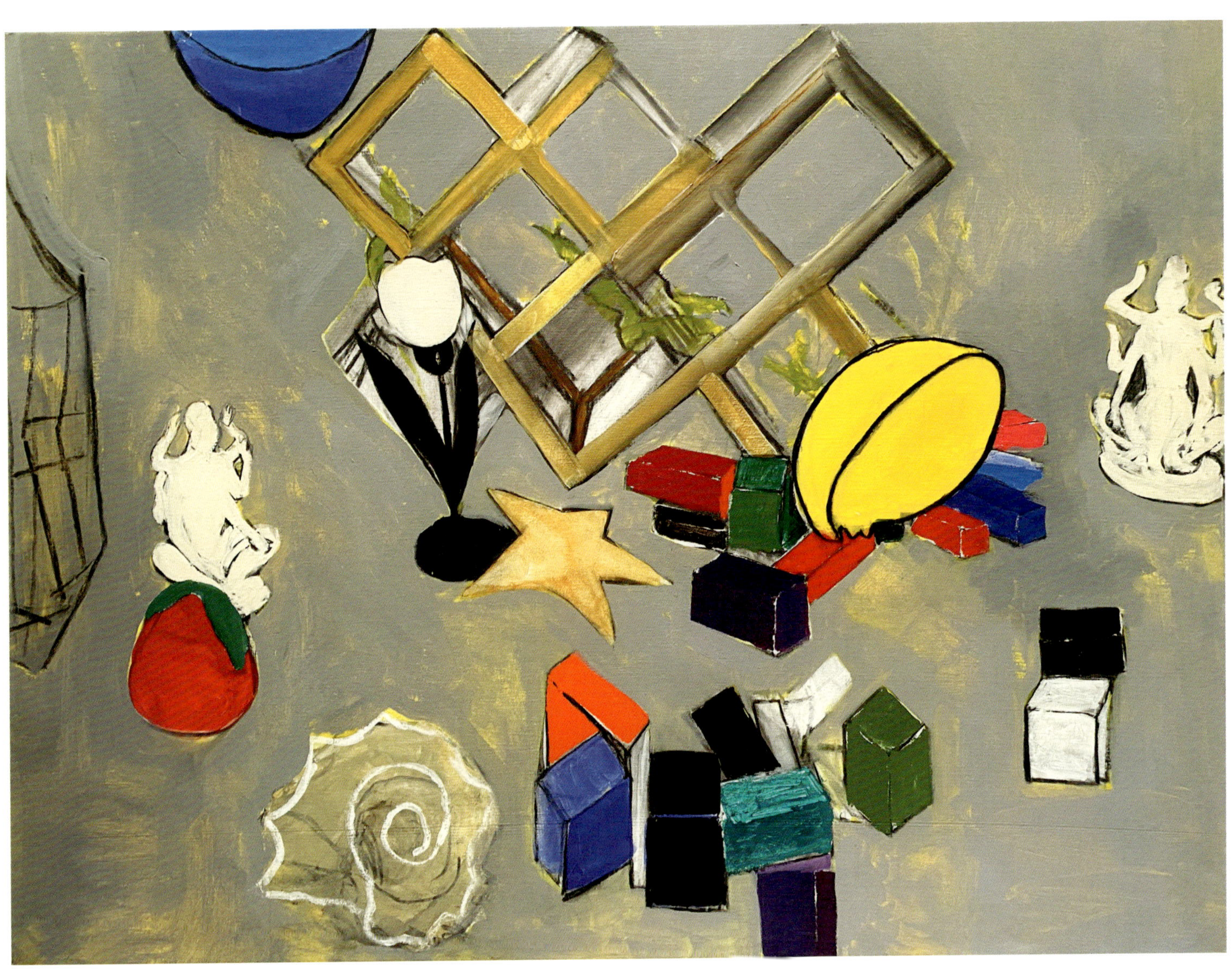

■ *Bright Boxes (Gates III)*, 1960s.
Acrylic and charcoal on canvas, 35 x 47 in. (88.9 x 119.4 cm).
Courtesy of Bookstein Projects, New York, NY.

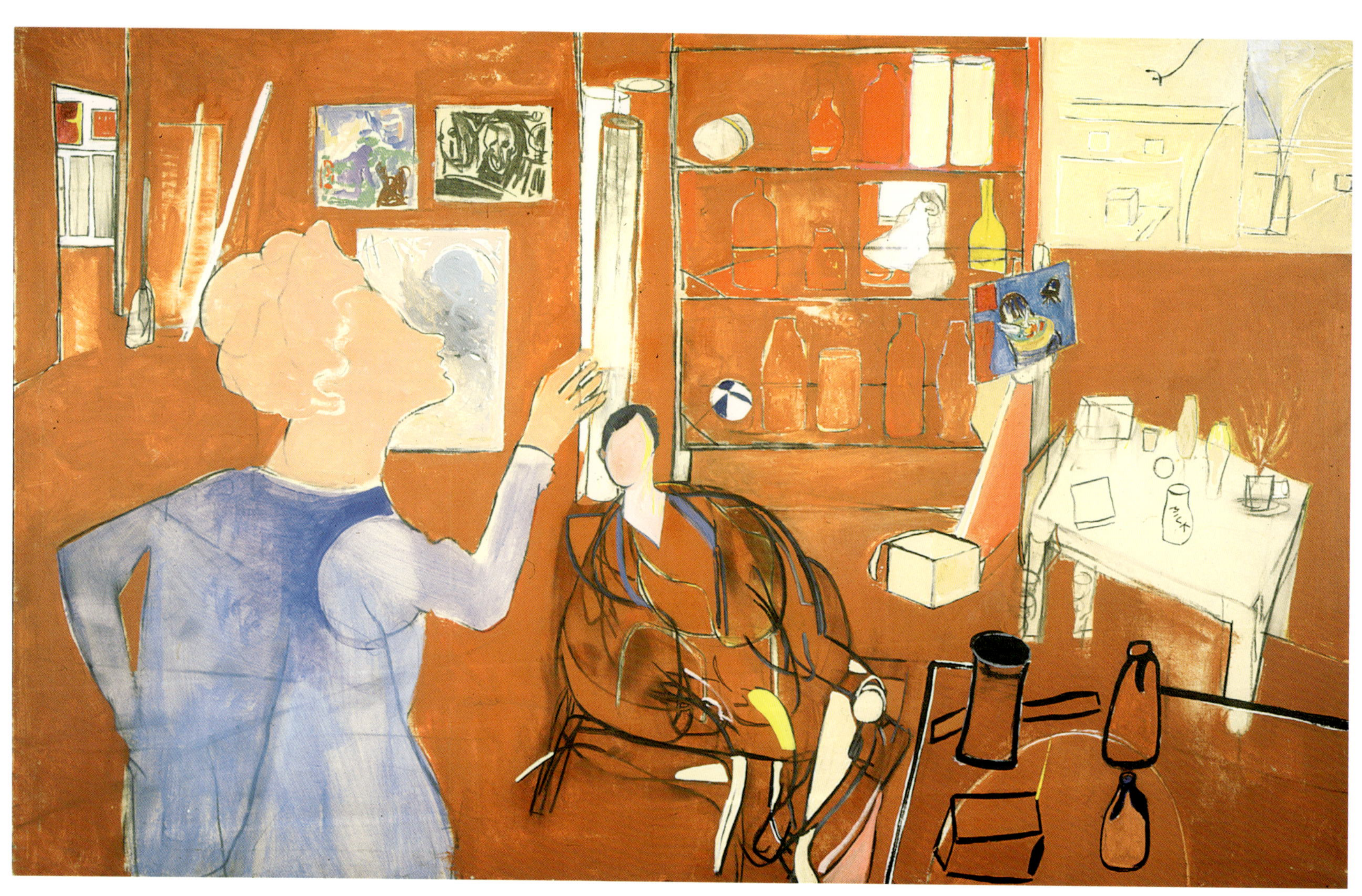

Studio with Artist and Sitter, c. 1965.
Acrylic on canvas, 49 x 79 in. (124.5 x 200.7 cm).
Private collection, NY.

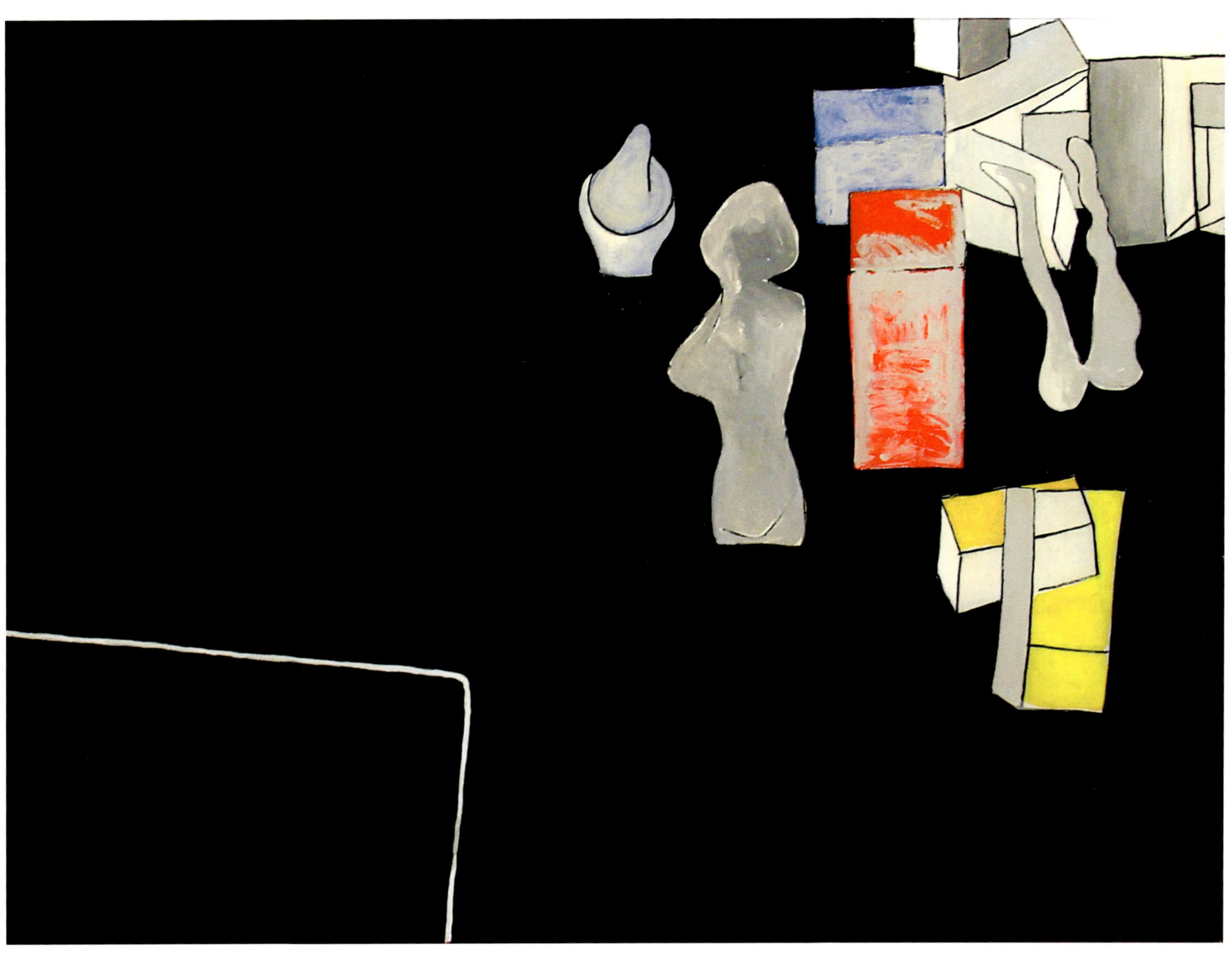

Untitled (Black Still Life), 1960s.
Acrylic and charcoal on canvas, 50 x 68 in. (127 x 172.7 cm).
Courtesy of Bookstein Projects, New York, NY.

Cambridge with Tulips and View, late 1960s.
Acrylic and charcoal on canvas, 38 x 48 in. (96.5 x 121.9 cm).
Courtesy of Bookstein Projects, New York, NY.

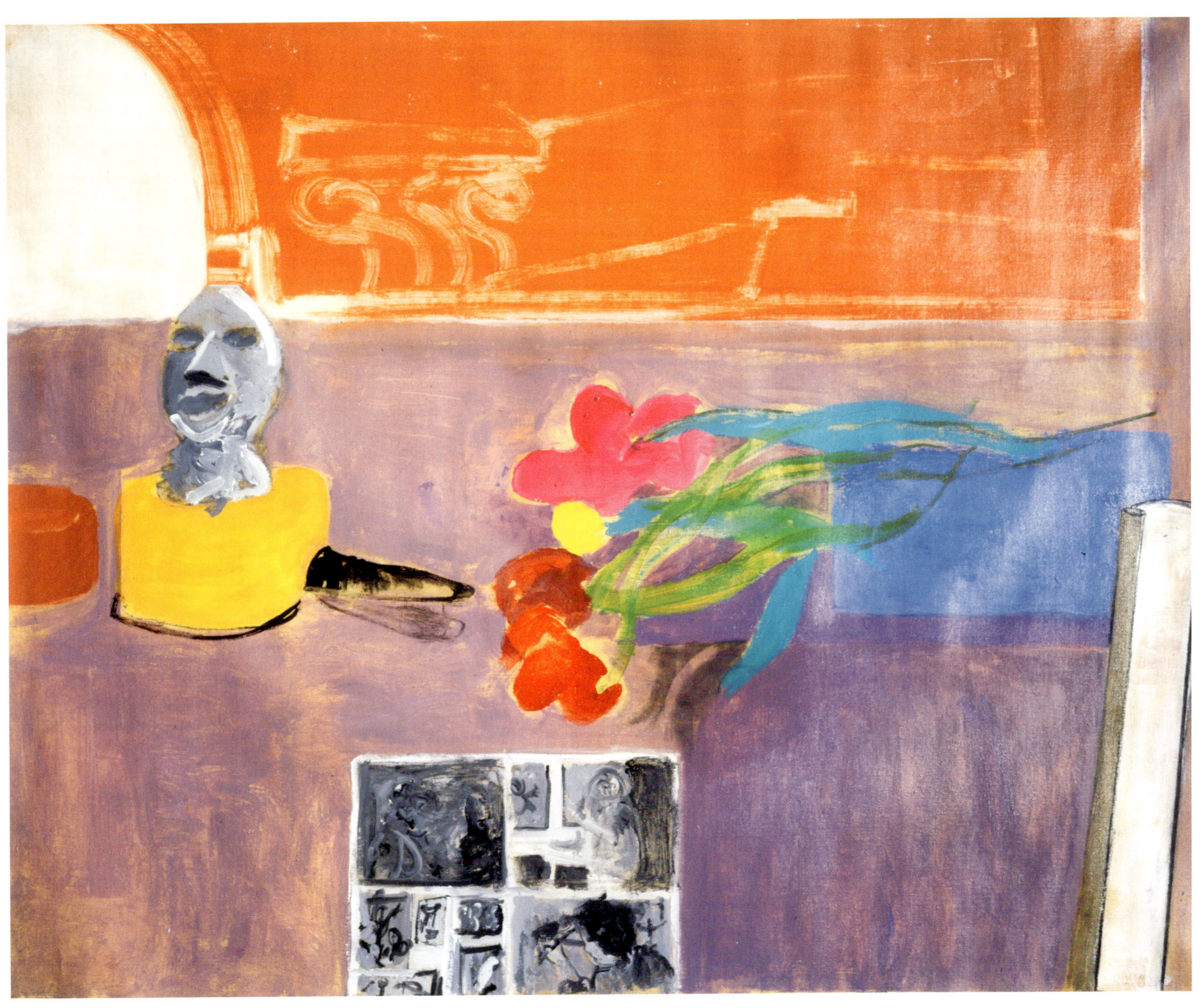

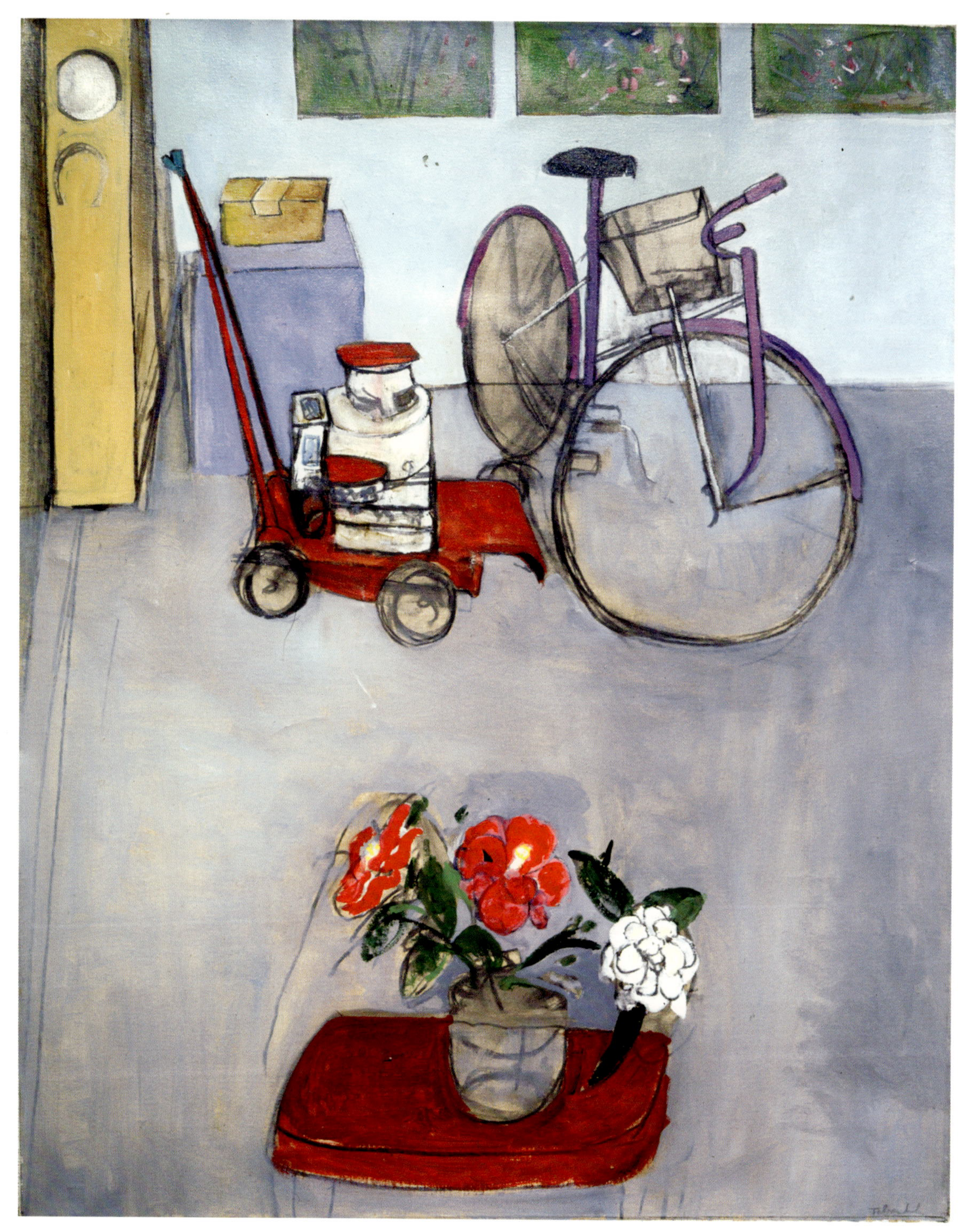

Anne Tabachnick, *Louisiana Bicycle*, 1975.
Acrylic on canvas, 47 x 37 in. (119.4 x 94 cm).
Courtesy of Bookstein Projects, New York, NY.

Robert De Niro, Sr.

Untitled (Still Life), 1960. Oil on canvas, 30 x 40 in.
(76.2 x 101.6 cm).

Portrait of a Young Man with a Red Face, 1961.
Oil on canvas, 40 x 30 in. (101.6 x 76.2 cm).

Three Women, 1968. Oil on linen, 64 x 70 in.
(162.6 x 177.8 cm).

Lois Dodd

Chickens, 1957–1958. Oil on linen, 42 x 54 in.
(106.7 x 137.2 cm).

Cows in Landscape, 1958. Oil on linen, 44 x 51 in.
(111.8 x 129.5 cm).

Jane Freilicher

The Electric Fan, 1957. Oil on canvas, 49⅝ x 56 in.
(126 x 142.2 cm).

Grey Day, 1963. Oil on canvas, 24 x 32 in. (61 x 81.3 cm).

Paul Georges

Lisette, 1958. Oil on canvas, 61½ x 50½ in.
(156.2 x 128.3 cm).

Artist in Studio, 1963. Oil on linen, 80¼ x 70¼ in.
(203.8 x 178.4 cm).

Grace Hartigan

Giftwares, 1955. Oil and charcoal on canvas,
63 x 81⅛ in. (160 x 206 cm).

Phoenix, 1962. Oil on canvas, 80 x 88 in.
(203.2 x 223.5 cm).

Wolf Kahn

Emily in 1958, 1958. Oil on canvas, 30 x 24 in.
(76.2 x 61 cm).

Self-Portrait, 1959. Oil on canvas, 42 x 40 in.
(106.7 x 101.6 cm).

Alex Katz

Landscape with House, 1955. Oil on Masonite,
10 x 11¾ in. (25.4 x 30cm).

Ada in Black Sweater, 1957. Oil on Masonite, 24 x 18 in.
(61 cm x 45.7 cm).

Red Rose, 1966–1967. Oil on board, 8⅞ x 8½ in.
(22.5 x 21.6 cm).

Albert Kresch

Brown Still Life, c. 1958–1959. Oil on canvas,
15 x 24 in. (38.1 x 61 cm).

Red Still Life, c. 1958–1959. Oil on canvas,
18 x 25 in. (45.7 x 63.5 cm).

Ten Trees in a Landscape, c. 1970. Oil on canvas,
18 x 23 in. (45.7 x 58.4 cm).

Paul Resika

*The Visitation (An Angel and a Painter in a Landscape
on Long Island)*, 1958. Oil on canvas, 14 x 28 in.
(35.6 x 66 cm).

Fairfield Porter Painting in Bridgehampton, 1959.
Oil on canvas, 16 x 12 in. (40.6 x 30.5 cm).

Boy with a Stick (Nathan), 1963–1964. Oil on canvas,
40 x 34 in. (101.6 x 86.4 cm).

Anne Tabachnick

Green Still Life, 1960–1962. Acrylic and charcoal on
canvas, 48 x 33 in. (121.9 x 83.8 cm).

Bright Boxes (Gates III), 1960s. Acrylic and charcoal on
canvas, 35 x 47 in. (88.9 x 119.4 cm).

This catalogue is published on the occasion of the Brattleboro Museum & Art Center's exhibition, *Figuration Never Died: New York Painterly Painting, 1950–1970*, from October 23, 2020 to February 14, 2021.

First Edition

© 2020 The Artist Book Foundation

Published in the United States by The Artist Book Foundation
1327 MASS MoCA Way, North Adams, MA 01247

Distributed in the United States, its territories and possessions, and Canada by
ACC Distribution
www.accdistribution.com/us

Distributed outside North America by ACC Distribution
www.accdistribution.com/uk

Publisher and Executive Director: L. Pell van Breen
Art Director: David Skolkin
Design: Irene Cole
Editor: Deborah Thompson
Proofreader: Nicole Barone

Printed in Canada

ISBN 978-1-7329864-3-5

Library of Congress Cataloging-in-Publication Data

Names: Wilkin, Karen, 1940- author. | Weber, Bruce, 1951- writer of
    foreward. | Brattleboro Museum & Art Center.
Title: Figuration never died : New York painterly painting, 1950-1970 /
    Karen Wilkin ; foreword by Bruce Weber.
Description: North Adams : The Artist Book Foundation, 2020.
Identifiers: LCCN 2020014944 | ISBN 9781732986435 (hardcover)
Subjects: LCSH: Figurative art, American--20th century--Exhibitions. |
    Modernism (Art)--United States--Exhibitions.
Classification: LCC ND212.5.F5 W55 2020 | DDC 759.13074--dc23
LC record available at https://lccn.loc.gov/2020014944

p. ii: Paul Resika, detail of *Fairfield Porter Painting in Bridgehampton*, 1959. Oil on canvas, 16 x 12 in. (40.6 x 30.5 cm). Collection of the artist.

p. iv: Alex Katz, *Lois*, 1957. Oil on Masonite, 24 x 18 in. (61 x 45.7 cm). Museo Nacional Centro de Arte Reina Sofia, Madrid, Spain. © 2020 Alex Katz / Licensed by VAGA at Artist Rights Society (ARS), New York, NY.

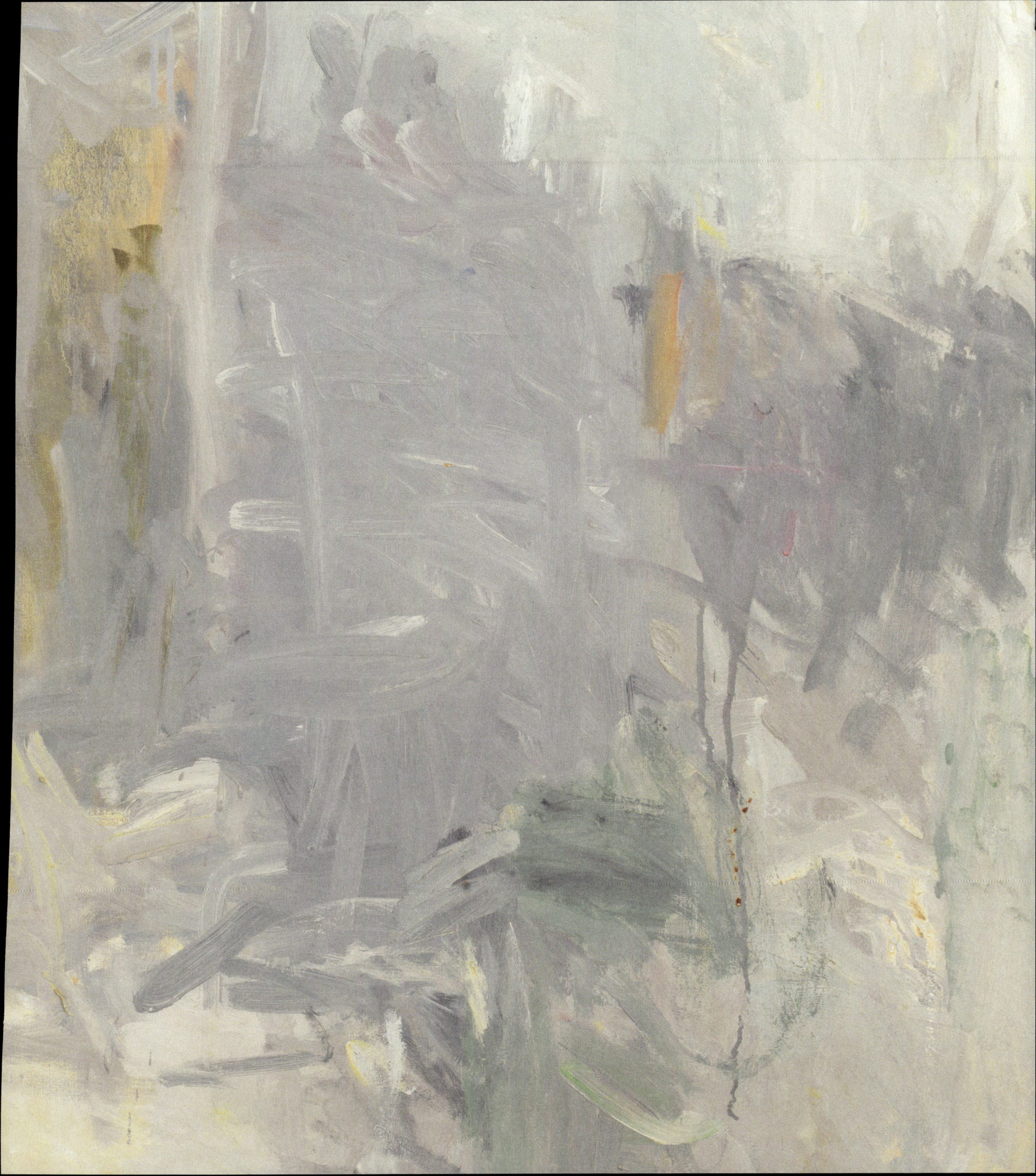

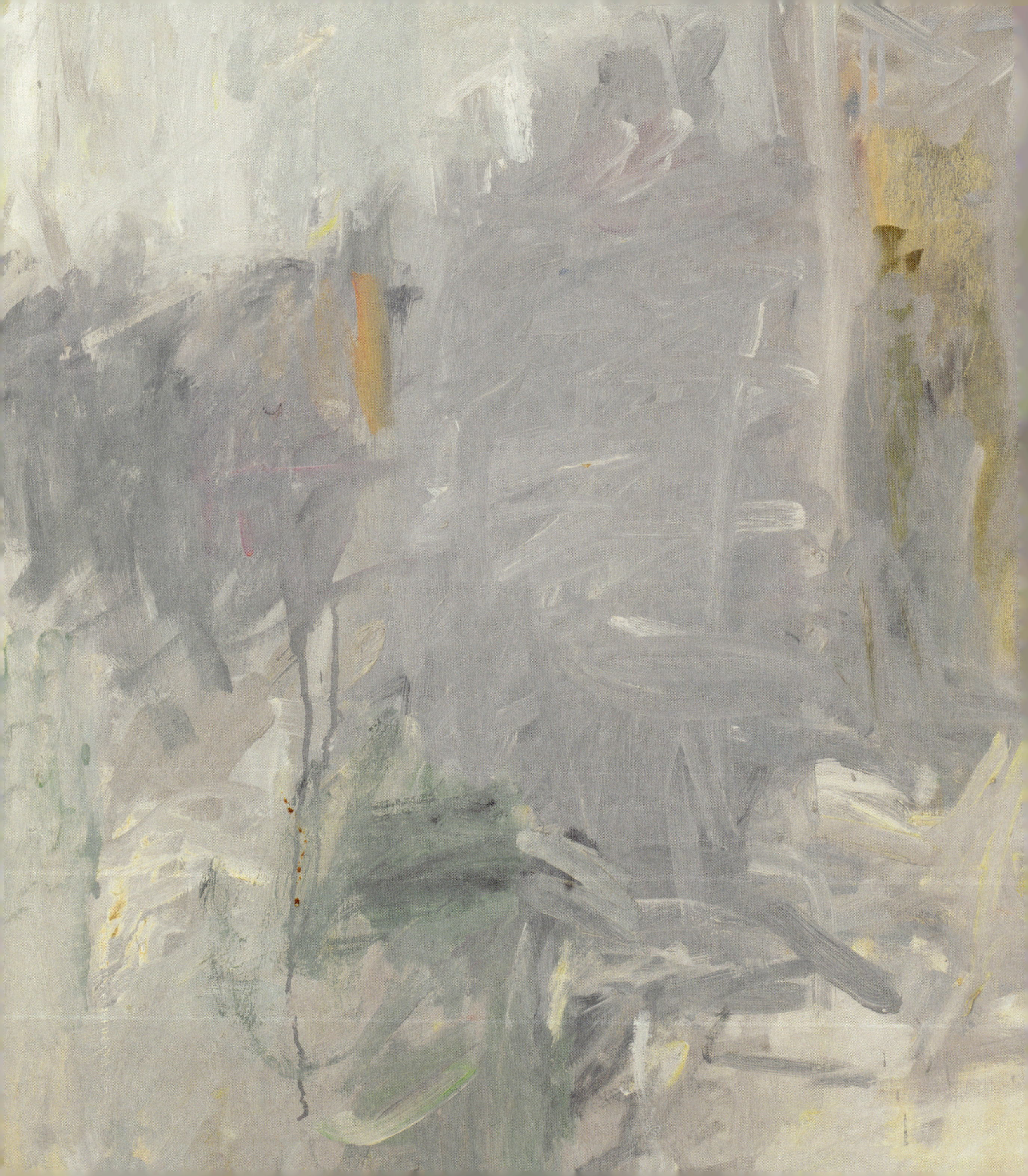